INTO THE HEARTS OF THE AMAZONS

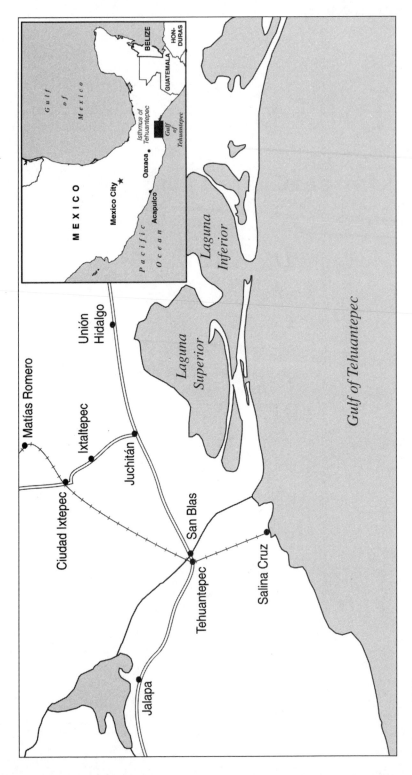

Isthmus of Tehuantepec

Into the Hearts of the Amazons

In Search of a Modern Matriarchy

Tom DeMott

THE UNIVERSITY OF WISCONSIN PRESS
TERRACE BOOKS

The University of Wisconsin Press
1930 Monroe Street
Madison, Wisconsin 53711

www.wisc.edu/wisconsinpress/

3 Henrietta Street
London WC2E 8LU, England

1   3   5   4   2

Printed in the United States of America

Library of Congress Cataloging-in-Publication Data
DeMott, Tom.
Into the hearts of the Amazons : in search of a modern matriarchy / Tom DeMott.
p.   cm.
Includes bibliographical references and index.
ISBN-13: 978-0-299-21640-5 (cloth: alk. paper)
1. Zapotec women—Mexico—Juchitán de Zaragoza—History.
2. Zapotec women—Mexico—Juchitán de Zaragoza—Social conditions.
3. Zapotec Indians—Mexico—Juchitán de Zaragoza—Social life and customs.
4. Matriarchy—Mexico—Juchitán de Zaragoza.
5. Juchitán de Zaragoza (Mexico)—History.
6. Juchitán de Zaragoza (Mexico)—Social life and customs.
I. Title.
F1221.Z3D44   2006
305.897´6807274—dc22   2005032818

Terrace Books, a division of the University of Wisconsin Press,
takes its name from the Memorial Union Terrace, located at
the University of Wisconsin-Madison. Since its inception in 1907,
the Wisconsin Union has provided a venue for students, faculty, staff,
and alumni to debate art, music, politics, and the issues of the day.
It is a place where theater, music, drama, dance, outdoor activities,
and major speakers are made available to the campus and the community.
To learn more about the Union, visit www.union.wisc.edu.

To
DARRELL
MAUREEN
DOLORES

You should see them arrive like walking towers, their windows open, their heart like a window, their nocturnal girth visited by the moon.

Elena Poniatowska

I am still of the opinion, that only two topics can be of the least interest to a serious and studious mind—sex and the dead.

William Butler Yeats

Contents

Acknowledgments

Thanks to Howard Campbell, whose research, articles, and books on the Isthmus provided a platform from which to launch this book. To Julin Contreras for introducing me to the right women and for providing insight and historical perspective to Isthmus customs. I also owe thanks to Julin's recently deceased father, Jorge Contreras, for inviting me to return to the Isthmus during the season of *velas* and for commentary about how men fare in the unusual culture of the Isthmus. To Magda Garrido, and both of her parents, Galaor and Hortensia, who were especially hospitable and informative whenever I came unannounced to their door.

I would also like to express my gratitude to Lugarda Charis, Delia Cruz, Gloria de la Cruz, Juana de la Cruz, Maureen Gosling, Florinda Luis, Obdulia Ruiz, Marinella Miano Borruso, Edaena Saynes-Vázquez, Jocasta Shakespeare, and Rosario Vialba for answering my many questions.

Maureen Heckman listened patiently to my book talk for the last five years and provided thoughtful criticism and careful proofreading under the pressure of deadlines.

I owe gratitude to Jody Rhodes, my agent, for believing in my book when there were few believers to be found. And to Adam Mehring, an editor at the University of Wisconsin Press, for making me feel I was more than just a first-time author. Raphael Kadushin, also of the University of Wisconsin Press, allowed me to reshape the book long after it was due. Carla Aspelmeier helped find a suitable cover photo.

Special thanks to my readers and reviewers, including Tony Cohan, Matt DeMott, Brian Deutscher, Michael Fosmire, Jim Laird, Nadia Mejia, Richard Roper, Linda Watanabe, and Sandra Zentner. My final thanks go to my mother for introducing me to books at an early age and for proofreading the final drafts of the manuscript.

Several of the names have been changed and places disguised to protect the privacy of the individuals described herein.

INTO THE HEARTS OF THE AMAZONS

The Blue Mortuary

MAY 1997. The only photo I have of Rosa sits unprotected on my basement desk, and fleck-by-fleck it is disappearing. This began a year ago, when the same humidity that soaked and rotted the basement door began chipping off the pale olive of Rosa's neck. And though I've been meaning to put the photo away for years, it has lingered, neither framed along with loved ones nor categorized in an album with other, less significant photos.

I met Rosa in Juchitán, a dusty, windblown town deep in the flatlands that lie along Oaxaca's Pacific coast. It was May, at the beginning of the rainy season, but the cloud cover had yet to yield its first drop. From my seat on the bus the only signs of life on the desert flats that surround Juchitán were gray shrubs and leafless trees. As we approached the outskirts of town, men in wooden carts drawn by oxen returned from the fields along a dirt road that ran parallel to the highway. At seven, we rolled into Juchitán, and I took a room at the Fortress Hotel on Calle 5 de Septiembre, ten blocks north of the plaza.

On Monday, my first day in Juchitán, I woke to learn that my hotel faced a mortuary. It was a two-story, Bauhaus building with a bleak angularity that brought to mind Druid structures before the invention of the arch. The color of the mortuary, however, rescued it from its dreary architecture with an optimistic blue that belied the true nature of the business. This cheerful effect was heightened with signs in white that gave warm welcome to the bereaved: OPEN: RING THE BELL and ECONOMIC COFFINS and SERVICE TWENTY-FOUR HOURS A DAY. Below the signs, an oversized showcase window was filled with coffins, one stacked on top of the other like cakes on display at a bakery.

3

Some of the coffins were wooden and plain; others were wrapped in satin with silver fringe and sagging ribbons. All were fitted with brass handles that caught and reflected the morning sun.

Some might have interpreted the location of the mortuary so close to their hotel as an ill omen, but for me it marked an auspicious beginning. Before all else, Mexicans are a spiritual people, and any attempt to understand them must begin with a look at the supernatural world of the indigenous people who inhabit the area. The Isthmus is heavily populated by Zapotecs; and the rituals they practice are far different from the Aztecs of Mexico's Central Valley or the Mayans of the Yucatan Peninsula. One constant, however, is the importance these Mesoamerican peoples give death and its attendant rituals. Although a saint's birthday is not shrugged off as unimportant, only the date of a saint's death can propel the extravagance of a Mexican feast day. Given this perspective, I saw the mortuary as a gateway to the spiritual world of the Zapotecs. Add to this the fact that spirituality was a part of the culture in which Isthmus women maintained exclusive control, and you will understand why I resolved to make contact with the owner of the mortuary in a day's time.

On the morning of my second day in Juchitán, I seated myself in the hotel restaurant where I could keep an eye on the mortuary. I ordered the Continental Breakfast: three slices of white bread with pineapple jam and a cup of instant coffee. Halfway through the toast, a blonde, fair-skinned woman in her early twenties emerged from the mortuary carrying a plastic bucket. She snatched a sponge from the bucket and began sloshing soapy water onto the hood of a silver hearse with a blue oval logo that said Laroche. I paid the bill and headed for the mortuary, rehearsing under my breath what I would say in Spanish: *No soy antropólogo* (I am not an anthropologist). This should come first, because as anyone familiar with the Isthmus knows, the Zapotecs have had enough of anthropologists. In the 1960s, American anthropologist Beverly Chiñas took up residence in the Isthmus, denouncing matriarchy as myth "because anthropologists have never encountered any truly matriarchal cultures." In the 1990s, a group of German feminists led by Veronika Bennholdt-Thomsen descended on Juchitán, renaming it "The City of Women" and insisting that Juchitán's society was — and always had been — a matriarchy. In between the Americans and

Germans, a slew of anthropologists had come and gone, each one with a fresh opinion about who held power in the Isthmus.

And so it was that I crossed the street with a certain amount of apprehension, and rather than entering the mortuary, I approached the young woman washing the hearse. "Is the owner in?" I said. She put the sponge into the bucket, drew a strand of hair off her face, and said, "My husband is inside." Through the glass door, a man with a potbelly that would have filled a wheelbarrow spoke to a young woman in black. He did not look like a mortician. A braided gold necklace swung conspicuously around his neck, standing in contrast to his otherwise casual dress. For a shirt, he wore a white, V-neck tank top; for pants, khaki shorts cut off above the knees. His eyes shone with a kind of restrained optimism, and his cheeks, which had become dislodged from his cheekbones, sagged with the onset of middle age, but he brought them into place when he smiled, and this was often.

When I entered the mortuary, he stopped midsentence and stared. This sort of reaction—a stunned look and a long stare—was something I would have to become accustomed to in Juchitán. Although it is less than 350 miles south of Acapulco, Juchitán is light years from contemporary culture. It has little tourism, and I would soon learn that I could stop conversations and turn heads no matter where I went—so rare were the features of my North American face to a town so removed from time.

The man held up his index finger as a signal to the young woman in black that he wanted a moment to deal with me. Then he approached me, grinning as though he had won the national lottery. We shook hands, and he introduced himself as Pablo Laroche. I waited for him to introduce the young woman. She wore a long, one-piece garment that was more T-shirt than dress, and it hung on her like it would have on a hook or hanger, revealing nothing about her shape other than an occasional bone. As soon as I looked in her direction, she turned away from us and fixed her gaze on the coffins in the showcase window.

When Pablo asked what brought me to Juchitán, I paused. I wanted to give him the long answer, but I was sure that this would take more time than he was willing to spend. I would have to explain that when I was a freshman at university and began pursuing the opposite sex, the women's movement was in full flux. In the newspaper I spread out on the kitchen table before going to class, I learned of the Equal Rights

Amendment and the inequity of women's salaries when compared to men's. Editorials written by feminists attacked not only the patriarchal structure of American society; they blamed patriarchs for bringing war, hunger, and corporate greed to America and the world. Senseless as it may seem, I took these attacks personally, and a question took seed in my mind: Would life be any better in a matriarchy?

Though I carried this question in the back of my mind for years, I assumed there was no answer; matrilineal and matriarchal societies had ceased to exist. But seven years ago, while reading Paul Theroux's *The Old Patagonian Express,* I came across a paragraph that caught my attention: "These Indians, the Zapotecs, were a matrilineal people: the women owned land, fished, traded, farmed, and ran the local government; the men, with that look of silliness that comes of being bone-idle, lounged around. The station showed this tradition to be unchanged: enterprising women, empty-handed men."

This passage rekindled my interest in seeking an answer to the matriarchy question, and according to my guidebook, I could catch a flight at noon in San Francisco and by nine the same day I would be in Oaxaca. On the topic of women, the guidebook went a step further than Paul Theroux. It described Tehuantepec—the second largest city in the Isthmus—as a matriarchal society "where the birth of a daughter is a cause for celebration, and the men turn their wages over to their wives, who control family finances."

But I felt suspicious. Paul Theroux took his stand on the matriarchy question while sitting in a train headed south. He never bothered to speak with the Zapotecs. He didn't even step off the train. And although my guidebook went one step further, guidebooks are notoriously unreliable. If I wanted the truth, I would have to travel to the Isthmus and speak with the enterprising women and the empty-handed men myself.

The time would come when I would tell Pablo this and more about the reasons why I had traveled to Juchitán. For now, however, I gave Pablo a shorter version. I explained that I was a writer, not an anthropologist, and that I had a personal interest in gender and a curiosity about matriarchal societies. But no sooner had the word *matriarchal* passed from my lips than Pablo's smile faded, and it was clear I had touched on a topic he was tired of discussing. "Isthmus women work very hard," he said. "They also work long hours, sometimes ten to twelve hours a day. If an Isthmus woman's husband doesn't give her any money, she doesn't care. If her husband runs around drinking, it doesn't matter to her, she keeps on working. I lived in Veracruz for a long time. The women there are lazy, but here they work hard. This doesn't make them matriarchs, but it gives them privileges that women from other parts of Mexico don't usually have. When tourists see our women enjoying these privileges, they jump to conclusions."

I knew this argument. It was a variation on what I will call the "tourist myth." For decades, Istmeños have blamed tourists for inventing and perpetuating the myth of Isthmus matriarchy. Isthmus men, the argument goes, rise before dawn to work in the fields while Isthmus women labor in the market. When tourists come to walk through the plaza, they see women hard at work in the market while the men are nowhere in sight. Based on what they see, the tourists falsely conclude that Isthmus society is matriarchal, and when they return home, they spread the word, and thus the myth was born.

But I told Pablo none of this. It would only alienate him, and this made no sense. He was articulate. He spoke Spanish rapidly, but clearly, and I felt lucky to have found him.

"So what exactly does your interest in matriarchy have to do with my mortuary?" Pablo said.

I explained to him what I knew about Zapotec rituals of death: that Isthmus women dominate the ceremonies, and in a society renowned for ancestor worship, I conjectured that this must lend them power. "Little is written about these rituals," I said, "and I had hoped you could answer some of my questions."

"Better than telling you," Pablo said, "why don't you tag along with me today and see firsthand. We'll be delivering a casket that Benita—the young woman in black—is picking out for her mother." Then Pablo put his big, Gallic nose in my ear and murmured, "I should warn you that the woman who died suffered from diabetes. She had gangrene on her legs, which is pretty common when diabetes reaches an advanced stage, so the smell will be strong, and the sight of her legs might sicken you. If you can help me lift her into the coffin, I'd be glad to answer your questions."

Soon, Benita had chosen a coffin for her mother, Victoria. Pablo and his teenage helper lifted it out of the showcase window. It was the smallest and simplest coffin and unlike any I'd ever seen. Someone, a seamstress, had tacked gray, pleated organdy to the sides of the casket, and the cloth on top was printed with tiny white marigolds against a black background. Benita followed the coffin with her eyes on its way to the truck, and as she turned toward me, I saw in her face the look of the trustworthy, of the child who assumes too much responsibility too soon. She wore no makeup or jewelry, and her black, shoulder-length hair was parted down the middle and tucked into place behind her ears. Her features were small and fine and—because of the recent past—fixed as a Toltec mask.

As I studied Benita, I wondered if she had foreknowledge of her mother's death. According to Zapotec tradition, a person who is approaching death will witness omens. There are the usual Mexican portents, such as the hooting of an owl and the presence of a great black moth in the house. To this list, the Isthmus Zapotecs have added their own: those about to die dream of falling teeth. When one or more of these omens occur, the person near death will often ask family members to remain with them as the date approaches.

I left Benita and joined Pablo outside, where his helper was loading a flatbed pickup with folding chairs. It was near ten now, and a blazing sun had risen over the top of the Fortress Hotel. And though I stood still in the shade, sweat rolled off my forehead and bled through my shirt. Many of the people brushing by me on the sidewalk carried a piece of cloth in their hands. Some carried handkerchiefs, others dishrags or washcloths, and it wasn't until a man took a swipe at his forehead with a terry-cloth towel that I realized that the cloths were intended to mop up sweat. Called *paliacates,* they are a permanent fixture of Isthmus life and a testimonial to Isthmus heat.

After Pablo finished loading several candleholders and a pair of silver crucifixes into the truck, he motioned to me to join him in the front seat. I got in and moved to the center of the seat to make room for Benita. Then I heard her high heels on the wooden bed of the truck behind me. Before I had time to ask about this unusual seating arrangement, Pablo had driven off toward the main plaza.

The buildings that lined the stretch of road between the mortuary and the plaza are divided evenly between homes and businesses. Unlike most homes in Mexico, with their protective walls to keep out intruders, the adobe homes in Juchitán do without them and are set back a good hundred feet from the road. Trust is a factor, and so is heat: the unwalled homes allow cooling breezes to pass over the bare-earth yards, which are often shaded by mango and tamarind trees. But the more we drove, the more it became clear that most of the buildings in Juchitán, especially those that housed businesses, were monolithic cinderblock structures, not much different from Pablo's mortuary.

As we neared the marketplace, the proportion of women to men rose dramatically; there were at least three or four women for every man. Many women balanced baskets on their heads that they had stuffed with fruit or tortillas or fish and called out what they had for sale in Zapotec, a tonal language that sounded more like Chinese than Spanish. The full-length skirts they wore touched the ground and hid their feet, creating the impression that the women floated rather than walked. Indigo, brilliant red, yellow, and purple were the colors of their skirts, and the women stood out against the cinderblock buildings like a flock of parrots crossing a twilight sky. "The full-length skirts you see the women wearing are called *enaguas*, and the blouses, *huipiles*," Pablo said. "Surprising as it might seem, these women are not dressed up. They are on their way to market in their everyday dress. Most are wearing what we call the *huipil de cadenilla*." The huipil is a sleeveless garment seen throughout Mesoamerica and can be sewn in minutes. A yard of muslin is folded in half, and a hole is made in the center for the neck. This is draped over the shoulders of the wearer and sewn at the sides, leaving two armholes in the measurements of the wearer's arms. "Unlike the *huipil de fiesta* where the flowers are embroidered by hand," Pablo continued, "the geometric patterns on the huipil de cadenilla are created with a sewing machine." *Cadenilla* is Spanish for chain, an appropriate name because the gold thread with which the huipil de cadenilla is embroidered creates the illusion that the women wore gold chains around their necks.

Frida Kahlo often wore Zapotec costume when painted by Diego Rivera and also in many of her self-portraits such as *Pensando en Diego* and *Dos Fridas*. "In another period I dressed like a boy with shaved hair, pants, boots, and a leather jacket," Frida wrote. "But when I went to see Diego, I put on a Tehuana costume." Aside from the obvious beauty of

Isthmus dress, Frida chose to wear it for what it symbolized to Mexicans. "The costume she favored was that of the Isthmus of Tehuantepec," wrote Kahlo biographer Hayden Herrera, "and the legends surrounding them informed her choice: Tehuantepec women are famous for being stately, beautiful, sensuous, intelligent, brave and strong. When she put on Tehuana costume, she was choosing a new identity and she did it with the fervor of a nun taking the veil."

Pablo crossed the bridge over the River of the Dogs and turned south onto a dirt road. We followed the river for another hundred yards until we hit a bad patch of road and stirred up something white and billowing that rose onto the windshield like snow. "Chicken feathers," Pablo said. As we drove nearer Benita's house, wooden shacks and lean-tos replaced two-story homes. Children, most of them around the age of ten, were everywhere. Gaunt young men with hollow cheeks and drug dealers' eyes watched us from their posts on the street corners, and every couple of blocks someone shouted Pablo's name.

"You have lots of friends here," I said.

"The majority of my customers live here. If I didn't have a network of friends, it would be a risky —" Here he trailed off because we had arrived. Pablo turned the truck off, and when the noise of the engine died, a chorus of bawling filled the morning air. Rather than rising, the voices seemed to fall, rolling toward us over a dirt lot that surrounded a one-room house without a door. The first one out of Pablo's truck was Benita. She walked a dirt path that ran straight as a plumb line to Victoria's house, a low, gray structure that encompassed a single room and a patio. The path had been worn smooth as old ivory by bare feet and crossed a quarter-acre of land where a random array of plants grew wild. Half the plants were dead, impossible to recognize from their stringy brown corpses. The other half, composed of flowers such as hibiscus and vinca, were barely alive, their growth stunted by a lack of water and the intensity of the Isthmus sun. Benita took no notice of the dirt lot or her menagerie of plants and passed by without inclining her head toward either side of the path. Then, as she approached the house, she slowed her pace, and when she crossed the threshold, the bawling stopped. Pablo and I looked at each other, then toward the house, ready for a vision or minor miracle — but then wailing began again, now with renewed force.

With Benita out of sight, the lot was still, unless you count the panting of a rust-colored mutt lying in the scanty shade of a papaya tree. A hefty man named Eulalio, who I took to be one of Victoria's sons, emerged barefoot from the house and leaned himself against a wood fence that appeared on the verge of collapse. Now and then a crowd of curious boys gathered on the driveway, and Eulalio would shoo them away with his arms as if he were swatting at flies.

I got out of the truck, and the mutt ran up to greet me from his spot under the papaya tree. His eyes were clear, without pigment, and you could see through them much like you can see through a cube of ice. He wagged his tail in a friendly way, but I didn't pet him. Instead, I climbed into the back of the truck and handed chairs to Pablo, which he lugged inside.

Soon it came time to carry the coffin to into the house. Pablo called out to Eulalio, who was still leaning against the fence. It took another minute before Pablo's request pierced Eulalio's grief. Then Eulalio reached behind him, grabbed a hold of his pants, and gave them an upward yank. He crossed the lot, swaying as if drunk. At last he climbed into the truck, and they got the coffin out and carried it toward the house.

Pablo returned from carrying in the coffin and paused for a moment, resting his sandaled feet on the tailgate of the truck. "Because Victoria died yesterday," he said, "you've missed some of the rituals. Benita has already collected sand from the banks of the River of the Dogs that she used to make a cross on the floor of Victoria's house. Then, with the help of her family, Benita laid Victoria out on the cross."

When the sorrowful racket from the house grew calmer, I grabbed an armful of chairs from Pablo's truck and entered the house. The smell of death was sharp, of sulfur or burnt matches, yet nowhere near as strong as Pablo had suggested. In the center of the room, laid out on a cot, was the corpse. To the left, the coffin rested on top of a four-foot metal rack, and to the right a handful of women knelt in prayer. At the foot of the corpse was a holy table, a household commodity in Juchitán generally the size of a coffee table, which Zapotecs pile high with religious icons and photos of ancestors.

I leaned the chairs against the wall, and as soon as I let go of them and lifted my gaze to take in the room, I felt the stares of the women to the right of the coffin. I could remain while working, the stares seemed to imply, but gawking was prohibited. The women were a stern lot, a choir of elderly matrons dressed in black from the scarves on their heads to the flat black shoes on their feet. All but one of them were on their knees, where they were expected to remain for hours, resting only for short periods on the chairs we were bringing in. Some of the women were sobbing, and in between sobs you could hear others murmuring the Hail Mary in Zapotec, fingering the black beads of their rosaries in unison.

When I had two chairs left to unfold, I took a closer look at Victoria. Wrapped in a white felt blanket that was marked with sand and mud, her body made no more of a hump in the blanket than a cornstalk would, and only her head, hands, and feet were uncovered. Her skin was more yellow than gray, pulled taut over her skull like the skin of an old conga drum, splattered with brown blotches of age. Her hands were folded together over her flat chest, and her wrists were bound with leather shoelaces, as were her feet. And though death had drained all life from her, there were still clear traces of warmth and intelligence in her face.

Outside, I found Pablo on the bed of the truck collecting the candleholders. As he handed them to me, I asked why Victoria's feet and hands were bound.

"So that a stray arm or leg won't fall out of place when we move her to the casket," Pablo said.

"And how did she get from the cross of sand to the cot?"

"When her friends and relatives arrived, they wrapped Victoria in a shroud, and moved her to the cot. The family and relatives will use the chairs we're bringing for the *primero,* the first of a nine-day funeral service called a *novena.*"

"And if the closest relative were a man," I said, "would he have performed these rituals instead of Benita?"

"No," Pablo said. "They would have chosen the nearest woman relative."

I reentered the house and set the candleholders on the ground near the door. Again I was met with the stares of the women, but when I turned to leave, Pablo sidled up to me with an armful of candleholders. "Did you see how her feet touch the holy table?" he whispered. "That means she was married. If she had been single, she'd be turned around the other way so her head touched the holy table."

"Why is this?" I said.

"No idea," Pablo said. "It's always been this way."

Pablo left the room, and I remained for a quick look at Victoria's holy table. On the Day of the Dead and other religious holidays, Zapotecs believe that photos provide a venue to which the spirits of ancestors can return. The only photo Victoria had placed on her holy table was a lone snapshot depicting a pale, distracted young man in a straw hat. Two spit curls, each one an inch in diameter, crept out from under his hat and hung like coiled worms on his forehead. Insignificant as this worn-out photo appeared at the time, it would play an important role in unraveling the mystery of Victoria's death.

From the bed of the pickup truck, Pablo handed me one of the two crucifixes, and we each carried one inside, stationing them on either side of the holy table. When we turned to leave, Pablo nicked one of the crucifixes with his belly, and it fell face-down into the dirt. As you might expect, the room fell silent as the women took in the blasphemy of the situation. But instead of looking at Pablo, the women glared at me, cursing me out of the corners of their eyes. I froze, and an admonition from my guidebook came to mind. "Tehuana women brook no nonsense from visitors." No one moved, and the hot silence continued. From outside came the sound of Eulalio chasing the boys off the driveway, now with the support of barking from the mutt. As I waited for someone to give in and breathe, it occurred to me that the women might have been picking up little pieces of evidence that were proof of my pagan heart. Unlike the faithful, I had not made the sign of the cross, nor had I kissed my fingers after handling the crucifix. Whatever their motives were, it wasn't long before the women began to look away, whispering among themselves between accusing looks.

Pablo snatched the crucifix off the dirt floor, and an arc of dust rose with it that hung in the air. He went to the door and called out to Eulalio. When he got no answer, he moved to the cot, where he unfolded the felt blanket in which Victoria was wrapped. He twisted the four corners of the shroud into ropelike handles and gave me the two handles at the head of the corpse. Then he returned to Victoria's feet and took hold of the other two handles. I looked at Pablo. He smiled, and we lifted. Stiff as the corpse appeared, it slouched to the middle of the blanket, and we had to return her to the cot, where Pablo stretched her out flat again. Then we lifted and got very near the coffin. But the width of the blanket prevented us from raising her above our waists. We had to lift our hands as far as they could reach above our heads to avoid slamming her into the side of the coffin. It took three tries to get her inside, and when we did, her neck rested on the front edge of the coffin and her head hung outside. We lifted her again, took a step toward the foot of the casket, and this time she rested inside.

Benita brought an armful of Victoria's clothes, which she tucked into the coffin near her feet. Next, she carried a large wooden bowl that held Victoria's soap, eyeglasses, jewelry, and a comb, which she placed near Victoria's head. All of this was an affirmation of the Zapotec belief in an otherworldly paradise, where Victoria would live on, wearing the same clothes, using the same articles of dress and adornment.

Benita untied the leather straps from Victoria's hands and feet, and she began massaging the arms of the corpse near the elbows and murmuring something so low I couldn't understand. "She is massaging Victoria's arms to get them at her side," Pablo said in a whisper. "Only then can they dress her." Benita brought a cotton skirt and an indigo blouse that had a shine to it. These were Victoria's best clothes. These were the clothes she would wear into the next life.

When Benita began undressing Victoria, the women turned and looked at us, and we knew it was time to go. "Can I show you something before I leave?" Pablo said. Benita stepped away from the coffin, and Pablo closed it. "If you want to see Victoria," Pablo said, "just open this little door where her face is. That way you can keep the coffin shut." Pablo demonstrated how this worked. His tone was cheerful. He could have been a gentle Santa Claus demonstrating how to open the lid of a toy chest to a group of children at Macy's. I say this not as criticism, because his good humor had a tranquilizing effect on the women and on me. Then we said good-bye. Once we were outside, we had to push our way through a crowd of fifteen or twenty boys who had taken advantage of Eulalio's absence to flood their way into the patio.

On our way back to town we passed a funeral parlor that displayed coffins in a showcase window, and I told Pablo how unusual I found it. "We're not afraid of death," Pablo said. "We are very accustomed to seeing it, living with it, and playing with it. When we attend a funeral, and we are drinking, we tell jokes about the person, whether he played around with women, if he was a drinker—we don't show him a gloomy respect that comes from fear. Here we say, 'Great that you lived, that you spent money, and that you're gone.'"

"You also have a strong belief in an afterlife," I said.

"There is another world, always," he said, "or why would we fill the wooden bowl that the dead man carries with him to the grave? Come to the Isthmus some Palm Sunday of any year so that you see what happens in the cemeteries—it's a completely different world at night. The whole town goes there to live with the dead, to dine, to sleep until three or four o'clock in the morning. Every inch of the cemetery is taken up with families." We drove for another five minutes, and I asked Pablo the question that to me mattered most.

"Do you believe women's control over the rituals of death lends them power?"

"No," said Pablo. "Not from my point of view." This was a disappointment, but it represented one man's opinion, and I wanted others.

Shortly after we had crossed the river and entered a thoroughfare, processions began appearing on the side streets that intersected with our route to the mortuary. The processions stretched for a block or two and were populated almost entirely by women and girls wearing full-length velvet dresses in deep vermilion and purple. At first, we saw one procession every mile or so. But later, as we approached the center of town, they multiplied and collided like velveteen rabbits in a maze. One procession would run into another, and the women in the colliding processions would point fingers at each other and laugh as though they were trading mock insults. I couldn't make out much detail; Pablo drove as if he were running a race to get home before we became trapped by the processions. Then, when one of the processions crossed the road directly in front of us, Pablo groaned and pulled to the side of the road to allow it to pass. "Ay, Juchitán," he said. Meanwhile, four old men in black pants and white shirts led the procession past us toting a wooden stretcher. Balanced on top the stretcher was a four-foot statue of San Vicente, Juchitán's patron saint. Women—wide hipped and corpulent—followed close behind carrying beeswax candles and white gladiolas they clasped tightly to their breasts. At the end of the procession, girls in red velvet rode in the back of a flatbed pickup truck throwing party favors by the handful from large black bowls with crimson interiors. A pack of boys without shirts or shoes ran behind, catching the party favors midair or scooping them up from where they landed on the burning asphalt. And though the procession that blocked our path frustrated Pablo, it was pure pleasure to me. It represented the first manifestation of the May festivals for which Juchitán is famous, and the principal reason I chose to visit Juchitán during this month.

"This town," Pablo said, "is filled with partiers and slackers—you know what I mean. It's impossible to get anything done, and this is just the beginning. Because for every procession you see here today, there will be a dance tonight. And for every dance, there will also be a mass and a *lavada de ollas* [cleaning of the pots] two days later."

"Cleaning of the pots?" I said.

"No one does any cleaning," Pablo said. "That's just an expression that Juchitecos use as an excuse for another party." Taken together, the procession, the dance, the lavada de ollas, and the mass constitute what Istmeños call a vela, or vigil. The velas began as candlelight vigils honoring the patron saints of Juchitán's many wards. In recent years, however, women have taken to running and organizing the velas, and they have become more akin to Zapotec rites of spring. The setting has changed from church to field, and the ritual drinking of mezcal is common. Any dancing that takes place usually involves one woman in the arms of another, and anyone leaving before dawn is a spoilsport. My guidebook described Juchitán's May velas as "some of the most colorful festivals in the country"; it failed to mention, however, that to attend a dance, an invitation was required.

"Is an invitation to a dance hard to come by?" I asked.

"I'm not sure," Pablo said. "I haven't attended one in years, but my sister goes to these kinds of things. Maybe she can arrange an invitation."

"What's she like?"

"Rosa is thirty-four. She's the youngest in the family."

"I once loved the youngest woman in a family. She demanded a lot of attention."

"Rosa married young. Now she's a single mother, living alone. She'll be there at the mortuary when we arrive, and I'll introduce you." Then, as if his conscience were bothering him, Pablo added, "She's also very restless."

As the day wore on, the cloud cover thickened and seemed to close in on us like an enormous gray tent whose roof pole had given way. The resulting pressure and humidity added to the tension that was building from the processions. Every third block we'd run head on into another. Pablo would groan, grind the gears into reverse, and drive backward until he found a street that offered at least the possibility of a detour. When we got nearer to the mortuary, the cloud cover darkened, and I asked Pablo what would happen if it rained on the vigils that were to take place that night. "Don't worry about that," he said. "If it rains, people will dance in it, or you'll see them sitting in the mud with a bottle of beer. No, don't worry about rain. If it rains, they won't run for cover. They'll keep on dancing."

As Pablo had suggested, Rosa was standing in the shade of the mortuary when we pulled up to the curb. Seen from a distance, she had a light, waiflike quality that she played up with a jagged haircut and furthered by twisting the hair in front of her ears into a sharp elfin point. This hairstyle would have looked annoying on others, but because of Rosa's beauty, it suggested that her good looks would stand out no matter how she styled her hair. As soon as we were out of the truck, Pablo introduced us and quickly disappeared inside the mortuary.

For a while, Rosa and I exchanged pleasantries, and I took in her clothing: a tight-fitting knit blouse the color of key lime pie, a blue Levi's skirt that rose an inch or two above her knees, and leather sandals. Her eyes were her strongest feature. As black and glossy as watermelon seeds, they darted across every part of me whenever it was my turn to speak. Her voice, which was her only detraction, had the beginnings of a raspy cackle.

Shortly before I returned to my hotel, Rosa steered the conversation to her accomplishments. She had worked as secretary to the governor of Oaxaca and later as assistant to the mayor of Juchitán. Recently, she had begun her own business: "I do hair and nails and facials and that kind of thing," she said. "These services aren't in demand in Juchitán just yet, but I'll be ready when they are. I also do cosmetics, but don't misunderstand me—I'm not vain. It takes me less than a minute to apply my own makeup." I considered asking about an invitation to one of the dances, which were considered the culmination of every vela. Instead, I counted on Pablo to relay my wishes to Rosa. Then the heat of the day was on us, and I returned to my hotel and slept.

The Politician

In 1859, sixty years before politician José Vasconcelos first referred to Isthmus society as matriarchal, French traveler and historian Brasseur de Bourbourg set the stage with his description of the marketplace in Tehuantepec. Not only did he discover the market dominated exclusively by women, but he found them to be the least reserved in America: "[They] chattered, laughed, conversed, screamed, and argued with an incredible animation. They openly made fun of their men, who they provoked in Spanish and Zapotec with a shamelessness hardly equaled by the green-grocers of Paris." Later in the same visit, Bourbourg came across a twenty-two-year-old Tehuana selling coconut candy and playing pool with soldiers in a barracks outside Tehuantepec. Her name was Juana Cata Romero, and Bourbourg found her so beautiful that he compares her to Isis and Cleopatra. "Some claimed she was a sorceress . . . and the Indians respected her as queen." Given the women's lack of respect for their men and the regal devotion toward Juana Cata Romero, it is not hard to imagine that outsiders might go away with the impression that something unusual was going on, and that they might label this role reversal as matriarchal. This leap of logic is even easier to imagine when you consider that the context for Bourbourg's observations was male-dominated Mexico of 140 years ago.

José Vasconcelos was born in February 1882 in the city of Oaxaca, not three hundred miles from the Isthmus. As was the case with many Mexican men, the bond formed at an early age with his mother was far more profound than that with his father. "My mother's deep voice gave direction to my thoughts, determined my impulses. One might say that I was bound to her by an invisible, psychological umbilical cord which endured many years after the breaking of the physical bond." His mother took charge of his early education, reading and discussing the classics from her private library. Vasconcelos began his formal studies in Eagle Pass, Texas, and graduated from Mexico's La Escuela Nacional de Jurisprudencia with a degree in law. In 1908, not long after he graduated, Vasconcelos made his first trip to the Isthmus on a political campaign where he crossed paths with the mature Juana Cata Romero at the peak of her political power. Though he is reticent about their meeting, she must have held his attention, because he described her glowingly as the local political boss of that "species of indigenous matriarchy." Oblique as the reference to matriarchy might be, it marked a beginning: The pro-matriarchs had raised their flag.

In 1922, when Vasconcelos began his term as minister of public education, he took it upon himself to find a new source of inspiration for Mexican artists. For too long, they had looked to Europe. Vasconcelos wanted an indigenous wellspring that would stimulate Mexican artists to create a purer form of national art. After repeated visits to Tehuantepec and Juchitán, he was convinced that he had found this wellspring in the people and culture of the Isthmus. He described the region as a kind of earthly paradise where "no yearning of the flesh went unsatisfied." And, at the center of this paradise, were the women of the Isthmus: "Dressed in red and yellow with white headdresses, slim shoulders and waists, wide hips, firm breasts and black eyes, those women possess something of sensual India, but without the religious overtones."

One of the artists who listened to what Vasconcelos had to say on this topic was the young Diego Rivera, who had recently returned from Europe and was busy painting one of his first murals, *La Creación*. Because the mural bore clear influences from European schools of art, Vasconcelos urged Rivera to look toward Mexico's indigenous cultures for inspiration. More specifically, he suggested Rivera visit the Isthmus, and he sponsored Rivera's first trip there in 1922. In Tehuantepec, Rivera sketched Isthmus women, dances, and landscapes. He also began an oil portrait of an Isthmus woman naked from the waist up who was washing in the Tehuantepec River, which he titled *The Bather of Tehuantepec*. Art critics consider the work the turning point in Rivera's search for a style free of European influence. Vasconcelos's plan had worked.

Jean Charlot, an American muralist who knew Rivera and his tendency to fabricate, gives us a glimpse of Rivera's excited talk when he returned to Mexico City. "[Rivera] came back with tall tales of a matriarchal society where Amazonian women lord it over wizened men, of Indian babies born white, left to brown to a permanent deep ochre in the scorching of the sun, of bathing beauties with skins dappled like leopard pelts." Rivera also joked about his obesity and how Istmeños received it differently than in other parts of Mexico. "There," Charlot reports, "Tehuana women coveting his substantial girth approached his wife proposing in barter any male she might in turn covet." In a show of appreciation for having financed his trip to the Isthmus, Rivera began painting a mural at the east patio of the Ministry of Education where Vasconcelos worked. The first two panels show a transformation in Rivera's style that features Istmeñas balancing suggestive black bowls with crimson interiors on their heads.

By the late 1920s, word had spread about Vasconcelo's paradise, and the Isthmus became a fashionable gathering place for intellectuals and artists that included Frida Kahlo, Sergei Eisenstein, and Langston Hughes. Photographers seemed especially drawn to the Isthmus women and their colorful dress. Henri-Cartier Bresson shot photos there, as did Tina Modotti and Charles B. Waite. Perhaps the most famous American photographer to describe the Isthmus was Edmond Weston, who wrote that "The women handle the commerce of the state; the men do the physical labor. Free love is common practice in spite of Catholicism."

Although Vasconcelos and his followers refer to Isthmus women as sexual libertines, they do not tell us why. There are, however, practices in the Isthmus that might have led them to think this. One is the fact that the women of Tehuantepec used to bathe naked in the shallow, brown waters of the Tehuantepec River without shame or effort to cover up—even when foreigners came to photograph, paint, or leer. We also know that in the Zapotec language of the Isthmus, conversations about body parts and bodily functions are not considered vulgar. In fact, some Istmeños say that Zapotec has no forbidden words. Zapotec women, for example, have been known to refer to their daughters playfully as "little vaginas." Vasconcelos and the artists he sent to the Isthmus might have overheard similar conversations or references. Or they might have picked up on the graphic language Isthmus women used as they bargained over the price of iguanas or mangos. In the end, how foreigners were inspired to create the tales they told back home is unimportant. What matters is this: The women of the Isthmus soon had a reputation as sexually liberated Amazons.

Honoring San Vicente

I had been asleep in my hotel room for less than an hour when I was jolted awake by the distinctive ring of a Mexican telephone. It was a sound that, despite my time south of the border, I'd never gotten used to, and hearing it again for the first time in half a decade conjured up the same old image: an Irish tenor gargling his way through a quart of motor oil, pausing at regular intervals to breathe. When I answered, Pablo spoke with an uncharacteristic formality that made me think he'd been fed his lines by Rosa. "My sister Rosa will be attending the dance for a vela tonight," Pablo said. "You are more than welcome to accompany her. But you won't get in unless you're wearing black pants and a white shirt," Pablo said.

"I don't have a white shirt," I said.

"No problem," Pablo said. "I'll lend you one."

At nine, I crossed the street to the mortuary and found Pablo running the palms of his hands over a newly lacquered coffin the size of a small rowboat. Pablo's daughters, Ramona and Elisabet, played together near his feet. "Ramona is two years old and very sweet," Pablo said. "Elisabet is four. The most important thing with children their age is affection. I work from home, so there are lots of opportunities to hug them. We even take baths together. The first time, Ramona stared at my penis, amazed at the sight of it. Then, a couple of days later she grabbed it and pulled, and that was it, her curiosity was gone."

Near ten o'clock, the sound of high heels scraping against the stairs that descended from the second-floor apartment interrupted our conversation. Then Rosa appeared at the foot of the stairs, and I bellowed, "Que guapa" (How handsome). She wore a matching crimson skirt and blouse made of a glossy satin embroidered with daisies in blue, violet, white, and yellow. The contrast of the olive skin above her breasts with the blood-red dress was striking, and she repeated this effect at her face with crimson lipstick. She wore a spray of flowers behind her right ear and two slender gold necklaces round her neck. I gave her a peck on either cheek. Pablo drove us to the vela in an old Ford Mercury station wagon that doubled as a hearse.

As we approached the site of the vela, the surrounding streets became so congested with traffic that Pablo dropped us off a block away from the entrance. Rosa and I walked along a cinderblock wall that skirted the perimeter of a dirt field where the vela was underway. Near the steel gate entrance, we merged with a crowd of elegantly dressed women in velvet and lace who were funneling inside. After their dark velvet dresses, what most caught the eye about the women were the layers of gold they wore round their necks. Some were draped in as many as three or four necklaces and an equal number of bracelets, earrings, and rings that were fashioned from gold coins. The coins date as far back as the California Gold Rush in 1849, when the Isthmus represented one of the shortest routes between the Atlantic and the Pacific. Rather than spending the coins that the Forty-niners left in their wake at hotels, bars, and brothels, the women held onto them and crafted elaborate jewelry that often represented the family fortune. In hard times, the women pawned the jewelry, and in this way many a financial crisis was avoided.

Given the flashing gold and elegant dress of the women, the dirt field setting seemed all wrong. But the women didn't seem to notice. Already they had fixed their attention on the concrete dance floor at the center of the field. There, under a circus tarp flapping in the wind, a small army of women danced in each other's arms. Those who weren't dancing lolled about in wooden chairs that were dug into the dirt surrounding the dance floor. Many of the unoccupied seats had names like "Maria" or "Isabel," or just the letter *X* scribbled on their backrest with a permanent black marker. In a far corner of the field, a brass band played sones and boleros and an occasional merengue. A crescent moon stalled overhead.

When we arrived at the steel gate, I sensed a nervousness in Rosa's movements. She walked more quickly and then broke pace with me to speak to a man who stood watch at the gate. She whispered something in his ear, he nodded, and a couple of blue bills slid from her hand into his. Then she returned to me and said, "We have a tradition here that an uninvited man must bring a case of beer to the vela." Then Rosa took my arm, steered me to a flatbed truck loaded with dozens of cardboard boxes reading "Corona—20 Bottles." A man standing on the bed of the truck handed me a case which, I carried under my right arm. "Not like that," Rosa said. "Carry it like he is." She pointed to a man who carried the case of beer on his shoulder, and I followed suit.

I remember a certain amount of disappointment after passing through the steel gates and entering the vela proper. Many of the rituals I expected to witness at the entrance were simply not there. In the past, a man wishing to attend a vela had to make a cash contribution at a holy table, much like the one I had seen at Victoria's. In exchange, a designated toast pourer would serve up a round of mezcal, which the man was required to drink before entering. Every time a new man appeared, all of the men inside the vigil were also required to drink another shot. A woman, on the other hand, received a toast of sweet wine or grape juice after she paid her contribution. Her hair was sprinkled with confetti or she was given a cigarette that she wore behind her ear as evidence that she had paid. But at the vela I attended with Rosa, there was no holy table, no mezcal, no ritual drinking. And though I did not know it at the time, these traditions were still practiced, but I would witness them only when I began traveling outside of Juchitán and Tehuantepec to the less populated Isthmus towns.

Inside the vela Rosa surveyed the area and walked along the perimeter of the dance floor to a spot where her friends, all of them women, were seated opposite the band. I fell in step behind her, in part because I was unaware of her destination, and because I felt underdressed walking next to her. My faded black Levis and Pablo's white cotton shirt could not compete with her satin and gold, and I imagined I looked like a busboy hurrying behind his matron to clean up something spilled on the dance floor. But Rosa was attentive, and soon made me forget the disparity of our dress. She brought beer for the both of us and food on a paper plate: macaroni and cheese, one quarter of a club sandwich, pickled *nopal* cactus, and a dirty yellow thigh of chicken. I picked at the food with a white plastic fork, and when it fell from my hands into the dirt, she was on her feet and had a fresh one in my hands within a minute.

She also brought a pair of fresh beers, and as we drank them, I asked Rosa to tell me about her parents. This is an old habit with me. Rather than ask a woman her zodiac sign, I ask about her family, which I believe is a much better indicator of who she is and how she'll treat me.

"My mother met my father when she was managing the Fortress Hotel, the same hotel where you are now staying." Rosa said. "He had a degree in Electronic Engineering from the University of Mexico and worked as a civil engineer. He was twenty-two years older than she was. My mother claims the difference was only eighteen years, but any way you look at it, the age difference was great. For several years, my father and my mother lived together in the Fortress Hotel and had three children, me, Pablo, and my older sister, Carmen. Years passed, my mother and father had problems, and he moved to Mexico City. Twenty years ago he died."

"Did your mother remarry?" I said.

"No. She had male friends, like Francisco, the mortician in Oaxaca who took Pablo in and taught him the trade. Even though she was well off and very good looking, she never brought a man home to us. She never said, 'I need a man to help me with my children.' No, my mother didn't put much emphasis on that kind of relationship. Like most Isthmus women, she succeeded on her own."

Rosa introduced me to her friends. Like the majority of the women at the vela, they were middle-aged or older. Their dark velvet dresses were heavily embroidered with flowers in bright silk and hemmed with six inches of stiff white lace that collected the loose dirt. But already many of them seemed too drunk to care. They shouted, laughed, mock flirted, and danced with one other. When one of the women would get up to go the rest room, another would say:

"Where are you going?"

"That's none of your business," the second would say. "And I don't like your tone."

"It will be my business if I catch you with someone else," said the first, holding back her laughter.

"No," said the second, "it will be your fault for having tormented me like this. I can't stand your jealousy. It's killing me."

The women would go on like this for fifteen minutes at a time. One would accuse the other or tell an erotic joke and the rest of them would laugh so loud you could hear it above the din of the brass band. The men at the vela, in their monotonous black and white, shared none of the women's good-natured fun. They leaned silently against the cinder block wall behind us, smoking cigarettes and drinking beer from miniature glass bottles. For most Isthmus men, velas are considered obligatory rituals that they go out of their way to avoid. Those that do attend grumble about the amount of time and money the women spend preparing for and participating in velas. In the days following the vela, I asked several men about the difference in dress, and most answered with a cliché: "Think of us as the black and white border that frames our colorfully dressed women." Although the men seemed comfortable with the disparity of their dress, I was not. Seeing the men at the vela dressed so poorly and separated from their women reminded me of the ragamuffin boys at the end of the procession and the girls in velvet throwing party favors. And I remember thinking: if this society is not matriarchal, then it is tilted in favor of the women.

I asked Rosa for her stance on the issue of matriarchy in Juchitán. "If you go to the market," Rosa said, "you'll see that our women do the selling. A man might bring home fish, but only the women can sell the fish in the market." She went on along these lines, reciting the tourist myth. But she added her own twist. "We are not afraid to tell our men, 'Look, if I'm bringing money home, and give you support when you need it, then I also have the right to have an opinion and do what I want.' As you know, this is quite different from other Mexican women whose husbands beat them, and who have nothing."

When the band resumed playing, Rosa asked me to dance. I ignored her and watched the dance floor to gauge the talent of the competition. At first, the dancing entertained me, particularly the Zapotec dances in which a woman would catch hold of her white-lace hem and draw the skirt up on one side to allow the audience to admire the intricate needlework. While the steps of the dance dictated that the woman flit in a circle around her male partner, he was choreographed to keep his hands behind his back, hopping from one foot to the other. Baryshnikov would have looked awkward dancing this step, and it didn't take an anthropologist to explain why 90 percent of the couples consisted of one woman dancing with another.

And we drank, bottle after bottle of Corona—and then came a man with his cardboard box, "Don't you want another?" he'd say, and Rosa would add, "Have another." I stocked up, despite a line of open beer bottles under my seat, and the more we drank, the more ribald Rosa's female friends became. I would say something like, "Rosa, is it okay to leave your purse open like that?" Then a screaming cackle would arise, making me want to join the men against the wall.

The beer was having its effect on Rosa too. Whenever she thought she'd get away with it, she'd peer inside my mouth at my teeth or rake her hyperactive black eyes across my genitals. Later, she began emphasizing the significance of something she was saying by squeezing the flesh above my knee. I, in turn, stroked the triangle of hair at the back of her neck. I felt aroused in an apprehensive way and reminded myself that as desirable as she might be, we'd only known each other for a couple of hours.

As time passed, I grew bored watching the dancers and asked Rosa to tell me something, a story from her childhood. "Just after I began high school," Rosa said, "a catastrophe occurred. It's something we don't speak about much at home. Among ourselves, yes. But in front of my sister Carmen's husband, never. You've probably guessed the catastrophe by now—my sister Carmen got pregnant when she was sixteen." When Rosa's mother found out, she sent Carmen to the best boarding school in southern Mexico, Colegio Esparza in Puebla. Tuition was outrageous, but her mother made the sacrifice. Time passed, and Carmen's boyfriend, the one who made her pregnant, returned to a former girlfriend, and they were married and moved to Orizaba. "Now I don't know if you know it," Rosa said, "but Orizaba is very near my sister's school in Puebla, so all of my mother's work to put distance between Carmen and her former boyfriend were wasted. They got in touch with each other, although how they did is still a mystery."

"And how did your mother react?" I asked.

"She lost control," Rosa said. "She closed the restaurant at the Fortress and started spreading rumors that my sister had a brain tumor. Then my mother took her to New York. They lived together with some Cuban friends on Long Island," Here Rosa laughed, slapped her knees, and took a long drink of beer.

"I was only seven at the time, so I didn't know about the pregnancy until many years later. I was convinced my poor sister had a brain tumor and that my mother was consulting the best doctors and praying for a cure. When my mother finally talked Carmen into getting an abortion, and they were inside the clinic, my sister said no, she couldn't do it, she wanted to keep the baby."

Rosa tipped a bottle of Corona above her head, and I said, "So then they returned here, right?"

"They returned," she said, "but not together. My sister went to Mexico City a couple of months later, right at the end of her pregnancy, eight days before she gave birth. By the time my mother arrived in Mexico City, my sister had admitted herself to a hospital and gave birth to a baby boy who is now twenty-one years old." Then Rosa looked at me accusingly and said, "I thought we were going to dance." I listened for a moment to what the band was playing. It was a country bumpkin's two-step merengue. Anyone can dance a merengue, I told myself. Tell her yes. Then let her know this will be the first and last dance, and that we needed to think about leaving. "Yes," I said, "let's dance."

No sooner had I grabbed Rosa's hand and stood up than I knew I had made a mistake. Although I felt sober sitting down, standing up was a challenge, and dancing—in terms of embarrassment—could prove to be the equivalent of a public flogging. But Rosa was so bright-eyed and sober-looking that my male pride drove me into the crowd of dancers. At the center of the dance floor, where all correct dancing must begin, I managed to slide my right hand around Rosa's waist and interlace my left fingers with hers. But as I raised my left foot to begin the dance, I lost my balance. And we took what would have been a certain fall onto the concrete had our descent not been broken by a virtual Amazon of a woman and her pint-sized partner. Not only did they break our fall, they shoved us so hard in the opposite direction that Rosa and I found ourselves once again upright and on our feet.

"Not a very good beginning," Rosa said.

"Then why don't you lead?" I said. And she did, beginning with a sideways trot from one side of the dance floor to the other, our arms extended in front of us like a lance. Now the other dancers made room for us, and Rosa's movements grew bolder and more dramatic until I realized that Rosa was deaf to the merengue, *she* was dancing a tango.

Soon, however, a pattern emerged. Rosa had a propensity to dance in a slow circle around the periphery of the dance floor, and I molded myself to this, and we managed fewer collisions with other dancers. I felt as though I were on a carousel, and many of the faces in the audience would light up with laughter whenever Rosa and I rode by.

When the merengue ended, we returned to our seats, and Rosa put her lips so close to my ear that her lower lip brushed my earlobe as she spoke: "Are we going to make love tonight?" Under most circumstances, I would have married Rosa for the right to take her dress off. But no one had ever pursued me like this, and her pursuit distorted everything and made me so wary I stopped touching her. In part, my apprehension had to do with her beauty, and how it, rather than she, held sway over me that night. Women have never described me as handsome, not even those who claimed to have loved me. "You're attractive," they'd say and quickly change the subject. So, in me, Rosa's beauty inspired paranoia. She had to be after something, most likely a ticket north for her and her daughter that would bring them out of the desolation of the Isthmus and into the land of green lawns and late model cars. But how to answer her question? Saying yes would have been dishonest; I was past the age of one-night stands. On the other hand, saying no to sex might mean she'd have nothing more to do with me, and—if she wanted to be vindictive—she could turn Pablo against me as well. Although I am not proud of this, I answered her question as ambiguously as possible. "I don't know," I said. "Zángano," Rosa said in reply, meaning "jerk." She said this, however, with a smile.

Hours passed in this way. We would dance, and drink, and when I became bored, I would ask Rosa to tell stories from her past.

"Go on with the story about Carmen," I said.

"After my sister had her baby, our economic situation in Juchitán became difficult because my mother had shut down the restaurant. My mother traveled frequently, and when she was at home, she treated us poorly, and we were happy when she left. But I don't think she treated us bad for nothing; it was because she was sick with shame about my sister. This is something I've just come to understand now, as an adult."

"Did she ever hit you?" I asked.

"She beat me. She beat me on the back with a length of rubber hose, like the hose you use to water flowers. She said ugly things to me, and she was very foul-mouthed, but I know now that the shame was beating me, and not my mother. She didn't want the same thing to happen to me."

"Have you ever confronted her about these things?" I asked.

"No," she said. "I couldn't do that."

Then Rosa fell into gossiping with her friends, and when my boredom became unbearable, I mounted a campaign to convince her to leave, but she turned away from me whenever I brought up the subject. She babbled on with her friends, dancing with some and joking with others, while I sat watching the moon cross the sky. When I estimated it was three in the morning, I turned to Rosa and said:

"What time is it?"

"Three," she said. "You Americans don't know how to relax. Have another beer, and loosen up." For a while, I gave up on convincing Rosa to leave, and dozed in my seat. When I awoke, all but fifty of the wooden chairs were abandoned, some of which sat cockeyed in pockets of mud that had formed from spilt beer.

"What time is it?" I said.

"Three," Rosa said. "Have another beer."

Her stubborn insistence on staying angered me. But my irritation with her never lasted long because she seemed to always follow her irritating behavior with something kind or considerate. Now, out of the corner of my eye, I watched her improvise a bed out of a couple of empty chairs for a young girl who couldn't seem to fall asleep in the limited space of her mother's lap. Rosa stretched the girl's legs out over the chairs and covered her with a borrowed sweater. I was touched. Nonetheless, I stopped speaking to Rosa altogether, and for the next hour, the moon held my attention as it descended into the red blossoms of a Flamboyan tree.

"What time is it?" I asked one of Rosa's friends. "Rosa tells me it's three. But I know it's much later. What time do you have?"

"Three," she said. By now, Rosa's friends were in on the joke and they laughed and poked fun at me openly whenever I asked for the time.

For a while, I considered leaving on my own. I would shake Rosa's hand, kiss her cheek, as was the custom in the Isthmus, thank her, and walk away. But I reminded myself Rosa and Pablo were my only contacts in the Isthmus, and I again bit my tongue. Rosa must have sensed my anger, because a moment later she turned to me and spoke.

"We're leaving together, all of us."

Then the sky whitened at the horizon, and the brass band kicked in with a slow, plaintive tune. It wasn't a dirge, but more along the lines of a hymn, and for the first time that night, no one got up to dance. The lead trumpet player pointed his horn at the steel gate and walked in time with the hymn, so slowly he seemed not to move. Those of us remaining—who couldn't have numbered more than twenty or thirty—rose to our feet. Then the brass band had become a marching band, and at last, we formed a procession and followed. As we walked, the women held up votive candles and chanted in chorus, over and over, "Que Viva San Vicente."

On reaching the street, we didn't step onto the sidewalk. We marched at the rate of a crawl down the middle of the road, ignoring the long line of cars behind us that lit our way with their headlights. I waited for horns to sound, but they never did. The cars crept along with us, until they reached their turnoff, or they made a U-turn and disappeared in the distance. It was as though the drivers were affording us a special respect for having honored San Vicente in dance and song.

And when we came to a road that led to one of the marcher's homes, they drifted away from the caravan without the long, Latin goodbyes filled with smiles and kisses. Instead, they slowed their pace, dropped back toward the end of the caravan, and disappeared around the corner without a wave of the hand or a word from their mouths.

We followed this pattern when it came our turn to go, and drifted through the swinging glass doors of the Fortress. Inside the lobby, Rosa reminisced about the days when her mother managed the hotel. "The entrance is the same as when I lived here as a child. But where the lobby is now, there was a restaurant, and here, below the stairs, were rooms where the employees slept. On the other side of the lobby was an open corridor with an almond tree where my mother parked her car. This is also where she met my father."

I climbed the red tile stairs ahead of Rosa to my second-story room, hoping to make it clear that if she was coming with me, she was coming of her own accord. Outside my door, in a coy voice, she made an announcement.

"I've been watching you," she said, "ever since you took a room here."

"What do you mean?" I said. "My room is on the second floor. You couldn't see into my room from the mortuary if you had binoculars."

"You can from the second floor," she said. To prove her point, Rosa went on in detail about my movements in and around the hotel over the last three days. Her account was so accurate that it unnerved me; I could not get the key in the lock. "Last night," she said, "you were at the desk in your room writing, and—" I stopped listening. Then the key slid in and the lock clicked open. Inside, it was cold; I had forgotten to turn the air-conditioner off. But this did not stop Rosa from making herself at home. She got under the covers of my bed and turned the television on. She rummaged through the things on my bed stand and ate the apple I was saving in case I woke up hungry in the middle of the night. I crossed the room to the sliding glass doors that faced the street and pulled the curtains aside. Not fifty feet away, on the mortuary's second floor, was a picture window.

"Close those curtains," Rosa said.

Rosa's confession helped me understand her rush to bed down. In her mind, our relationship had begun when she started her watch three nights before. This gave her time to imagine a friendship, then a romance. Now she was ready to seal the relationship with sex, and in the reflection of the sliding glass window, I watched her peel off layers of clothing: necklaces and earrings and bracelets and high-heels and petticoats and slips and garters and stockings and bra and pantyhose. She got in bed and waited for me to follow suit. But the room was too cold to undress all at once. So I took off my shoes and socks, pitched them into a corner, and got in bed with her. She fumbled with the top button of my shirt and slid her warm tongue in my mouth.

"Our first kiss," she said.

Though I've given it much thought, I'm unsure why this phrase spurred me out of bed and onto the cold tile in my bare feet. I don't like soap operas and have never read a romance novel, so a distaste for the flowery must have played a part. About the truth of the phrase, I can't argue. It was our first kiss. Yet the implications were more than I could bear on an empty stomach and an emerging hangover. If this were the first kiss, I heard myself reason, there would surely be a second, and a third, and when there wasn't a fourth, how would she make me pay? Sex wasn't sex with any of the women I'd ever known. It was the beginning of a lifetime commitment.

"I can't do this," I said. "Not now." Her lips still parted from our kiss, Rosa stared at me for several seconds with the look of a starlet who's been spit at by her chauffer. But I stayed put, and let the chill from the tile rise and cool my blood. A moment later, when it became obvious that I wouldn't rejoin Rosa in bed, she clamped her mouth shut, biting down hard as if my tongue were inside and she was about to swallow. Then she spoke: "Walk me home."

I put on my shoes and socks, and Rosa got dressed. I followed her out of the room and down the stairs, past a sleeping desk clerk in the lobby and onto the sidewalk that was already reflecting the sun. When, for a moment, I regretted what I had said and extended an arm around her shoulder, she was quick to push it away. "Don't touch me," she said, "and don't tell my brother about any of this." In another minute, we had crossed the street, and Rosa had her key in hand. I began walking backward toward my hotel, keeping an eye on her until she was safe inside. I tried to memorize her profile, her figure, her movements, because this, I was convinced, would be the last I'd ever see of her.

The Apologist

When he was still a teenager, the insider who would be the first to rise and defend the reputation of Isthmus women stood with his horse at Juchitán's train station, weeping into its neck. His name was Andrés Henestrosa, and his mother, Tina Man, had been urging him to leave home for months. "Better yourself, go see the world, study, be somebody." And though Henestrosa had begun learning Spanish the year before, he followed orders, selling his beloved horse to pay for his train trip to Mexico City. When the deal was done, he was left with 30 pesos and two sets of clothes that he carried in a pillowcase. On his arrival in Mexico City, Henestrosa arranged a meeting with José Vasconcelos, then dean of Mexico's National University. Fearing Vasconcelos wouldn't understand his Spanish, Henestrosa brought a translator to the meeting. "I'm here on account of you," Henestrosa told Vasconcelos. "Because you said in the newspapers that when the revolution triumphed, there would be education for the poor, the orphaned and the Indians. I believed you, so I hope you don't turn out to be a liar." Vasconcelos kept his word and enrolled Henestrosa in the Escuela Normal de Profesores.

Eight years later, when Henestrosa was twenty-four and his Spanish had improved, he began his defense of Isthmus women with his essay "The Forms of Sexual Life in Juchitán." At the opening of the essay, Henestrosa lists the assertions made by what he terms foreigners, tourists, and superficial men. The two most important assertions are sexual promiscuity and free union, the latter referring to common-law marriage. With a tone of indignation, Henestrosa denies both: "There is no sexual looseness of any kind, nor can there be in a town that scrupulously follows ancestral custom." Given the kind of stories spread by Vasconcelos and followers, Henestrosa's indignation is understandable. Nonetheless, the position of "no sexual looseness" in Juchitán is as untenable as the claim of widespread free love. Here—as would happen with many who followed—Henestrosa had been drawn into the illogic of the controversy. Later in the essay, he fields other claims by foreigners more evenhandedly. He acknowledges nude bathing but explains convincingly that it does not stem from a lack of modesty. All Isthmus life obeys customs rooted in ancient tradition, he writes, and bathing naked in the river is one of those traditions. At the same time, another custom running just as deep dictates that a man should avoid passing by the river when a woman is bathing, but if he must pass by, he should never stay and watch.

Midway through the essay, Henestrosa describes the unusual custom of Isthmus matrimony called *rapto*, or rapture. The nonviolent form of *rapto* takes place when the groom asks for the woman's hand in marriage, but her parents deny it. If this is the case, and the woman is willing, they elope. The violent form of *rapto* occurs when the woman is not willing. In this case, Henestrosa writes, "the man may take her by force, literally 'dragging her away.'" As scandalous as this sounds, the many scandalmongers who visited the Isthmus during this period never reported *rapto* to the world.

To further convince us that the rules he outlines in the essay are followed scrupulously, Henestrosa tells us how they are enforced. Throughout the year, anyone who transgresses the rules faces public satire. But during the Christmas season, especially a day or two before the celebration of the birth of Christ, a pagan enforcement takes a bolder form when Isthmus men stand in front of the home of the transgressor. Rather than singing carols, the men speak at the top of their voices about the violator's sexual improprieties. "They finish by saying that the flower—the woman—which is the most pure, should know these things and so should the townspeople."

At the end of the essay, Henestrosa backpedals about the supposed sexual looseness: "I recognize that [in Juchitán] there may be a degree of moral or sexual perversion as is natural in all cities," he writes. Still, labeling the least egregious forms of sexuality as perversion sounds puritanical to the modern ear, and one must keep in mind that "The Forms of Sexual life in Juchitán" was written over seventy years ago. And though Henestrosa addresses the promiscuity charge at length, for the moment he is silent about matriarchy.

Lavada

Two days after the dance, Rosa surprised me with an invitation to a *lavada de ollas*. The *lavada* is an event hosted by the *mayordoma*. It celebrates the elderly women who cooked and served the food at a dance associated with one of the many velas that take place in May or December. The *mayordoma* makes sure the elderly matrons eat, drink, and dance until all traces of responsibility are gone. The *lavada de ollas* has the reputation as being the only occasion when Isthmus women could drink to the point of drunkenness. Many of the women, I was told, take advantage of the fact that their men are working, and so they drink what they will.

My immediate reaction to Rosa's invitation was that I had underestimated her. With this invitation, she was brushing off my rejection two nights before as though it had never happened. This made me admire her in a way that I can't fully explain. I agreed without hesitation, and at two in the afternoon I boarded a taxi with Rosa and her daughter Ana. Rosa wore a dark but flowery enagua and a huipil de cadenilla, and Ana, like most Isthmus girls, wore a school uniform: a pleated skirt and a white blouse stiff with starch.

The physical layout of the *lavada* was much the same as it was at the dance. Two hundred chairs surrounded a concrete dance floor with wooden poles at the four corners. Rather than supporting an overhead tarp as they had at the dance, the poles provided anchorage for wide swaths of white cotton that were decorated with gold moons in various phases ranging from full to crescent. Two bands, one brass, the other marimba, took turns playing on stages in opposite corners of the grounds. Both played Zapotec hymns and ballads, as well as merengues

and popular dance tunes. The same joking, dancing, and marathon eating and drinking I'd seen at the *baile* (dance) were in evidence everywhere. Now, however, they were exposed to the unforgiving light of the
midday Isthmus sun.

At the entrance to the *lavada*, I purchased a case of beer and carried
it inside on my shoulder. We seated ourselves with the same group of
women who attended the *baile* honoring San Vicente. Rosa sat to my
left, her daughter to my right. Rosa soon engaged the women around
her in conversation. Ana kept to herself. She was a somber, reserved
child who rarely laughed. Ana and I were two of a kind: both of us
shared the angst of separation. I was isolated by culture; Ana, by her
age. We grew bored quickly, and when I failed to draw Ana out with
conversation, I gave her my notebook. A house, a tree laden with mangos, and grass blown by wind soon appeared, and underneath the shade
of the mango tree were Ana and her mother, both with arms extended.
Ana's sketch contained what you might expect from any Isthmus eight-
year-old, except for a pair of telling details. Rosa hovered a good foot or
two above the grass; Ana had arms but no hands.

To pass the time, I walked around the periphery of the dance floor.
Halfway around, I spotted a man in huipil and enagua dancing with an
elderly matron. He was clearly a transvestite—called *muxe* in Zapotec—
and both he and his dance partner seemed to be enjoying themselves.
After Isthmus women, *muxe* are the subgroup of the Zapotec population to whom visiting anthropologists have paid closest attention, and
the news is good. Most anthropologists agree that *muxe* enjoy a level of
acceptance in Zapotec culture rarely seen in other parts of the Western
world.

"In effect we find the *muxe* playing prestigious and socially recognized roles as much in the family as in the public and community arenas," writes social anthropologist Marinella Miano Borruso. In Juchitán's political sphere, the *muxe* are particularly active and for decades
have aligned themselves with the conservative Partido Revolucionario
Institucional or PRI. This alliance began when Juchitán elected a PRI
gay mayor in the mid-1980s and has continued into the present. Some
in the gay community argue that *muxe*'s support of PRI has nothing to
do with their conservative political platform. Instead they attribute the
preference to PRI's open courting of the *muxe* vote with fiestas over-
flowing with beer.

When I returned from my walk, I asked Rosa to tell me what she knew about the *muxe*. "Here in Juchitán," Rosa said, "the *muxe* have a status more or less equal to our heterosexual men. This stems from their physical strength when compared to women. Now is a time when homosexuals are more visible than before, and you'll often see them on the streets in women's clothes. Some even wear huipiles and enaguas to the market to sell cheese or bread. At other times, especially in spring, you'll see a mother walking with her arm around her homosexual son or holding his hand on the way to a fiesta where she drops him off and then returns home."

According to Beverly Chiñas, Isthmus Zapotecs consider *muxe* children to be the brightest and most gifted of children. When a choice must be made about which child receives costly advanced education, most Zapotec families consider the child who is *muxe* as their best bet.

"They even have their own vela," Rosa said. "It's called Vela de las Intrépidas. A group of *muxe* organized the vela fifteen years ago, and it's been up and running ever since."

"If all of this is true," I said, "why haven't I ever come across a *muxe* on the street?"

"The *muxe* tend to live in our poorer wards such as the six, seventh, or eighth, and the people who live there feel very proud of this fact. The Isthmus mother tends to love her *muxe* son deeply because she knows that he will never marry and that he will always be there to help his mother in caring for her sons and daughters and even her husband." Then Rosa paused and said:

"Have any of them ever flirted with you?"

"I told you—that other than here—I've yet to even see a *muxe*," I said.

"No one on the street ever said, 'Adios, handsome?'"

"I'm going for another walk," I said. I handed her my camera, which she put inside her purse. She turned away from me and began a conversation with a woman seated behind her. The beer bottles under Rosa's seat were accumulating faster than they had at the *baile*, but I brushed this off as unimportant. She was an adult, and Ana's presence might make her act like one.

The wind had kicked up, and the swaths of cotton above the dance floor flapped violently in the dusty air. I bought a bottle of water from a blind man and approached the stage where a marimba band was playing. A man with a microphone approached me.

"We are here reporting live for Radio Equis. Can we ask you a couple of questions for our radio audience?" he said.

"What kind of questions?" I said. He didn't respond. He sized me up, and when he saw that I was sober, he handed me brandy in a plastic cup. I sat with him for a while and listened to the brass band that alternated with the group playing marimba music. The musicians—twenty-nine in all—wore uniforms with white shirts and blue collars. They played horribly out of tune, and before long, I felt the urge to leave the *lavada*.

When I returned to where Rosa and Ana were seated, Rosa patted my chair with the palm of her hand, indicating she wanted me to sit down.

"I'm going to leave now," I said. "You have a good time, and we'll see each other soon."

"No," she said. "Sit down." I saw a fight brewing, so I turned quickly and walked toward the entrance. My exit didn't seem to phase Rosa. She didn't follow me, and this was a relief. Once I'd passed through the gate, however, I looked back to see that Ana was running down the sidewalk in my direction, calling out at me to wait. When she caught up with me, I explained to her that my leaving had nothing to do with her. I walked her back inside the gate and said goodbye. Once again I turned in the direction of the Fortress and began walking away from the *lavada*. At the corner, a young Juchitecan balancing a basket on her head passed in front of a turquoise taqueria, the perfect subject against the perfect background. I instinctively reached for my camera and realized I'd left it with Rosa. I returned to the *lavada* and approached the group of women where Rosa was seated. A hefty man with cheeks like stuffed pork chops and the vacant look of a bouncer sat next to Rosa. When he saw me, he walked to the front of the group of women and stationed himself directly in my path.

"What's happening?" he said.

"I'm collecting my camera," I said. "Then I'm leaving." I tried to sidestep him, but he again put himself directly in front of me, his breath reeking of cheap tequila.

"What's the rush?" he said. Rosa was smiling, looking mildly entertained, and I wondered what she had told the bouncer. The women in my life, it seemed, were always one step ahead of me when it came to arguments. Rosa knew she had my camera. She knew that I wasn't going anywhere without it, and now she'd arranged this scene with the bouncer.

"Come and have a seat with us," the bouncer said.

"No, thanks," I said. "I want to leave." I walked a wide circle around the bouncer, and Ana, sweetheart that she is, fetched the camera out of her mother's open purse and handed it to me in one swift motion. Without thinking, I spoke to her in English: "God bless you."

Once again, I turned and left. I hadn't passed through the gate and taken six steps down the sidewalk when I heard Rosa's voice. "Tom," she shouted. It was the first time I'd ever heard her say my name. It startled me. I stopped and swung around. What happened next is not clear. I only know that when I roll the film of our scene on the sidewalk that afternoon, the volume is down. I see Rosa, her arms stiff at her sides, her fists clenched, her mouth open. One word—*ingrato*—is the only one that comes through. "Ungrateful," she shouts, over and over. Then, unexpectedly, she turns and leaves. When she rounded the corner, and I could no longer see her, I too turned and fled.

There was a time on my first trip to the Isthmus when every second Juchitecan I spoke with suggested I read a magazine called *Guchachi' Reza*. The title, which means "sliced iguana," is a light-hearted reference to an Isthmus delicacy that, like the magazine, is uniquely Zapotec. Founded by a group of Isthmus intellectuals with a decidedly leftist bent, *Guchachi' Reza* often includes articles on Zapotec history, ethnology, songs, and poetry. In spite of its humble origins, many in Juchitán consider *Guchachi' Reza* trendy and chic. The editors demonstrate their awareness of worldwide literary trends through translations of Brecht and Neruda into Zapotec. In 1983, PRI came to believe the magazine was subversive, and it burned down the only bookstore that offered *Guchachi' Reza* for sale.

Fortunately, they did not torch the copies at the local library, which I visited on the fourth day of my stay in Juchitán. The librarian, Gloria de la Cruz, was a small, nervous woman whose face assumed a look of righteousness when she saw me heading in her direction. I asked her if the library had back issues of *Guchachi' Reza*. "We do," she said, "but not all issues. Wait here, and I'll see what I can dig up."

Juchitán is one of the only cities in the region that has two libraries, one at the Casa de Cultura and the one in which I stood on Calle Hidalgo. The latter was opened in 1981 bearing the name of a university professor who had been "disappeared" by the Mexican military. It has an inventory of eleven thousand books, and unlike most libraries in Mexico, readers could borrow them three at a time for as long as a week.

When Gloria returned, she carried a small stack of recent issues of *Guchachi' Reza*. She handed me the magazines and agreed to answer a few questions. On the topic of matriarchy, Gloria recited the tourist myth, but she had ideas of her own about Isthmus men. "Nowadays, Isthmus men are very macho," she began. "They don't even enter the kitchen, they don't help out with the affairs of the household no matter what. In addition to selling, the Isthmus woman takes responsibility for everything else, including taking care of her children and cleaning."

"Are the women of Juchitán involved in politics?"

"Here, many women are in politics, especially during campaigns for mayor. This happens every three years. The women form committees, and their participation is enormous."

"Would you say women's participation is greater than men's or equal?"

"Equal. Or at least it should be, because the women work very hard."

"But isn't that the same as in other parts of Mexico?"

"No, no, no. Here women participate much more. It's the woman who marches in front during demonstrations and campaigns."

"In other parts of Mexico, men are known to flirt with women passing by on the street. Do they do that here?"

"Very little. No, the only thing that Isthmus men can say to our women—and more than anything to the young women—is 'Bye-bye, precious' or 'See you later, beautiful' or 'Farewell, handsome'—but in Zapotec, of course."

"Nothing vulgar?" I said.

"Nothing vulgar," she said. Then her face stiffened, as if to warn me that if I had any thoughts about a word-by-word review of vulgar phrases, I'd be in deep trouble. She stood up, and I knew our encounter was over.

I paged through the pile of magazines until I came across a cover photo that held my attention. It was a wartime photo, easily eighty or ninety years old, that might have been taken in the Mexican Revolution. In the background of the photo, a troop of soldiers stands at attention, shoulders thrown back and chests puffed up, rifles held in front of them, pointed skyward at a forty-five-degree angle to their torsos. Seated in front of the soldiers are two women. Both are barefoot and dressed in polka dot blouses that must have been in fashion at the time. Both wear full-length skirts, one flowered, the other plain, and both skirts are hemmed with ten inches of fancy lace. What makes the photo special was this: In the women's laps—where babies should have been—are Winchester rifles and cartridge belts.

And lest you think the rifles were there for decorative purposes, know that the women clutched the wooden bodies of these weapons with a familiarity that suggested that the Winchesters *were* their babies. The woman on the left, with a murderous look, fingers the trigger of her rifle and glares in the direction of the camera. The woman on the right has a colder but no less dangerous look on her face. What was it about this photo that made me feel I had made an important discovery? Although the identity of the women would remain a mystery for years, the photo showed that the stories about the bravery of Isthmus women who fought and died alongside their men was in all likelihood true, and that Isthmus women had assumed the role of women warriors long before other civilized societies. And though the photo did not resolve the matriarchy question, it convinced me that Isthmus women were *special*. They were women worth knowing and writing about, matriarchy or not, and I was pleased to have made this discovery.

When, in addition to the cover photo, I had found several articles I wanted to take with me, I asked Gloria if I could make photocopies. The library had no photocopy machine, she said, and she looked at me skeptically, asking herself if I could be trusted to leave the premises with a copy of *Guchachi' Reza*. Her face said no, and she looked around the library for someone she trusted until her eyes lit on a girl with a demeanor as sour as Gloria's though she was only eight or nine years old. "Angelica," Gloria said to the girl. "Would you go with this man to make photocopies?" Gloria showed Angelica what I wanted copied. We left the library and walked east on Calle Hidalgo toward the marketplace. The photocopier's, it turned out, was closed. Angelica suggested another shop around the corner. It was crowded. We waited fifteen minutes, made the copies, and left. We were halfway back to the library when I realized I had left the magazine in the photocopy machine. We walked back and collected it.

When we were approaching the library, I realized that what should have taken five minutes took twenty-five. Gloria stood in the street in front of the library, her arms folded over her chest. A man who looked like a security guard with white hair and liver spots and black horn rim glasses stood behind her, also looking in our direction. Their faces were strained and worried.

"You've been thinking malicious thoughts about me, haven't you?" I said.

"No," Gloria said. "Not at all." I thanked her for her time and walked back to the Fortress with my prize.

I next saw Rosa on the weekend. She had organized a trip with three of her friends to Playa Cangrejos, a beach that lay half an hour north of Juchitán. Juan and Maria, a married couple who drove a late model SUV, left fifteen minutes ahead of us with Ana. Lucia, Rosa, and I followed in Lucia's rusty Toyota sedan.

Twenty minutes into the trip, we left the paved highway and drove west along a sandy road lined on either side by dense jungle that vaulted forty feet into the air. We rounded a bend and were passing through a tiny pueblo when a teenager in blue jeans and a yellow T-shirt darted into the road and stopped directly in front of us. Lucia punched the brakes, and we skidded to a halt no more than ten feet away from where he stood, his face blank as cement. Then he reached for the zipper on the front of his Levis, pulled it down, and exposed himself. Lucia screamed and bent her fingers backward in a display of revulsion. Rosa laughed and covered her eyes with a towel. I thought: What would the flasher's family say on finding him with tire tracks across his face and his penis in his hand? Then he turned and ran. The last I saw of him was a glimpse of the white and rubbery soles of his tennis shoes as he sprinted into the surrounding jungle. Rosa expressed shock, but Lucia knew better. "I know you, Rosa," she said. "And I saw you. You only covered one of your eyes." Lucia mimicked Rosa, putting the towel over her left eye. To demonstrate how little the towel impaired her vision, Lucia put the car in gear and drove away. Rosa only laughed, but Lucia's insight was valuable to me. It let me know that I had not exaggerated Rosa's love of the bawdy. The way in which Rosa and Lucia reacted to our flasher also had an effect on me. In the States, at least in California, Lucia would have been in tears, and Rosa would have collapsed, but not before delivering a lengthy diatribe on male sexuality in which the word *perpetrator* would have figured greatly. The more I spent time with Isthmus women, the more I found that they bore no grudge against men—even when we were at our worst. In everything, it seemed, they found humor.

We arrived at the beach well before noon. Lucia pulled into a parking lot behind a row of restaurants that lined the beach. Each of the restaurants had a single adobe hut that served as a kitchen and a thatched roof that shaded several tables and chairs and a couple of hammocks. Juan and Maria joined us from the other end of the parking lot, and we followed Rosa into Enramadas, her favorite restaurant. We were waiting to be seated when from behind us, a television blared the voice of a long-winded sportscaster screaming, "Gooaaalll." We turned round in unison. In the adjacent restaurant, twelve men dressed in military khakis and closely-cropped hair sat huddled around a television, engrossed in a game of soccer. This was a breakthrough. Since my arrival in Juchitán a week prior, I had visited cantinas, farms, tourist agencies, parties, cemeteries, libraries, restaurants, and churches, but I had never been in a situation in which the men outnumbered the women. As a male, I would have preferred that the force that brought the men together that day had been something loftier, say a passion for art or philosophy, but this was not the case.

The popularity of a career in the Mexican military accounted in part for the absence of Isthmus men, but a much greater force was men's emigration northward in search of better wages. Unskilled farm workers in the Isthmus earn anywhere from $3 to $4.50 per day. In spring and fall, when competition for laborers is highest, the price is driven up to a meager $10 per day. The situation is not much better for skilled workers. Entry-level railway workers—even when they belong to a union—earn little more than $7 a day. Compare this with the wages in the United States, where unskilled laborers earn between $6 and $10 per hour in cash, and you will understand the strength of the force that drives men northward.

The same force exists at the professional level. It is more difficult to compare salaries here, but the loss at any socioeconomic level is always felt by Isthmus women. "This emigration pattern," writes anthropologist Beverly Chiñas, "of long duration, has serious consequences not only for the marriageable girls left behind but also for the pueblo as a whole since the more ambitious, enterprising, better educated, and perhaps more intelligent young men of each generation, who might otherwise have made the greatest contributions to their home and community, are forced by economic circumstances to leave."

Some take jobs in Mexico City, others in U.S. cities where there are substantial Zapotec communities. Once they are established with work and dwelling, the men begin sending home a portion of their earnings, usually on a weekly basis. On Friday evening across the southwest you can see these men crowding Western Union offices to wire a portion of their earnings home. Taken together, the money they send is one of Mexico's largest sources of foreign income—second only to tourism.

Many Isthmus men travel to the central valleys in California seeking farm labor. "Sixty to seventy percent of farm workers in California's San Joaquin Valley are Zapotecs from Oaxaca who send money across the border to their homes," writes Pam Burke. "In September 1994, the Zapotecs from Oaxaca and the Mixtecs joined forces to represent their peoples in California as well as in Mexico. This organization is called the Bi-national Indigenous Front of Oaxaca. They call for better migrant workers' rights, sustainable economic development; construction of infrastructure, and respect and preservation of indigenous culture and tradition. This organization links the Zapotecs of Oaxaca to those in California."

We seated ourselves in white lounge chairs that surrounded an old wooden table whose brick red paint was peeling off in strips. We studied the menu and spent a half hour negotiating over what we would eat before we ordered. A squat woman in a red and white checked apron took our orders. When Rosa and I ordered fish, the waitress asked us to pick which fish we wanted from a red cooler that stood in a corner. Inside were a couple of red snappers, along with shrimp, and some sleek silver fish I'd never seen before that lay like medieval swords packed with ice.

When I looked over my shoulder in the direction of the soldiers, they had gone, and the television screen was blank. The silence was short lived. Someone in the kitchen turned on a radio that blared a current hit with a bizarre refrain: "Qué sabe de colesterol?" (What do you know about cholesterol?) Then the food came, and it came in quantity. Shellfish and shrimp and red snapper arrived on white platters served with tortillas. As we ate, Rosa stood at her place and satirized the upper-class Mexican teenager. This was a time when any children whose parents had money invested in braces for their children whether they needed them or not. Rosa's sole prop was a band of tinfoil she wore over her front teeth like braces, and she had only to open her mouth and criticize our table manners, and we knocked our beers over and cried with laughter. Yes, she was funny, and some part of me envied her. At the same time, however, something about her repelled me, which I tried to piece together as I watched her perform for her friends. Soon, I reasoned, she would be a woman too hard, too tough for any one man to put up with. Too willful. Her voice would lower another octave and grate against the nerves from constant smoking and talking, and there would always be a drink close by.

I felt my mood change as the meal progressed. The eating and drinking made me sleepy, and it was hard for me to follow Rosa's jokes and double entendres. I would laugh, but never in rhythm with the rest of the group, who eyed me surreptitiously as they kicked their heads back and roared. And, as is often the case in Latino culture, everyone seemed to talk at the same time.

I walked to the restaurant where we had seen the soldiers. In the back of the adobe hut that housed the kitchen was a transport vehicle, an army-green Hummer. The soldiers were camped out behind the kitchen where a six-foot hedge served as a clothesline that held their freshly washed uniforms. I turned away from them and hunted up a hammock where I could lie quietly and write. Before my pen touched paper, however, Rosa was at my side, her breath reeking of beer. "If I'm too much for you," she said, "say the word, and I'll disappear." From the worried look on her face, it was apparent that she took my separation from the group as a rebuke. "It's not like that," I said. "I'm a northerner, and northerners need time alone." This reassured her. She smiled and left.

One other event worth mentioning marked this trip to the beach. When I returned to our restaurant, Lucia explained that the others had taken a walk to swim in a nearby sweet-water lagoon. Lucia suggested a walk along the shore. When we set out, the sun was directly overhead. It had bleached the sand linen-white, and in the distance, a blue triangle of the ocean touched a mountain that came down to the sea. The beach was deserted, Lucia explained, because most everyone feared wading into the three- to five-foot waves, which in my mind were small. On our way back to the restaurant, Lucia searched for a certain kind of stone that was common on Mexican beaches. "If you press the stone into the eyes of someone suffering from cataracts, it will cure them." Being with Lucia brought insight. I found her easy to be with and her conversation enjoyable. She was observant, kind, a fellow traveler in a mysterious universe, and I felt that given the opportunity, I would gladly strike up a relationship with her. Rosa's constant sarcasm and soap opera monologs reminded me all too much of my father.

Shortly before sunset, we collected our things and headed for the parking lot. Lucia bought a whole coconut with a straw protruding from it. She drank from it, passed it around to others in our party, who drew on the long paper straw, but the coconut seemed bottomless. "Where did all that water come from?" I said. "I was thinking exactly the same thing," said Lucia. Rosa stared at her. She could sense my interest. Juan drove his SUV alone to Juchitán. Maria, his wife, drove Lucia's car with Ana in the passenger seat beside her. Lucia, Rosa, and I rode in the back seat. As we drove along the sandy road, herds of goats made way for us under mango trees.

When the conversation died, Lucia fell asleep. I too leaned back in the seat, resting my head against the window, wishing I would doze off, if only for a couple of minutes. I gave up after a time and without moving my head, I opened my eyes to find Rosa staring intently into Lucia's mouth, her face so close to Lucia's I was surprised her friend didn't wake. Rosa seemed to be examining Lucia's teeth as if she were a dentist and Lucia the patient. She sniffed Lucia's breath, lightly but audibly. She raked her eyes over Lucia's breasts, her incipient potbelly, and squinted as she examined the inside of Lucia's ears. She went on in this way on until she reached Lucia's feet. One of Lucia's sandals had fallen off, and Rosa explored her toenails. Throughout the exam, Rosa smiled.

Later, when Lucia woke, she talked of love. "If you were given your choice of a woman from any country in the world," Lucia asked me, "from what country would you choose?" I told her I had never been with an Asian woman and that I found their seriousness stimulating. Lucia laughed; the usually jovial Rosa did not. I soon regretted what I had said. In the space of minutes, Rosa's mood was no longer bubbly. In fact, I believe that I had seen the real Rosa for the last time at Playa de Cangrejos. After that, she gave up on the idea that I might fall for the freewheeling Rosa, the lover of vulgarity, low satire, and booze.

As much as I enjoyed my time in Juchitán, there came a point at which the urge to leave became overwhelming. The simplest transaction, buying a pen or a loaf of bread, stretched into an ordeal that seemed to last hours. In the Fortress restaurant, for example, I would attempt to pay the waiter with the equivalent of a $10 bill. On seeing the $10 note, he would let out a little groan and say:

"No traes cambio?" (Don't you have something smaller?)

"No," I say, and then, jokingly, "so I guess the meal was on you."

Then we would argue, and finally he would come up with the change—but only after a long delay. Sometimes he would have to go to the travel agency across the street, or to another restaurant a block away. Of course, there is no written law about who is responsible for bringing change to a transaction, it's only a matter of tradition. But I was too old to shake myself of the anger that rose within me every time someone would ask "No traes cambio?"

The music playing in the hotel restaurant had also begun to irritate me. Every morning for a week I ate breakfast to a techno-pop number with this refrain:

> Boom Boom Boom,
> Let's go back to my room.

At lunch, I ate chicken enchiladas to a Musak version of "I Did It My Way." The music might have been bearable had not the service at the restaurant deteriorated so profoundly. Despite 15 percent tips, the waiters seemed to ignore me, and I began serving myself coffee refills from the bar rather than asking a waiter. I am sure that they found me as annoying as I found them, and they must have laughed at me behind my back.

But the worst of the annoyances were the phone calls. In my room, when I would lie down and try to recover from the heat, the phone would ring and a man with a deep voice would say, "Te la mamo?"

(Shall I suck it for you?) I would hang up, but several hours later he would call again and repeat the same tired phrase.

And so it was that I began to make arrangements to take a two-day train ride, which I always find therapeutic, across the Isthmus and back. Because trains have a reputation for eating journals, one of the first things I did to prepare for the trip was to make a photocopy of what I'd written so far. I then considered what luggage to bring. The trip would take two days; there was no sense in bringing my suitcase along when I could carry everything I needed in my backpack. The only problem I faced was where to leave my suitcase. I didn't trust the Fortress staff, so I called Rosa, and she agreed to take charge of it for the time I was away. In return for this favor, I invited her to eat at the restaurant of her choice.

At six, Rosa called from the lobby. My room was chaotic with clothes and equipment and half-eaten apples, so I performed triage, grabbing an armful of clothes that were strewn across the bed and dumping them in the closet. In putting up this false front, it occurred to me that some part of me cared for Rosa more than I would admit. Once the chaos in my room was under control, I opened the door. Rosa had just reached the top of the stairs wearing a baby-blue summer dress and black heels, and she was as beautiful as I'd ever seen her. She strode past me and into the room, knowing full well the extent of her beauty and the effect it was bound to have on me. I sat on the bed and watched her pace. "Have you ever eaten at Viandas?" she said. I hadn't. She described the restaurant, and as she spoke, she neared the bed and sat down. I smelled her breath. She hadn't been drinking. She looked at my feet and said, "You don't use socks, do you?" Then she was sitting beside me, lifting my pant legs.

"Who asked you to look at my ankles?" I said. My comment did not discourage her. She moved closer so that our thighs touched. She began massaging the muscles between my shoulder blades, moving closer as we spoke, and then she was kissing the side of my neck. I was aroused.

"Have you ever had an orgasm?" I said.

"No," she said. "Maybe once, but how would I know?"

"You'd know," I said. "Trust me, you'd know."

I got up, collected my wallet and hotel key, and turned toward the door.

"What's wrong?" Rosa said.

"Nothing's wrong," I said. "But I should tell you something. I've been faithful to the same woman for seven years. For me, this is an accomplishment. I can't throw that away without a little forethought." We were silent for a moment, and then I said, "Are we going?"

She didn't answer, but got up and followed me out the door. At the foot of the stairs, I noticed that she was clutching my journal to her breasts.

"What are you doing with my notebook?" I said.

"I'm using it as a prop," Rosa said. "I don't want the receptionist to think I'm chasing you, or that anything unprofessional is going on in your room. If she sees me with your notebook, she'll think I'm working with you."

"I doubt it," I said.

Viandas was a disappointment. It had a pretentiousness to it that didn't belong in honest, function-over-form Juchitán. The wooden ceiling was rustic and the knick-knacks antique: black and white portraits of Zapotec families in Victorian suits and ruffles, antique coffee grinders, and terra-cotta toy dolls painted red and white and blue. Rosa was quiet, serious, the opposite of what she was at Cangrejos, where she joked nonstop all afternoon. We ordered pizza. Rosa blessed herself when it arrived, something she did often, whenever we passed a church and at times when a statue of San Vicente or the Virgin was carted by in a procession. I asked Rosa to write words of the Zapotec anthem "Llorona" in my journal. "No," she said, "I can't stand doing two things at once. Eat your pizza." And then, "That's what's wrong with you Americans. You're forever doing too many things at once."

We talked about relationships. About Pablo and his first wife. I told her that I dreamed often of my first girlfriend though I hadn't seen her in twenty years. I asked about her previous boyfriend.

"He's a pilot in the Mexican Air Force," Rosa said.

"When did you break up?"

"We haven't broken up."

"Why haven't you mentioned him before?"

"I don't know," she said. "Maybe it's over, maybe not. I only know that he hasn't returned any of my calls for a week. We used to talk three times a day, but now he's grown silent."

"What's he like?"

"He's thirty, five years younger than I am. He treats Ana well and has always said that he wants to marry and spend the rest of his life with me."

"So what's the problem?" I said.

"I don't know," she said. This was hard to believe.

"One good thing about him," Rosa said. "He likes me as I am." I tried to think of something helpful to say. "You might try *not* calling him for a couple of days," I suggested. The role of counselor suited me. I felt comfortable in Rosa's presence for the first time in a week. I patted her hands, assuring her that the pilot's disappearance was probably just a break that he needed.

"Men are like that," I said.

"I still love him, but I'm afraid he'll leave me when he has his midlife crisis. It would be much more prudent to marry a man who is over forty, who's already past his difficult years. I don't want to go through another divorce. When he is forty, I'll be forty-five. Who in their right mind would want a twice-divorced forty-year-old with a child?" Rosa knew I had passed the forty-year mark, and her comments were directed to me. I again assured her that given enough time, the pilot would once again come around.

It was dark outside when we returned to the mortuary, and the walk was up and down. Every house in Juchitán has its own opinion about what height a sidewalk should be, and often the opinions varied by feet rather than inches. We labored in the heat toward Calle Hidalgo, and Rosa paused every now and then to pad the sweat off her forehead with her red *paliacate*. When we passed a fence with metal bars that stretched half a block, Rosa told how she used to drag a coin across the bars every morning on her way to school and how the music she made stayed with her throughout the day. This memory made her think of Ana, and she told a story with a certain amount of pride in her voice. "When I came home after giving birth, I was determined not to have to get up in the middle of the night to feed Ana. So I didn't. She made a hell of a racket for the first two weeks, but after that, she learned that last call for milk was eleven. She never woke me up after that." I remembered Ana's self-portrait without hands, and how I never heard her laugh, and I wondered which was worse, the occasional beating with a rubber hose or the sense of abandonment in a child's first weeks of life.

At the mortuary, Rosa waited in the lobby while I went to the hotel to collect my suitcase. The Fortress restaurant was devoid of waiters, and I climbed the stairs to my room without passing anyone along the way. I tucked the photocopy of my journal inside the suitcase for safe-keeping, snapped it shut, and lugged it across the street. In the mortuary lobby, I found Rosa staring through the display window at the traffic passing by. "Maybe you want to move on because you're tired of me," she said. I said nothing, but it was true, I needed a little distance. The story about Ana made me wonder whether any kind of emotional relationship with Rosa would be healthy, and the hypocrisy of her new, ultra-serious personality had worn me out. I also needed a fresh perspective. Much of what I experienced in the Isthmus was colored with Rosa or Pablo's way of thinking. I needed to hear the voices of other women, other men.

After saying goodbye to Rosa, I returned to my room. I stuffed clothes and toiletries into my backpack and thought about the possibility of moving on to Tehuantepec rather than returning to Juchitán. Both Rosa and Pablo had bad-mouthed Tehuantepec, but this was to be expected. Juchitán and Tehuantepec had a fierce rivalry that dated back to the previous century. The rivalry began in 1862 when Napoleon III sent French troops to collect on a debt that Mexico had suspended. The French formed an alliance with Mexican conservatives and occupied the Isthmus. Both Tehuantepec and Juchitán remained loyal to Mexico—until a captain stationed in Tehuantepec shifted his support to the French-conservative alliance. When the Juchitecos learned of the captain's betrayal, they stormed Tehuantepec but were defeated, and half their troops were slaughtered. Four years later, led by the same conservative captain, Tehuantepec attacked Juchitán. After a bloody battle in which both Juchitán's men and women took part, Tehuantepec and the conservative alliance were defeated. The Juchitecans took full revenge for the slaughter in 1862. For five days, they burned and looted Tehuantepec, and the ugly rivalry was born.

Although there has been no bloodshed between the two towns since these initial battles, not only did the rivalry remain, but it spread. Juchitán and Tehuantepec competed over who sponsored the greatest number of festivals, and who could throw the most lavish velas. "Tehuantepec doesn't have festivals like we have here in Juchitán," Pablo told me earlier in the week. "All of May is dedicated to festivals in Juchitán. In Tehuantepec, they celebrate just one vela in the whole month." Outside observers such as Helen Augur noted the spread of the rivalry even further. "There is great bickering between the towns about good looks, hairstyles, and clothes. In any rivalry of manners the Tehuanas are clear losers; their market women are often strident, bawdy, and deliberately rude." But the more I heard Tehuantepec bashed, the more I wanted to go there. By the time I was finished packing I was sure. On the return trip I'd get off in Tehuantepec rather than Juchitán. If all went well, I would be in Tehuantepec in two day's time.

The Russian

At the same time insider Andrés Henestrosa was writing his defense of Isthmus women, the father of Russian film and director of *Potemkin* was traveling south to Tehuantepec. Once there, he would film Isthmus women for one segment of his documentary *Que Viva Mexico*. Since his childhood at the beginning of the twentieth century, Sergei Eisenstein had fallen in love with the images of Mexico presented in the Russian circus with clowns and sets borrowed from the opera *Carmen*. In 1920, his fascination with Mexico led him to begin his creative career by designing sets and creating costumes for a theatrical version of Jack London's *The Mexican*. Several years later, Eisenstein's interest in Mexico was rekindled by the silent film *The Mark of Zorro,* which he described as "stirring and incomprehensible." But it wasn't until 1926, when Rivera met Eisenstein in Moscow and spoke excitedly to him about a matriarchal paradise, that Eisenstein began investigating the logistics of a film set in Mexico.

In 1930, the Soviets approved Eisenstein's request to visit the United States, where they hoped he could learn about the new techniques of making movies with sound. He spoke at several Ivy League schools before moving on to Hollywood, where he hoped to make a film for Paramount. When this failed, Eisenstein turned to socialist writer Upton Sinclair for help in realizing his dream of a film on Mexico. Eisenstein, along with a vast number of Soviet moviegoers, was enchanted by the movie version of Sinclair's novel *The Jungle*. In like manner, Sinclair had been profoundly moved by Eisenstein's *Potemkin*. Due to this mutual admiration the two began exchanging letters. In November 1930, they agreed to collaborate on a film set in Mexico that would include an episode on the Isthmus. Sinclair's brother-in-law, Hunter Kimbrough, would accompany Eisenstein to Mexico as business manager.

Eisenstein's outline for the Isthmus segment suggests how deeply he was taken with the idea of a matriarchy in Tehuantepec: "The moist, muddy, sleepy tropics. And the dreamy eyelids of girls. Of girls. Of future mothers. Of the fore-mother. Like the queen-bee, the mother rules in Tehuantepec. The female tribal system had been miraculously preserved here for hundreds of years till our time."

On arriving in Tehuantepec, Eisenstein and his film crew had experiences with the Tehuanos that did little to broaden this narrow image of Isthmus women. In a letter to Sinclair, Kimbrough described the difficulties convincing the Istmeñas to pose before the camera. "[They] were not sure whether it is modest or not. A couple of pesos apiece helped them decide that it is proper." A problem with men also cropped up. They became convinced that the filmmaker's cameras enabled them to look through the women's clothes. That night a festival was to take place in San Blas, a small town adjacent to Tehuantepec with a reputation for rebelliousness. Escorted by police, the mayors of Tehuantepec and San Blas accompanied Eisenstein to the festivities to shoot film. The mayors attempted to assure those at the fiesta that Eisenstein and company were in fact making a film with an episode devoted to the Isthmus. "But the police and both [mayors] got drunk," Kimbrough wrote, "and the people who were already drunk, would pay no attention to them." In the long run, only the elderly Tehuanas consented to pose at two pesos per photo.

In all, Eisenstein spent over a year in Mexico, but never completed *Que Viva México*. Not until 1979, when one of Eisenstein's assistants edited the raw footage and gave it a sound track, was the film released. The episode that focuses on the Isthmus is a love story that portends to teach us about a more primitive but better form of courtship and marriage. At the opening of the story, Istmeños Concepción and Abundio are already boyfriend and girlfriend. Concepción is a fruit vendor in Tehuantepec's market; Abundio doesn't seem to have any particular profession other than lying about in a variety of hammocks. Almost immediately, you know you are being fed one of the oldest clichés about the Isthmus: the men are lazy louts, and the women, through their industriousness, run the show.

The second major fabrication concerns the film's repeated suggestion that women of the Isthmus buy their husbands with gold necklaces. In the film, Concepción has such a necklace, but lacks one last coin that would complete the agreed upon dowry. "Concepción needs one more gold coin—just one—for her dream to be realized," the narrator says. As the film proceeds, Concepción is shown laboring under a tree selling fruit to make the additional amount of money needed to buy the last coin. Once Concepción has the required number of coins, the camera turns to a full-face shot of Abundio at an Isthmus dance sitting next to Concepción. He is smiling and licking his lips uncontrollably and his hair is falling into his eyes. Then Concepción has a moment of lucidity and questions her resolve to marry Abundio. "Isn't this what you wanted, Concepción?" the narrator says. "What you dreamed of for so long?"

The scene shifts to Abundio's patio, where he is asleep in a hammock, this time lying face down with his feet wiggling in front of the camera. Abundio's mother haggles with two elderly women seated on the ground cross-legged. "The matter passes into the hands of the mothers and matchmakers," the narrator says. This scene has an element of truth to it. According to Isthmus tradition, once the bride and groom's families give their assent to a marriage, a delegation is sent by the groom to the bride's mother to negotiate the terms of the marriage: who will pay for what, when the civil marriage and church weddings will take place. Isthmus matchmakers, however, are a rarity.

Come the wedding night, we see Abundio unfasten the necklace of gold coins and pour it from hand to hand much like a tropical version of Dickens's scrooge. Then the bride begins to undress, and the next thing we know, Abundio's mother is on the balcony announcing to the world that Concepción was in fact a virgin, and that all had gone well. In the final scene, Abundio is again sleeping in a hammock, this time on a strip of sandy beach. Concepción approaches with their child in her arms, wakes Abundio, and all three face the camera and smile.

Quintessential Isthmus Women

Juana Cata Romero—the young beauty Bourbourg discovered playing pool in the barracks outside Tehuantepec—rose far from selling candy to soldiers to become a role model of excellence for Isthmus women. She began her flight from poverty and anonymity by becoming fast friend and ally of one of the pool-playing soldiers, Lieutenant Colonel Porfirio Díaz. A Mixtec Indian charged with protecting Tehuantepec from conservative plots and rebellions, Díaz often camped on the banks of the Tehuantepec River, waiting for a chance to cross the shallow water and open fire on the enemy. Juana Cata proved her loyalty to Díaz when she lit fires on the opposite bank to indicate an opportune time to attack. When the ploy succeeded, Díaz made Juana Cata head of his intelligence service, and they began an affair that would last four decades, even though both would later marry other partners. In a show of love, Díaz ordered that the trans-Isthmus railway be built so that it stopped within steps of the front her house. "When my grandfather visited her,"—Lila, Porfirio's granddaughter, said—"the engineer reduced his speed and whistled a signal; Juana Cata would half open her door and without the train even stopping, Porfirio would jump out as soon as the first step . . . came even with the running board."

In her middle years, Juana Cata became the leading figure of the region both socially and economically. Her business sense was impeccable; she owned sugar and coconut plantations that stretched across the Isthmus and a variety of the best-stocked stores in town. She purchased a state-of-the-art sugar mill from Germany and used it to produce prize-winning sugar that drew attention to the Isthmus at the World's Fair in 1904. In terms of administration, Juana Cata proved herself to be a hands-on manager; she visited her holdings personally with a pistol packed into her belt. Some say that Juana built her wealth through her alliance with Porfirio Díaz, who in 1876, when Cata was forty-five, became president of the country. Others suggest it was her association with Isthmus warlord Remígio Torres, who she met after her first acquaintance with Díaz.

Socially, Juana Cata needed no alliances, but she did have to face up to the fact that at thirty, she was illiterate. She learned to read, and the first book she attacked was a manual of etiquette that she soon put to good use. She hosted her own vela, called Vela Bini, that she celebrated under a canvas canopy supported by wooden columns in gold and white and lit with crystal chandeliers. The women flocked to the vela in lace and gold fringe; the men in black suits and stiff white collars. According to Miguel Covarrubias, "Juana Cata gave out little *carnets* with pencils attached for the guests to write beforehand the partners with whom they would dance polkas, waltzes, and lancers. A great supper was served, with rows of roast turkeys, platters of cold cuts, and rivers of imported wine."

Not all that Juana Cata did was noble. A pious Catholic, she insisted that her servants and field workers and all her other hirelings attend mass and take communion every Sunday. She was also known to exploit her contact with Díaz—who murdered and cheated his way into the presidency—to obtain special pardons for her friends. To those who knew her, she was a calm but determined political boss who could depose chieftains and strip warlords of their power.

Juana Cata was in her sixties when she began her career as a philanthropist. Tehuanos prefixed her name with *Doña*—a sign of respect not everyone is afforded—and Juana Cata became Doña Cata. Her first act of charity was the rebuilding of Tehuantepec's cathedral. Next, she instituted a college for women run by Teresian nuns, and then a Marist college for young men. In her last days, she remodeled the cemetery, and for herself, she constructed a large chapel located in the cemetery's center. She also reconstructed the Convento de Santo Domingo, which the last Zapotec king had erected himself. "After that reconstruction," wrote Enrique Krauze, "she was venerated as a saint by the people of

Tehuantepec." Doña Cata and Porfirio Díaz died in same year, 1915, when Doña Cata was eighty-four. The entire town came to her burial, which was carried out with great ceremony in the chapel Doña Cata had built for herself. Porfirio Díaz's life ended in Peru, deposed from power, far from Juana Cata, whose name he cried out while dying.

On my arrival in Tehuantepec, I walked along the railway tracks until I came to Doña Cata's house, which at the time it was constructed was the only two-story building in town. Built to resemble a French chalet, Doña Cata's mansion both dwarfs and stands out against the eighteen-century Spanish style architecture that surrounds it. Because of this, some refer to it as an eyesore, asserting that Doña Cata built it only to establish her superiority over the rest of the townspeople. Although no evidence seems to support the claim, this much is true: at first glance, Doña Cata's white mansion gives the impression of a presidential palace, with north and west wings that ramble down the block off a circular entryway. Still, like everything else in Tehuantepec, closer inspection revealed decay. The once white eaves are blackened with soot, and the blue awnings that unfolded like tongues from every window drooped with age. Even the wrought iron gate, loose on its hinges, had worn grooves into the cement below it.

When I turned away from the mansion to leave, a small crowd of women were watching me.

"Whose house is this?" I asked.

"Long ago," one said, "it was Doña Cata's."

"And who was Doña Cata?"

"A woman," one said, "and a leader."

When the women turned away from me, I walked to the main plaza, one block away, where the city of Tehuantepec had erected a controversial bronze statue of Doña Cata. The statue depicted a stern, conservatively dressed woman who looks as though she is about to quote a passage from an open book she holds in one hand. Many claim the statue is a misrepresentation. Helen Augur, in her book *Zapotec,* is one: "The inscription on the bust praises Doña Juana for the works of charity that marked her old age, and the brassy portrait makes her look like a severely pious sodality sister. That is well enough for public purposes, but the Tehuanas cherish her as their secret ideal, a woman who used her beauty to amass great riches which she administered shrewdly, a Tehuana always fiercely loyal to her town." Seated on benches on either side of the statue was a small group of elderly men, some bald, others with cowboy hats, who seemed to be drifting toward sleep. Without introducing myself, I said:

"So how is life in Tehuantepec?"

"Sad and poor, mister, very sad and poor," came the reply.

And so it seemed. But once, during Tehuantepec's Época de Oro (Golden Age), Tehuantepec was neither sad nor poor. This time of riches began in 1907 shortly after the inauguration of the trans-Isthmus railway, which provided the shortest trade route between the Atlantic and Pacific Oceans. Tens of thousands of travelers in fifty trains per day crossed the Isthmus, making it one of the busiest railways the world has ever known. With these travelers came money, and Tehuantepec flourished. José Vasconcelos, then campaigning in the region for Mexican president Francisco Madero, recorded his impressions in his *Ulises criollo:* "The new rich spent their time speculating; yesterday's small landowners had seen the value of their properties soar a hundredfold, and either sold or rented them to foreigners so everyone had a good time working up a sweat." Lamentably, the wealth evaporated as fast as it had appeared when the Panama Canal was completed in 1914. Since then, the people of the Isthmus, and in particular the people of Tehuantepec, have fixed their gaze on the past, and more than one guidebook on the area refers to Tehuanos as, "backward looking, although enough remains for a traveler to occasionally catch a glimpse of its former glory."

Part of this glory is the sprawling, two-story city hall that occupies an entire block and towers over every other building on the square. Built in provincial neoclassic style, the massive columns and arches of city hall are as impressive as any in the Isthmus. But the backside of city hall is another story. The cynics in Tehuantepec like to refer to it as the coliseum, because the irregular pattern of brickwork makes it appear that decay has demolished the back half of the building. But in reality, the construction was never completed, and since 1906, every mayor to hold office has made and later reneged on promises to finish the project. In 1975, Mexican president Luis Echeverria got involved. He sent a group of architects to restore city hall as the historic center of Tehuantepec. The architects not only drew up plans to finish city hall but also sketched improvements to rebuild churches, and plazas. But in the end, the cynics won out, and as time passes, city hall looks more like the *coliseo* every day.

For a time, I lingered with the old men and sleeping dogs under city hall's grandiose arcade. On the northern side of the plaza lay Tehuantepec's brick and cement marketplace that was as large as city hall but without any of its appeal. The remaining sides of the plaza were occupied by single-story, colonial-style structures that once housed the wealthy but are now subdivided into shops such as stationery, music, and clothing stores.

When the sun set and the street lights came on, I was reminded that I had not yet rented a room for the night. It was approaching eight, and I feared I might end up sleeping on the ground floor of Pablo's funeral parlor. I walked one block north from the plaza along Calle Ocampo until I spotted the chalk-white Oasis Hotel rising four floors above the buildings that surround it. With its balconies and balustrades, the hotel fits well into the predominately colonial architecture of the buildings that surround it, but the wall that skirted the parking lot, with its vertical sections of concrete shaped like rocket fins, quickly dispelled any illusions that the hotel had been built in colonial times.

Seen from the parking lot, the Oasis is shaped like a horseshoe with a fifty-foot gum tree at its center. To the right was the hotel restaurant, and to the left the hotel proper. I entered the restaurant and was greeted by a tall, serious young woman who identified herself as Mari-Magdalena—or, as I came to think of her in English—Mary Magdalene. She wore a pleated skirt and bright white blouse, and her movements were precise. She flipped through a receipt book, wetting her index finger on every third turn of a page. Within a minute, she found a room on the second floor that she rented to me for $8.60 a night.

The following morning, I was eating breakfast and catching up on my journal in the hotel restaurant when a small, cheerful-looking woman with skin the color of dark ash approached my table. She introduced herself as Julin Contreras and said that her family owned the Oasis. "I'd be interested in knowing what you are writing about," she said. This seemed forward to me, so, rather than telling her, I asked her what kind of work she did. "Poorly paid work seems to be my specialty," she said. "I'm director of the Casa de Cultura. I also work for the Instituto Nacional de Bellas Artes." I put my fork down and wiped my mouth with my napkin. If I could convince her to do so, she could prove very useful for making contact with the women of Tehuantepec. "I'm writing about Isthmus women," I said. Then, in an attempt to impress her, I opened my journal and fanned the 250 pages that were filled with tiny, insectile notes. When she didn't react, I handed the notebook to her. She flipped through it until her eyes lit on a phrase that held her attention. She read out loud, "Zapotec expression: '*Un par de tetas jala mas que cien carretas*'" (A pair of tits pulls harder than a hundred oxcarts). This was not the phrase I would have wanted her to read as an introduction to my writing. I waited for what seemed a long time before she spoke. "This is not a Zapotec expression," she said. "It's a Mexican expression." I tried to think of a question that would impress her and make her want to spend time with me. But the only topic that came to mind was one she'd probably heard too much of.

"What's your stance on Isthmus matriarchy?" I said. The question did not seem to bother her as it had the Juchitecans, and she did not recite the tourist myth.

"Matriarchy here in Tehuantepec is commercial, nothing else," she said. "Women control the marketplace and, as a result, administration of household finance." In the context of the family, Isthmus women regard men as benign figureheads and, at times, as adopted children rather than partners. "I'll give you an example," Julin said. "At a dinner party, the hostess will say, 'First the men.' She sets the table and serves him bread and chocolate and chicken and tortillas. As he eats, the women ignore him. Then, there is a great cleaning up, and the party gets rolling for the women and only the women."

"I should add that in my own family," Julin said, "the power structure has always been matriarchal. This is the way it should be because the women in the family have always worked much harder than the men." Julin paused here. She studied my face for a moment, checking it for signs of trustworthiness. Than she leaned back in her chair and began relating the story of her family, beginning with Jorge, her father.

"My father was born into a family that was considerably poorer than my mother's." Jorge never met his parents; his mother died while giving birth to him, and his Arab father was forced out of the country before he was born. In those days, shortly after the Mexican Revolution in 1910, there were many nasty repercussions for foreigners. As a consequence,

Julin's father stayed with his paternal grandparents, who registered his birth with the name Jorge Contreras. When he was fourteen years old, he fled the house because his grandparents died. Eventually, he made his home in Minititlán, the site of Mexico's richest oil fields. He worked like a peon in a number of jobs. "First as a mason, and later as a tailor, then as a baker, you name it," Julin said. "He put together a lot of money and made a victorious return to Tehuantepec."

"My father first saw my mother, Emilia, at a dance," Julin said. Rather than approach her directly, Jorge learned what he could about her family. Mutual friends informed him that the family owned a sugar refinery and that her father had died recently, leaving his family in debt. "My father saw an opening here," Julin said. "He began sending gifts, not to my mother, but to my grandmother." At first, he sent practical gifts such as oil for the machines that ground the sugar cane. Then came packages of wine and tobacco and fruit so that little by little, he made his way into the house by way of gift giving. Jorge explained all this generosity as being borne out of sympathy for a family grieving the passage of its patriarch, and who could argue? "In a matter of months," Julin said, "he conquered my grandmother, and through her he gained access to her daughter." When Julin's grandmother died several years later, at the age of fifty, it was only natural that Emilia should turn to Jorge, and that he should marry her. But any dream he had of a handsome dowry soon faded. All of the land was heavily mortgaged. Nonetheless, he assumed the debts and paid the mortgages in Emilia's name, including land and buildings her family owned. All of this he did before he was twenty-five.

And though at first Jorge was the sole breadwinner in the family, he always turned his salary over to Emilia. What she was able to save she used to make tamales that she sold in the market. Jorge worked 130 miles away in Minititlán, and Emilia lived in the old house that was on the land where the hotel was later built. Every time Emilia was going to have a baby, Jorge would return from to Minititlán to help. He stayed three months before and three months after the birth of the child.

"But my mother was driven," Julin said. "She wanted to be rich and to live in the style her family did when she was little." And so, in the early days of her marriage, Emilia worked very hard and looked for opportunities to make money without being employed full time. When the Mexican government began spending enormous amounts of money to construct the Pan-American highway, Emilia saw gold. The engineers and workers who were building the highway and the bridge over the Tehuantepec River had set up camp on the opposite bank. Once, there was a huge flood that threw itself against the bridge. Everyone—engineers, workers, cooks, caretakers—were forced to cross the river in small boats because the flooding had swamped the camp and left it underwater. Emilia took advantage of this mishap. The highway workers needed a place to stay, and she offered them hammocks and cots and cooked for them as well. The money the highway workers paid her she saved. One day, Jorge came home to find that his wife had subdivided some of the rooms in the family home. He asked what was going on. "The more rooms I have, the more I can rent. I'm making your savings grow," Emilia said.

After the flood, Emilia constructed a little restaurant in which she fed and attended to the highway workers, and all the other people who traveled through Tehuantepec—and there were many. When the demand grew past the available rooms, she had an idea. Why not knock down the house and build a hotel in its stead? Jorge, however, opposed this notion, so Emilia had to wait until her husband was away. The opportunity arose several months later when he was hospitalized for a minor health problem. Emilia quickly hired a crew that demolished the family home. By the time Jorge returned, the house was gone, and the work on the hotel had already begun. "In the end," Julin said, "my father was always an obedient husband, and he would have given in sooner or later."

"Over the years, in her capacity as businesswoman, my mother attended to governors and even presidents of the republic," Julin paused here, thought a moment, and began again. "I always say 'my mother' rather than 'my family' because she was the one who took the initiative with respect to our family business." But through it all, Emilia never neglected her family. "She loved us so much," Julin said, "that every day she served us fresh bread that she had made herself." At her peak, Emilia owned a commercial mill, a cattle ranch, a grocery store, and a community center named El Cairo that she ran on the weekends. As she approached middle age, Emilia had amassed a small fortune. She then began giving back to the community in much the same way as

Doña Cata did, by establishing a school for children who lived in the vicinity of El Cairo. The school she founded had one of the highest attendance rates in the Isthmus and has won many academic prizes.

"When my mother was sixty-three," Julin said, "she suffered a cerebral stroke." Shortly thereafter, she gave her keys to Julin and then died quietly without complications. Although Zapotec custom dictates that Isthmus women should be clothed in black for the funeral, Julin dressed her mother in her best huipil and enagua and emptied her perfume bottles into the casket before it was taken to the cemetery.

When Julin completed her story, she explained that she was scheduled to greet the members of the Oaxacan State Orchestra when they arrived later in the afternoon for a concert. I was sorry to see her go. Like Rosa, she was opinionated and bright, and this made for good material. She was also supportive and kind, characteristics Rosa lacked. Before she left the table, I asked if she would be available for more questions. "Maybe tomorrow," she said. "It would be wonderful if you could come to the Vela Zandunga tonight and sit at my table. I'll give you a running commentary on the different activities and rituals you'll see. Do your best to attend. It's an event that goes to the very heart of who we are."

The Kid

Miguel Covarrubias was born in Mexico City in 1904. Like many who would come to study the Isthmus, Covarrubias came from the privileged class. His parents and relatives were high-ranking civil servants. "I came from a family of diplomats," Covarrubias said, "but I was not one of them." From the moment of his birth, two of his aunts were devoted to him. "They overfed him and showered him with gifts and treats," writes Covarrubias biographer Adriana Williams. The aunts also liked sewing and clothing him in dress that at times masked his gender in the same way that Hemingway's mother had done for him.

In early adulthood, Covarrubias could often be found in Los Monotes, a café where painters and writers of the Mexican New Wave such as Diego Rivera, Clemente Orozco, Lupe Marín, Rufino Tamayo, and others would gather to socialize. "He reminded me of a small boy," Elena Poniatowska wrote, "his pockets filled with the fruits of life, which he would abandon without a second thought to grab what was going by." Covarrubias had a knack for caricatures, and everyone who went to Los Monotes was sooner or later the subject of one of his cartoons. Diego Rivera gave lessons to the young Covarrubias, who became mascot for the New Wave with the nickname of El Chamaco (The Kid).

Although the exact date of Covarrubias's first visit to the Isthmus is unknown, he told a reporter for the *New York Sun* in 1938 that he had been there at least twenty times. "I was attracted by its violent contrasts—its arid brush, its jungles that seemed lifted from a Rousseau canvas . . . the majestic bearing and classic elegance of the Tehuantepec women walking to the market." For more than a year, Covarrubias traveled the Isthmus by train, gathering information on Zapotec sexuality, courtship, marriage, velas, work habits, and rituals of death. His knowledge of archeology and anthropology resulted in a cool-headed analysis of Isthmus society, giving his voice an authority his predecessors lack. They rarely cite evidence or provide details; Covarrubias almost always does. The resulting book, *Mexico South*, is structured along the lines of an anthropologist's case study. First published in 1945, *Mexico South* is comprehensive and voluminous. It answers many of the questions his predecessors raised, and also disproved some of the more outlandish accusations. On women's sexuality, he writes: "The sexual life of Isthmus Zapotecs is as simple as their general mode of life and as direct as their character. The relations between the sexes are natural and uninhibited, free of the puritanical outlook on sex of the Indians of the highlands, and of Spanish feudal concept of the inferior position of women, so characteristic of other parts of Mexico. Outside of the conventions observed by the upper classes of the larger Isthmus towns, sex does not represent the mysterious taboo that weighs down the provincial, conservative, and intensely religious communities of the Mexican plateau."

On the topic of matriarchy, Covarrubias is less clear. In one chapter of *Mexico South*, he implies that Isthmus society is ruled by women: "It is these women, from the age ten to eighty, who run the market, which, in a woman's town, is the most important of Tehuantepec's institutions." One hundred pages later, he reaffirms his stance, "Theirs is a society of women, run by and for women." Later in the book, however, Covarrubias contradicts himself, arguing that women's social and economic independence gave them "a position of equality with men." Nonetheless, the general impression Covarrubias conveys is that Isthmus women enjoy more than a fair share of the power in the Isthmus. In daylight, he tells us, Tehuantepec is a woman's world, no matter if their men work in town or in the fields. With the money they earn during those hours women can purchase land, houses, jewelry, or whatever else they might wish. Neither their husbands nor relatives have any authority over the management or disposal of these purchases.

About free union or common-law marriage, Covarrubias disagrees with Henestrosa. "These unions are known as *ti'iziga*, or 'marriage behind the door,' and there is no particular stigma or social taboo against them." He also takes aim at some of the frequently repeated stereotypes.

"It is a commonly expressed fallacy that the women do all the work while the men relax at home or get drunk with their equally worthless cronies." Covarrubias blames the stereotype on "superficial observers," a clear echo of Henestrosa's "superficial men." In this way, Covarrubias provides a perverse example of an outsider blaming outsiders for the controversy swirling around Isthmus women. Nevertheless, Covarrubias's careful fieldwork and attention to ethnographic detail won him favor with Istmeños who consider *Mexico South* the most accurate and complete representation of their culture.

Vela Zandunga

With my departure two and a half days away, I began feeling edgy about the fact that my luggage was still in Juchitán under Rosa's watchful eyes. I also felt that a face-to-face goodbye was in order, so I walked to the public telephone at Papelería Esferas and called her. Her tone was upbeat; she seemed glad to hear from me. I invited her to lunch, thinking we could eat in a public place that didn't serve liquor and afterward I would retrieve my luggage from the mortuary. This was not to be. When she asked what I was up to, I made the mistake of mentioning Vela Zandunga, sure that she would not want to enter into the rival territory of Tehuantepec. I was wrong. Almost immediately, she latched onto the idea that we could attend the vela together, and I found myself swallowing the anxiety that rose in my throat when she promised she'd be in Tehuantepec before nine.

I was shuffling through the photos of my train ride across the Isthmus when Rosa rapped on the door of my room at the Oasis. She wore a Levi's dress and carried a purse large enough to be an overnight bag. She smiled and kissed me on the cheek when she strode past me and into the room. There were no chairs, and I watched her take in the two queen size beds, one near the window in which I had slept the night before and the other against the adjacent wall. I motioned toward the bed that was still made, and we sat down. I spoke to her with enthusiasm about the train ride, and when she showed no interest I got out photos I had taken of a diesel-powered locomotive and Guatemalan illegals riding in empty boxcars, and the jungle that grew back as fast as the Isthmus trains could knock it down. She simply wasn't interested.

But when I told her my back ached from the twelve-hour train ride, she became suddenly very attentive. She gave me a forceful massage that relieved much of the pain. Soon enough, however, the massage turned into a wrestling match until I said, "I can't do this." She stopped and sat up. We talked. I told her that in all likelihood we would never have sex. She said that she had called her pilot boyfriend the day before, and again that day, and that she was doing her best to keep the relationship with him intact. She would give him time, she said, to get over his work-related problems. Rosa was honest with me, and I with her. I felt reassured that I was not using her in some dysfunctional way. "If you don't want that kind of relationship," she said, "then I have to respect your decision." Then she said that she admired my firmness with her, my refusal to bicker. She gave me a long talk about how she hated weak men and the abuse they put up with. Her cousin's husband was one such man. If he were a real man, she said, he wouldn't put up with the fighting, the personal insults, the abusive language her cousin doled out.

When we finished our little talk, she got up from the bed and rummaged through her bag until she found a new pair of fingernail scissors. She grasped my left hand and went at my cuticles like a *machetero* at sugar cane. I felt as though I were a dog being groomed by a loving owner until I felt a sharp jab under a toenail from her scissors.

"Rosa," I said. "That hurt."

"There's something stuck under one of your toenails I'm trying to snag."

When she finished with my toenails, she returned to her purse for Q-tips.

"Hold these," she said.

"What are they for?" I asked. She looked at me like I was playing stupid.

"Don't you know?" she said. "They're for cleaning out your ears."

"Are my ears really that dirty?" I asked. She didn't answer. Then I felt a Q-tip enter my inner ear. I tried to remember when she might have had the opportunity to look inside my ears. I came up blank until I remembered the ride home from the beach, and how she had inspected Olga from head to foot.

She asked if she could trim my mustache, and I gave her a pair of scissors I had brought from home for this express purpose. When she finished my mustache, she lay across me and said, "Now I'm going to cut something off that's been bothering me for a long time." She poked the scissors up my nose and snipped. She got lotion out of her bag and began massaging my feet. She pulled on my toes so hard it hurt. "I'll bet this is the first time anyone has given you this kind of attention," she said. I told her she was right. I read the newspaper. Why was she doing this? I think she wanted to make it clear, that in case I changed my mind about her, I would reap many benefits. The manicure, the nose cleaning, the mustache trimming, and the back rub were advertisements for herself. "Look what I bought you," Rosa said, smiling the smile Pablo used to comfort the bereaved. She handed me a pair of blue socks and a red paisley *paliacate*. I accepted the presents, and thanked her for them, especially the *paliacate*. Inside, I worried. These were not the kinds of gifts one friend might offer another, at least not the socks.

I stripped off my shirt and hung it on the bathroom door. I got into the shower in an attempt to get rid of the sweat and revive myself for the vela. On the way out of the shower, Rosa gave me a look as she pulled mounds of hair out of my hairbrush, as if to say, "Do you see how well I treat you?" Then, when she noticed that I was putting on a green shirt rather than the white one I had borrowed from Pablo, she became belligerent.

"Don't be stupid," she said. "They won't let you into the dance with a green shirt. Change it now." I ignored her, and she repeated the same remark three more times. Instead of returning fire, I took a close look at her. As dark as her skin was, she had circles under her eyes that were darker.

"You look tired," I said.

"I left in a hurry," she said. "I had to put my makeup on in the taxi." She turned away and a minute later got into the shower. She came out wearing a towel. Rather than dressing in the bathroom as I had, she dropped the towel and began dressing slowly, piece by piece. Women who dress in front of me have always annoyed me, and there she was, going from naked to bloated in full Isthmus regalia with matching huipil and enagua. A minute before we left, I glanced in the mirror, saw a beautiful woman, and thought: "Jesus, she's gorgeous." Then, of course, I realized the woman was Rosa. I told her this. "Te vi en el espejo y pensé que tan bella es esta mujer."

On our way to the vela, we crossed the courtyard behind city hall. When we came to a brick planter on the courtyard's western perimeter, Rosa stopped abruptly and said, "Sit down on the bricks." I did, and she knelt and tied the lace on my right shoe, which had come untied. There was nothing submissive in what she was doing. If I felt like a prize dog in my hotel room, now it seemed I was a pure-bred horse with a loose saddle, and I remembered what Julin had said earlier in the day: that women regarded their husbands as adopted children. "Later on," Rosa said, "We're going to have to do something about your hair."

The vela was held on Calle Juárez, the street that runs along the southern end of Tehuantepec's main plaza. At the entrance, an orderly line of well-dressed men and women were buying tickets from an ancient Tehuano standing inside a small white ticket booth. As Rosa and I waited in line, I remember thinking how different the velas in Juchitán were. There, the entrance was wide enough to allow a platoon of women marching through in rows of twenty, and the idea of an entrance ticket would have provoked derision. Already, even before we had entered, I missed Juchitán's happy disorder and the case-of-beer ritual required on entry. In the end, I handed over a blue, 100-peso note to the ticket seller, and learned that price of entrance for the two of us was $10—roughly the same as it was in Juchitán for a case of beer. The ticket seller gave each one of us a stub that we handed over to a dark giant of a man who guarded the entrance.

The mood inside the vela was hot and somber, in part because the chain link fence that surrounded it was covered with banana leaves that blocked the cooling winds. The women at the vela made up for the lack of breeze by fanning themselves with ornate white fans embroidered along the top with yellow lace. The men simply sweated, wiping their foreheads now and then with *paliacates* already limp with moisture. Unlike the velas in Juchitán, there were no wooden folding chairs with women lolling about in them half drunk; instead, only white plastic chairs and matching tables covered with gaudy red and green tablecloths. Seated at the tables were two hundred women, and a few men, and both sexes were impeccably dressed. The men wore black and white, but the quality of the cloth the Tehuanos wore was finer and newer than the black and white pants I saw on the men in Juchitán's velas. The women wore huipiles and enaguas de fiesta in colors unimaginable to Juchitecas: white or off-white seemed to be the color of the year, and gold fringe decorated the modest neckline of all but a few women. At the center of the vela was a dance floor, and above it a live band played Mexican pop music so loud that conversation was impossible. In itself, loud music was not unusual for an Isthmus vela. What was unusual was that even when the band stopped playing, the crowd remained eerily silent.

"Where are we sitting?" Rosa asked. In the distance, roughly half a block away, I spotted Julin at a table near the bandstand. Her table was packed so tightly with people that everyone seated there was rubbing elbows with their immediate neighbors. There might have been room for me, but clearly not for the two of us. Even worse, it appeared that from our vantage point at the entrance, all of the other tables were taken. Rosa was quick to notice this, and quick to complain. "I thought we were going to sit at Julin's table," she said. I asked Rosa to wait at the entrance. I crossed the dance floor, forcing my way through the sweaty, writhing bodies. On reaching Julin's table, she greeted me warmly. We spoke for a few moments, and I shifted my weight from foot to foot while I waited for her to offer me a seat until it was clear that the offer would never come. Somehow, I preferred it this way. Like everyone else at the dance, those who shared Julin's table seemed grim. No one spoke, not even to immediate neighbors. Fighting with Rosa seemed better than this silence, so I excused myself and left without mention of the promised seat.

Rosa was no longer standing near the entrance where I had left her. I scanned the crowd, and after a couple of worried moments, I spotted her sitting alone at a table squeezed into a far corner of the grounds. Her table, and the one next to it, were the only ones without tablecloths. As I got nearer, I noticed gray scars cut into the white plastic tabletops which gave both of them a worn out, punished look. I was sure Rosa felt some degree of humiliation about sitting there, and I braced myself for more quibbling. I sat down next to her and explained that Julin's table was full. She turned away from me so that I could not see the anger that was already darkening her face. "There's something else," she said, and turned to face me. "We can only order beer by the carton and whiskey by the bottle. Why did you even bring me here?" I was about to answer her complaint when from out of the banana leaves along the fence, an odd creature, clearly male, trudged toward our table. Everything about his looks was uniformly flat: his face, eyes, nose, and mouth, as though he had come out of a rectangular can rather than a womb. His hair was combed forward into his face, and his bangs were fashioned into five or six points that nearly touched his eyebrows. His overall impression was that of a depraved king wearing his crown upside down, and I came to think of him as Mr. King.

When he was within three feet of our table, he exchanged a single, knowing look with Rosa as if to tell me that they had already discussed our seating problem. Then, rather than speaking, he turned toward me. He shrugged his shoulders and turned his palms upward as if to say, "What in the hell is going on here?"

"Who is this guy?" I said to Rosa.

"He works here. He says we don't have an assigned table."

"Does it matter? You were with me when we bought the tickets."

"It *does* matter. They never gave us a table number, and these tables are for the workers." This kind of confusion was a common occurrence in Latin America. Those who knew the ropes fare well enough in situations requiring a ticket or a license or a permit. But the innocent newcomer is seen as fair game for anyone willing to milk him for a bribe. My guess was that the ticket taker had purposefully failed to give us a table number. Then he informed Mr. King of our transgression and how he might take advantage of us.

"What are we going to do?" Rosa said. "You said we would sit at Julin's table. If you don't do something soon, I'm leaving." I knew that if I were to hand over a few dollars, say five, Mr. King would go away. I wasn't, however, in the mood for bribing anyone. I also knew that if I spoke, no matter what I said there would be trouble. And so it was that I stood up and walked toward the elevated sidewalks to the right of the entrance. I seated myself on the steps of Papelería Esferas and offered up a prayer: Thank you God for helping me to restrain myself from having sex with this woman.

For a while, I sat and watched the vela progress. From this heightened perspective, my first impressions were confirmed: Vela Zandunga was a dry, humorless event. Unlike the velas in Juchitán, no one was milling around cracking jokes or knocking their beers over into the dirt—in fact, there was no dirt—asphalt and cement covered everything. None of the women flirted or tipped their beer bottles into the air, though most of the dancers were women. No one chanted "Viva San Vicente" or made any reference to a patron saint at all. Lamentably, the velas in Tehuantepec had been stripped of their religious origins.

When the band took a break, I returned to sit with Rosa, reassuring myself that her anger had passed in the thirty or so minutes I had been away. As I approached our table, I noticed that the table next to Rosa was no longer unoccupied. A pack of light-skinned, overweight thugs sat drinking a fifth of El Presidente brandy from tiny plastic shot glasses that they downed in one gulp. Their chunky forearms rested on the table as they waited for their turn with the bottle. For a moment, I wondered if Mr. King had extorted money from them, and just as quickly discarded the idea. These men were in a different class of misfits. They had the faces of seasoned criminals and it would take more that Mr. King's block-like face and his ridiculous hairdo to make them feel uneasy.

Rosa took no notice of me when I sat down. Two beer bottles rested in front of her, and she held my notebook open with both hands, smiling as though she were reading a comic book. This disturbed me. I had written about Rosa in ways that I was sure would displease her. I reached for the notebook and asked, "Do you mind?" Still smiling, she handed me my journal.

Now that she had a couple of beers in her belly, she was looking for a way to appease me, and it didn't take long for her to seize upon the idea of introducing me to the men at the next table. The majority of them might look like thugs, she said, but one of them she recognized as the mayor of Tehuantepec. During a lull in their conversation, she asked the mayor if he could spare a couple of minutes for an interview with me. "No," he said. Then she asked if he would allow us to take a couple of photos, and got the same answer. Julin would know who the men were, and why they kept their distance.

While the others at the vela crowded onto the dance floor, Rosa and I were content to drink and exchange disparaging comments about the Tehuanas and their dress. It wasn't until eleven that I noticed a tall, attractive woman with yellow hair who circled the dance floor with a camera in one hand and an incandescent light in the other. Although she wore a huipil and enagua, her features were European, and I saw in her an opportunity to speak English—something I had not done for two weeks. When she neared our table, I said hello, and she lowered the camera from her face. A photographer by trade, Diana was on assignment for *Geomundo*. She learned about Isthmus women through a class taught by Howard Campbell at University of Texas, El Paso.

I introduced Diana to Rosa, and she sat down at our table. Before speaking any further to Diana, I asked Rosa if our conversing in English would bother her. Rosa said no, and Diana described the frustration of being a photographer in a foreign country: "I won't know until I get home and develop the film how the shots will turn out." She asked me how I came to know Rosa and what our relation was. I explained. I also remember telling her about Andrés Henestrosa, whose sober style of writing I admired. She asked for the name of one of his books. I reached for my journal where I had copied down the names of some of his works. When I could not find the titles, Rosa snatched the journal out of my hands, and flipped immediately to the page in question. I was amazed. She seemed to know my journal better than I did.

Diana suggested that the three of us eat at one of the portable, outdoor cafés that appeared late at night on the plaza and disappeared before dawn. Rosa said she wasn't hungry and that Diana and I should go together. The cafés were run by women who invited us to sit at the long, rectangular tables with red-checkered tablecloths that were the centerpiece of each establishment. We sat down at the first table we came to and ordered *tlayudas*, the Isthmus equivalent of pizza. As we ate, Diana and I spoke of what we had learned about the Isthmus, and we passed half an hour in this way, eating and talking and drinking beer. When I suggested that we return before Rosa became upset, Diana laughed. "How can you possibly worry about any trouble from such a little woman?"

Inside the vela, we found Rosa busy tilting a bottle of Corona toward the sky. There were two empty bottles at her feet, and two more stood empty on the table in front of her.

"She's pissed off," I said as we approached the table. "And *you* are exaggerating," Diana said. Before we could seat ourselves, however, Rosa flashed her black eyes at me and said, "We're leaving." I thought this was premature, but I agreed, provided she gave me time to say good-bye to Julín. As I turned to leave our table, Rosa and Diana began an animated conversation. When I returned, I wrote the number of the Oasis on the back of one of Diana's business cards, and we parted ways.

Rosa and I had exited the vela and walked no more than thirty steps toward the Oasis when the complaints began. "This has been the worst experience of my life," she said. "We go to a dance together. You ignore me. You spend all of your time sitting alone on those steps and then talking to a woman you don't even know." I said nothing. Challenging her accusations would only make matters worse. She went on: "When you went to say goodbye to Julín, Diana grilled me about who you were, your age, if you were married, what kind of work you did. Do you think for a moment that this wouldn't make me jealous? It would make anyone jealous." Half crying, half raging, Rosa drew attention from the people on the street around us as she sputtered water from her eyes and nose and mouth. They knew the tune and attempted to repress their smiles, but it was clear that they appreciated the late-night, commercial-free soap opera.

At the Oasis, I fumbled with the keys to my room. When the key clicked, I gave the door a shove with my foot and welcomed the rush of cool air churned out by the noisy air conditioner. I knew exactly what I wanted. Without taking my shoes off, I lay face down on the bed by the window and let the exhaustion of more than two weeks of work and play flow out of me and into the bed.

"How will you get home?" I asked Rosa.

"It's too late to find a taxi," she said. Why hadn't she told me this before?

"You can stay provided we keep to our agreement," I said, "and you stay out of my bed." She nodded her head in compliance. I closed my eyes and fell asleep. Fifteen minutes passed.

"Take those clothes off," Rosa said. I opened my eyes.

"Didn't you hear me? Take those clothes off."

I ignored her. I closed my eyes, but before I fell back to sleep, she spoke again.

"How could you have done that to me? You were with that woman for half the night. You left me alone. And when you were with me, you weren't even there."

"I was hungry," I said. "I asked you if I could spend a couple of minutes with her. You said it was okay."

"So go on," she said. "Go on, be with her now."

When I didn't respond, she said:

"You are so ungrateful. Men don't know how to appreciate the kind of woman I am," and so on. I said nothing. Instead I waited. I was so exhausted that within minutes the fan, air conditioner, and Rosa's voice became background noise and I slept—but not for long. My bed shook as if it had been hit by a car. I opened my eyes. Rosa had slammed her way into my bed, wedging herself between me and the wall. Her blouse was on the floor. She wore a bra that cupped her breasts with cloth woven into concentric circles that gave her the look of a virgin from the South Pacific. "What are you doing?" I said. She said nothing. I rolled away toward the edge of the bed to make more space for her. She didn't touch me. She just kept inching over in my direction until I had no more room to move. "I'm going to fall out of bed if you don't stop," I said. She looked at me in my precarious position on the edge of the bed and laughed. I again fell asleep. Then the bed began shaking. Rosa was facing the wall, nowhere near me. Her body was moved by trembling.

"Are you okay?" I said. I touched her cheek. It was wet.

"I am so angry," she said. "I can't get rid of this anger." Her tone indicated that this was more of an explanation than an accusation, and I believed her. Whatever she suffered from wasn't something she willed upon herself, it was a passion she couldn't shake off that probably had little to do with me. Hers was a passion for intimacy and romance, and she'd realized that in me she'd come to another dead end. I sympathized with her, but at the same time I knew that if I didn't get any sleep, my neurotic tendencies would blossom and possibly overshadow hers.

I waited until she stopped crying, and said:

"Let's go. Somehow, I don't exactly know how, we'll find a bus or a taxi and take you home."

"Are you throwing me out?" she said. "What will my brother say if he hears that you threw me out of your hotel room at two in the morning?"

She had it right, I didn't want to jeopardize my friendship with Pablo. Like all of the women I'd ever been involved with, Rosa was one step ahead of me when it came to strategy. I moved to the other bed, the one she had started the night in, and read the paper.

"Turn off that light," she said, "and come to bed. I won't bother you anymore. I've lost interest."

"I don't believe you," I said. I had run out of ideas. If she stayed, I wouldn't sleep, and if I took her home in a taxi I wouldn't return till dawn. Then, above the sound of the air conditioner, I heard the voice of the hotel's night receptionist speaking on the phone. I had an idea. I got out of bed. I put clothes and shoes on. Rosa was asleep, or pretending to be during the time it took me to find my wallet and keys. But she must have sensed the finality of what I was about to do, because by the time I opened the door and turned to go, she had taken her clothes off and was kneeling at the foot of my bed, howling like a banshee into the mattress.

In the lobby, the receptionist continued the conversation I had heard in my room. He was tall, almost gaunt, and his hair was graying at the temples. When the conversation ended and he hung up the phone, he asked what I wanted.

"I'm having a problem with the other occupant of my room," I said.

"I understand," he said. "Mum's the word. Just leave the key with me when you go." I looked him in the eyes and realized he must have thought I had planned a rendezvous with another woman who was waiting for me somewhere outside of the hotel. "I'm not making myself clear," I said. "I only want to go to sleep. Do you have another room you can rent me?" It was easy to see that he didn't believe me. But he gave me a room on the second floor, and I hit the bed sleeping.

I woke the following morning far later than I had planned to. Earlier in the week, I'd told a priest in Juchitán that I wanted to witness a wedding. He said it would be difficult to arrange an invitation, but I could probably slip in unnoticed for a ceremony in Juchitán's cathedral at ten o'clock on Sunday. When I rose to dress, I remembered the disturbance with Rosa and I descended the steps to the first floor. I unlocked the door to my room and pushed it open a couple of feet. The room was empty; Rosa and her belongings were gone.

The bus I caught to Juchitán did not leave until nine-thirty. I had come to dread the long bus rides between Tehuantepec and Juchitán. The road was so poor and the busses so dilapidated that the violence of the ride made it impossible to read or write. In Juchitán there were no taxis to take me to the cathedral. I gave up waiting for one and walked, but by the time I reached the cathedral, the bridal party had already departed. This was a great disappointment, in part because a line from Andrés Henestrosa kept coming to mind. "If there is one institution the Zapotecs have preserved," Henestrosa wrote, "it is the wedding."

I left the cathedral and went directly to my favorite *licuado* shop, where I planned to improve my mood with sugar and caffeine. *Licuados* are a combination of fruit, milk, ice, and several large tablespoons of sugar thrown into a blender. I ordered two papaya *licuados* and a coffee. Halfway through the second *licuado,* a midget in a three-piece suit sat down next to me. I'd seen him before, coming and going from the Fortress. In fact, he had the room next door to mine, and I'd long suspected that he was behind the obscene phone calls. Despite his three-piece suit and the suffocating weather, he wasn't sweating. After he ordered a coffee, which he left untouched, I felt his eyes on me.

"Aren't you the guy who has the room next to mine?" he said.

"I'm the guy," I said. "Are you here for a convention?"

"No. I'm a PEMEX consultant." PEMEX is Mexico's state run oil monopoly.

"Interesting," I said. "But what are you doing at this end of the world?"

"Inspecting the PEMEX pipeline that runs from Minititlán to Salina Cruz." Here I handed him my notebook, and he drew a map that showed where the pipeline ran across the Isthmus. He explained that the pipeline carried both crude oil and gas.

"You have an unusual accent," he said. "Where are you from?"

I told him.

"San Francisco," he said and smiled. "Do you know the song 'Are you going to San Francisco, and will you wear a flower in your hair?'" He sang a few stanzas for me, and I had the urge to hit him.

"And how do you spend your spare time," he said.

"I write letters," I said. "Long letters."

"Have you ever been to Casa Verde?"

"Never heard of it."

"It's the nicest brothel in the Isthmus. You won't believe this, but the girls sit on your table and spread their legs. You really should visit it sometime. It's in Espinal, just outside Juchitán."

I drank my coffee and boarded a bus back to Tehuantepec. In the Oasis restaurant, I found Julin eating a late breakfast. I asked her for a time when we could meet. "At seven," she said. "*Maybe* at seven." This hurt. She was probably angry about the fact that I was late for the vela and that I didn't sit at her table. I returned to my room and read.

At seven, feeling optimistic about the possibility of meeting with Julin, I seated myself in the Oasis restaurant and waited. At seven thirty, I asked Mary Magdalene if Julin was punctual. "No," she said. "She's not." At eight, I gave up and wrote Julin a note: "I'm heading to Espinal to do an interview there. I'm sorry I wasn't able to wait longer, but I've got the whole day tomorrow if you'd like to meet. If I offended you by not sitting at your table last night, I apologize. I think the formality of the velas in Tehuantepec made me feel like the outsider that I am. Could you slide a note under my door tomorrow telling me when you're available?"

I didn't say in the note whom I wanted to interview because I intended to speak with a prostitute at Casa Verde, and this might not be to her liking. At eight thirty, I boarded a bus to Juchitán. As the driver waited for the bus to fill with people, I parted the curtains and watched children playing in the shallow water of the Tehuantepec River. A dog with three legs ambled down the left bank, his nose to the ground. Then the sky darkened, and it rained violently. The dust became mud, and the river, a torrent.

On arriving in Juchitán, I asked a taxi driver to take me Casa Verde. "There is no service on Sundays," the taxi driver said. I cursed my luck and boarded a bus back to Tehuantepec for the second time that day. At the hotel, I asked Mary Magdalene if she'd seen Jorge, Julin's father. I had spoken to him before and wanted to follow up on some of his observations about Isthmus women. "He's in Colima," she said. I remember this day as black Sunday.

On the morning of my last day in the Isthmus, I woke at eleven. The failures of the day before were the first thoughts that came to mind, and I might not have made it out of bed until late in the afternoon had I not noticed a slip of paper laying on red clay tiles inside my door. "Tom, Sorry about yesterday," it read. "Let's eat lunch together in the hotel restaurant. Julin." No time was specified. But my bus didn't leave until six in the evening, so I had the better part of a day to speak with Julin. I also had to collect the suitcase I had left with Rosa before my trip across the Isthmus. I called her, and we agreed to meet in the mortuary at five.

It was near noon when I seated myself in the Oasis restaurant to eat a late breakfast of pancakes drowned in honey. I was chewing on the last bite when Julin appeared at my table. Her face was drawn.

"The son of a close friend drowned in the river yesterday," Julin said. "He was sixteen years old. I have to attend the funeral."

I asked if I could tag along. "Yes," she said, "but I'm in no mood for any questions."

For the first ten minutes of our drive to the church, Julin was silent. Then, without my prompting, she spoke. "All of this reminds me of my brother, who also died at the relatively young age of twenty-eight. He was painting at home when someone who was staying at the hotel invited him to the movies. My brother didn't want to go, but my father encouraged him to do so because he hadn't taken a break from his art in days. When my brother and his friend were returning from the movies, a heavily loaded truck just ahead of them stopped suddenly. The car skidded under the truck and both he and his friend were killed."

Again we drove in silence, past city hall, past the plaza where children played in the shade of a jacaranda tree.

"It was a great loss," she said. "My brother was an unusually good painter, a genius with charcoal and brush. I've never met anyone who could paint animals so perfectly, without so much as a photo in front of him. He knew the figure and expression of many animals and painted them with skill. As a portrait painter, he knew no equal in Oaxaca. His friends loved him dearly. Imagine the patio of the hotel full of his friends, some from other countries, who came for the funeral."

"I'd love to see something he painted," I said.

"I'm afraid that's not possible. Several days before he died, he lent the entire collection of his work for display at an art exhibition. A week after his death we realized that he was the only one who knew the name of the exhibition and the curators who ran it. We waited for months before we finally faced the fact that his work would never be returned. My mother suffered so much that we thought she'd die. She was diabetic, and my brother's death worsened her health."

"I too had a brother who died in his twenties," I said. "He also painted, but he wasn't well recognized like your brother. Since birth, he was contrary. One of my earliest childhood memories has to do with his crying. When my grandmother visited us one day and heard him crying, she made a prediction. 'That child will have problems, I can tell by the way he cries.' And she was right. By the time he reached adolescence, he was diagnosed with severe manic depression. He was angry and turned his anger on my parents, often cursing and railing against them without reason. His illness went into remission when he met a young woman from France at a community college where he was studying art. They fell in love and moved into an apartment, where my brother and his art flourished. Then one day his girlfriend left him, for reasons I do not know. Within a month he was living at home, and his insanity returned with a vengeance. Without telling anyone, he purchased a Smith and Wesson pistol on a payment plan. When he had made all of the payments and the pistol was his, he shot himself in the temple and died. In my gender-obsessed mind, he killed himself because his girlfriend had left him, although other family members think it was a combination of factors. His death came at a time when I too was struggling with a relationship, and I've always believed it has affected the way that I see women. I value women highly, possibly too highly, and I believe it is one of the reasons I've traveled here to the Isthmus. I'm still trying to figure out my relationship with the opposite sex."

Julin drove us to a mosquito-infested church that lay in the crook of the Tehuantepec River, the same river that had drowned the sixteen-year-old boy. We crossed a bridge that gave us a view of the river, which was once again shallow, and I remembered the torrential rain that had fallen the day before as I sat waiting for the bus to take me to Casa Verde. And though no one I met that day said anything, it must have been clear to everyone that without the rain, the boy would never have drowned. There just wasn't enough water in the river to drown anyone. But then it rained.

Like all of the churches in Tehuantepec, the church in which the funeral mass was held had been painted an ultra-pure white with columns and cornices in blue. In the church's courtyard, a mother gently chided her youngest, who threw handfuls of dry dirt that hung in the afternoon air. Inside the church, mass was underway. The responses of the mourners to the priest's prayers were mumbled when not absent altogether. As if to show his contempt for a God who allowed a boy of sixteen to die,

an elderly man spat on the floor whenever the priest paused in his sermon or prayers. Even more contemptuous was the early exit from the
church of nearly everyone but the boy's family.

On the way back to the Oasis, Julin said, "Did you notice the men
who were seated at the table next to yours last night?"

"Yes," I said, "I couldn't have missed them. They looked like thugs."

"Not a bad guess," she said. "But the truth is they were politicians,
mayors of a number of nearby cities, including Tehuantepec. All of
them belong to PRI, and what they do is stupid. They put up a fence
that seals themselves off from other people. If you remember, they were
light skinned and had Arab or Spanish features. The people they represent are dark-skinned Zapotecs, and the mayors consider them inferior."

We arrived at the Oasis restaurant shortly after two. Julin ordered a
hamburger with fries and encouraged me to do the same. I remembered
the gristly chorizo burgers laced with chilies I had eaten in other parts of
Mexico. I waited for more encouragement, and when it didn't come, I
ordered pancakes with honey. While we waited for the food to arrive, I
asked Julin why Isthmus women attracted so much attention from
foreigners. "You are in a better position to answer that than I am," she
said, "but I'll tell you what I think." Long ago, writers and anthropologists such as Bourbourg or Covarrubias visited the Isthmus and idealized
the women here as the most sensual, the best dressed, the most independent, and so on. The writers from Juchitán took hold of this idealization
and gave it form and polish. "Oh, yes," they wrote, "the women of the
Isthmus are erotic, splendidly dressed, and fiercely independent." Then,
when our women read this, they began posing as if it were true, which
led to a competition. "If before, a woman wore one flower," Julin said,
"this year it has to be ten. Now she can't be happy if her necklace is not
real gold, if she doesn't have the finest lace. Every year, the dresses become more exquisite, more this and more that. In the end, women's traditions are losing their essence and our culture has become distorted."

When the food arrived, we paused and ate a few bites. Julin spoke
about the reasons Isthmus women dance together rather than with their
men.

"Until the forties, when beer arrived," Julin said, "women danced
with men just like they do in any other part of the world." Then a war
broke out between Corona and Carta Blanca, two of Mexico's biggest

breweries. Both brands gave away rivers of beer; they put on variety shows and concerts and presented popular artists who played folk music. "All of this was free and very common," Julin said. And in this way, these kinds of corporations began distorting the minds of Istmeños. They changed their taste, the things they loved and liked, even how they danced. "Women dance with women," Julin said, "because our men are often too drunk to stand."

Julin's explanation brought to mind an incident on my train ride that I described to her in detail. An hour outside of Tehuantepec, two women boarded the train in traditional Isthmus dress. After seating themselves near a window, one of the women retrieved two bottles of beer from a bag she was carrying. They drank the beers openly, enjoying themselves as if they were at home. Had the women been American, or European, I wouldn't have given the experience a second thought. But this was the first time I had ever seen Mexican women drink beer in a public place, and I found it somewhat shocking.

"That's a normal reaction," Julin said. "I've traveled all over Mexico, and nowhere more than here is the power of women more deeply rooted. I'd really like you to see my father's drawings of this kind of Istmeña. One shows a group of women at a vela dancing in a circle with bottles of beer balanced upright on their heads. The first woman who loses her balance and lets the beer bottle drop from her head must drink a beer and then rejoin the group. He also has a series of watercolors depicting Isthmus men who drag their drunken wives home from a vela."

I told Julin about a claim Pablo had made involving the French soldiers who had been defeated by Juchitecan warriors in 1866. According to what he said, the residents of Juchitán invited the French soldiers still alive to bed down with their daughters. "My father," Julin said, "once sketched a caricature of Juchitecans carrying a dying Frenchman to their barracks to cure him, and they are saying, 'Let's save this man. He'll give us some good seed to clean up the race.' His caricature is accurate. We believe, with all the complexes the Spaniards put in our heads, that we are ugly, that we are Indians, that we are black. Yes, to a certain degree, we are racist with our own people. We say, for example, 'Ay, *pobrecita*, that girl is getting married to a *negrito*.'"

Julin talked nonstop. Whenever I asked her a question, she'd take a bite out of her hamburger or eat a couple of fries, but she couldn't keep up. By the time our conversation wound down, it was three in the afternoon, and her food was cold and uneaten. I explained to her that my bus left at six, and that I had to pack and retrieve a suitcase I had left with Rosa. We promised to write each other and then parted ways.

At four thirty, I took a bus to Juchitán. I arrived at the mortuary at five, as Rosa and I had agreed. Yet neither Rosa nor Pablo were there. Had Pablo talked Rosa out of our last meeting? Sonia, Pablo's wife, brought my luggage to the lobby of the mortuary and promised she would thank Rosa and Pablo on my behalf. On the way to the bus station, I checked inside the suitcase I had left with Rosa. Everything was in order except the photocopy of my journal. It was smudged with grease and some of the pages were out of order, and I realized why Rosa knew my journal better than I did.

By the time the taxi reached the bus station, night had fallen and a yellow moon rose over Juchitán's low roofline. I bought a ticket and took a seat at the back of the terminal. In front of me were five rows of seats occupied entirely by Zapotecs engrossed in a soap opera on an overhead television. Several minutes before my bus arrived, a young woman peddling frozen mango popsicles from a corrugated washbasin entered the room. She wore a solid colored, wrap-around skirt that identified her as a resident of San Blas, the ultra-liberal community that sided with the Juchitecos in the war against the French. Like all Isthmus women, Blaseñas are noted for their commercial aptitude. At many of the velas and bus stations and plazas I had visited in the Isthmus, even those ranging fifty miles from San Blas, I often saw a pair of young women in solid colored skirts working a crowd with some kind of trinket or food.

As the young woman worked her way toward my seat at the back of the terminal, I began to see in her the kind of beauty Brasseur de Bourbourg must have seen when he discovered the young Juana Cata selling cigarettes and coconut candy in the barracks of Tehuantepec. Like the picture he painted of Juana Cata, the young woman had bronze skin and lively black eyes, and she wore her hair in two braids that were tied at the end with a ribbon. She offered her popsicles to men and women alike, perfectly at ease when they refused, though to some degree, her manner was proud. Soon, she stood in front of me, offering a popsicle in her outstretched hand. I paid her thirty cents, laid the popsicle on my suitcase and asked if I could take a photo of her. "Yes," she said, "but outside." I followed her out of the station to the parking lot where the busses came and went. We were alone. I took several photos of her, and as the automatic lens zoomed in and out, the experience became somehow erotic. Sensing this, she left and returned with her opposite, a young woman so fair skinned she could have been a descendent of one of the defeated French soldiers. Emboldened now that her friend was beside her, she spoke.

"Are you going to Oaxaca?"

I told her I was. She fixed her black eyes on my camera.

"You've got fifteen minutes until your bus arrives," she said, "why don't you show me how to take photos?" I handed her the camera, and when I showed her how to work the shutter release, my shoulder brushed hers, and for a moment, I wished my bus would never come. Rather than taking a photo of me, or her friend, she stepped into the parking lot and pointed the camera at the moon. The flash went off repeatedly, illuminating her dark beauty again and again until the camera ran out of film. Then a bus pulled into the station, and she hurried back to where I was standing.

"That's your bus, mister," she said.

"It says Mexico City."

"Yes, but it stops in Oaxaca," she said. I stood still, staring at her. "And you'd better get on it before it leaves."

I went into the station to retrieve my luggage. The popsicle had melted and streaks of the juice ran down the fake leather sides of my cardboard suitcase. I waited until the young woman wasn't looking, and threw what was left of the popsicle into a trash bin. Then I got into the bus, and when it pulled away from the curb, I looked at her, hoping for a wave of her hand, but she had already moved on to a newly arrived customer, the only other foreign male I'd seen in Juchitán.

The Spy

Two weeks after anthropologist Beverly Chiñas arrived in Tehuantepec for her first field study, the women of the market denounced her as a spy. She had been sent by the government, they said, to gather information for the purpose of increasing taxes. Chiñas explained to the women that she had come to study Isthmus markets and vendors as part of her thesis. But to the women, it didn't ring true. Why would a rich gringa come all this way to study such a poor, simple thing? Several weeks later, things got worse. A story on the front page of an Isthmus weekly accused Chiñas of being a Yankee imperialist spy sent to explore the possibility of a new, inter-ocean canal.

On reading about Chiñas's trial by fire in the preface of her case study, *Isthmus Zapotecs,* you drop your guard, you know what follows will be honest—although why Chiñas chose to study Isthmus markets is unclear. She does, however, drop occasional hints. "Women's roles," she writes, "have been one of my great preoccupations since I became aware of some of the ambiguities of such roles in our culture at the age of about twelve." Another factor in the believability of her analysis is that between 1966 and 1990, she spent over two years living in the Isthmus. This might not make her an insider, but I'd be willing to bet that if the women she came to know and write about were approached, they would bestow upon her the title of Honorary Insider.

At the time Chiñas's book was published in 1973, it was an anomaly. Until then, those who came to observe and write about the Isthmus Zapotecs had been male. *Isthmus Zapotecs* was also a groundbreaking book because it represented the first field study that focused on Isthmus women rather than the society as a whole. In her preface, Chiñas complains that too often women in field studies are depicted as part of the background or, as she describes them, "mindless creatures as colorless as fog." She also explains why she chose to focus on Isthmus women: "Not because I believe women are more important than men in Isthmus Zapotec culture but because they seem as valid a focal point as men, and one too long neglected." From a masculine perspective, this might sound as though Isthmus women will be portrayed with a feminine bias. But on reading her book, you soon learn that Chiñas writes what she sees and hears with unfailing accuracy. Her rendition of Isthmus women rings true to all but the most radical combatants involved in the controversy.

In *Isthmus Zapotecs*, Chiñas's stance on matriarchy is buried at the end of a section devoted to Isthmus women's role in history. Unlike Mexico's national historians, Chiñas tells us, who tend to slight women by not giving their names, Isthmus historians specify the exact names and even the kinship relations of the heroic women who fought beside their men: "Perhaps this is no more than history personalized, but it may be another manifestation of that elusive quality of relationships between the sexes which has led more than a quarter century of casual observers to perpetuate the myth of an Isthmus Zapotec matriarchy."

At first glance, Chiñas's stance seems unequivocal: Isthmus matriarchy is myth. But on repeated readings, the phrases "elusive quality of relationship between the sexes" and "casual observers" begin to stand out. The wording, especially her term "elusive" is unusual. It is not a word you would expect to find in a field study. I believe this phrase is Chiñas's way of acknowledging that although she believes matriarchy a myth, any attempt to capture or categorize relations between men and women is a tricky business and that the reader must beware. The phrase "casual observer" also merits attention. It has the familiar echo of Covarrubias "superficial observers" and Henestrosa's "superficial men," and the message is clear: Any talk about matriarchy or the reputation of Isthmus women should be blamed on outsiders.

Having identified the originators of the myth, Chiñas gives us an idea about who is propagating it. In large part, she blames travel guides, where exaggeration and distortion about the Isthmus and Istmeños is abundant. One of the most exaggerated examples comes from *Terry's Guide to Mexico:* "Like certain other native mothers, [Istmeñas] nurse their youngsters until they are three or four years old, and it is no un-common sight to see a child descend from a mother's knee after a lacteal repast, repair to an easy chair, light a cigarette and enjoy an after-dinner smoke. Children are sometimes seen smoking a cigar as fat as their own little legs."

In general, the travel guides recommend avoiding the Isthmus, and this serves them well. If no one travels to there—which is generally the case—then no one will ever call them on their exaggeration. "Visitors traveling overland to or from Chiapas will have occasion to pass through this area," one writes, "and the best advice is to stay on the move." Or, "It's a hot and steamy region long run-down and not in any way im-proved by the 1980's oil boom."At times they single out cities: "we tried very hard to view the ugly, dirty streets of Tehuantepec as the picturesque remains of an old civilization." About Juchitán, which is in no way a port, they are less kind. "[Juchitán] has a sleazy tropical port atmosphere."

In the same passage, Chiñas explains why she considers Isthmus ma-triarchy a myth: "I use the word myth because anthropologists have never encountered any truly matriarchal societies, i.e., cultures in which the women's roles are mirror images of men's roles in patriarchal cultures."

In a later edition of *Isthmus Zapotecs,* Chiñas reaffirms her matriarchy-is-myth stance. She also presents an alternative model that she feels better describes Isthmus gender relations than does matriarchy or patriarchy. "Not until the 1970s," Chiñas writes, "was a type of culture recognized where women do hold a central, but different, place than men: the matrifocal culture." Ann Tanner first proposed the matrifocal model after extensive cross-cultural studies in Indonesia and Africa in the early 1970s. In Tanner's model, a society or culture is matrifocal if the mother is considered culturally central to the family. Although mothers across the globe are considered structurally central, Tanner tells us, few are taken to be culturally central. Cultural centrality requires that "the people of the culture hold an *ideal* of the mother role as central to the functioning whole of the culture." A mother in a matrifocal culture must also be "affectively central"—the emotional bonds that tie the mother to her children must be the strongest and most enduring in the family.

Other key characteristics of a matrifocal culture are egalitarian rela-tions between the sexes. "The father is almost always living in the matri-focal household, and relations between husband and wife tend to be highly egalitarian," Chiñas writes. "It is not only *acceptable* for women to exercise power and authority in their everyday lives, it is culturally expected and encouraged." In addition, both sexes in matrifocal culture must have roles that are important, especially economic and ritual roles. Girls must be taught to become bold, energetic, and decisive in preparation for their roles as wives and mothers.

According to Chiñas, Zapotec culture is a classic case of matrifocality, and she fully embraces it. "Earlier social scientists had recognized that some cultures and subcultures produced a number of matrifocal families, but these were seen as aberrant family types caused by the absence of a father figure and a result of extreme poverty in urban environments, especially among Blacks in the United States." No one—until Tanner proposed her model in 1974—had suggested the existence of societies where a matrifocal structure is considered legitimate rather than an aberration from the patriarchal pattern.

The Other City Hall

DECEMBER 1997. If there is a single issue upon which insiders and outsiders agree, it is their appraisal of women's role in politics. Women might provide the political muscle for strikes, highway blockades, sit-ins, and marches, but they are poorly accounted for as mayors or members of city councils. And even when a woman is appointed to a city council, the seat she holds is inevitably less than essential to the functioning of city government. Both the liberal COCEI (Worker-Peasant-Student Coalition of the Isthmus of Tehuantepec) and the conservative PRI have had the habit of appointing women to lesser posts in culture and education, while the job of city labor leader or treasurer went to men. Only in one case, I was told, did a woman hold a position of real power in the Isthmus. Her name was Rosario Vialba, and she was the mayor of Ixtepec.

Like Matias Romero, Ixtepec is a small town that was built around a railway junction that was all but abandoned when the Panama Canal was opened in 1914. Since then, Ixtepec has taken on a lethargic pace and a sleepy mood that inspired other Istmeños to rename it Tristepec, or Sad City. Covarrubias, who visited Ixtepec thirty years after the opening of the canal, wrote: "Listless, sun-baked Ixtepec comes to life only in the early morning and afternoon and at midnight, train times when for a half hour the main street rustles with the sound of full skirts and bare feet."

But there is a volatile underside to Ixtepec that does not get much attention, and every so often it flares up and catches all of Mexico by surprise. In 1978, for example, an incident involving Ixtepec's women began taking shape on January 15, when the local news reported that demonstrators in Ixtepec had decided to wrest control of city government from PRI. Demonstrators claimed that PRI was attempting to impose rule at Ixtepec's city hall even though they had lost the municipal elections on November 20 of the previous year. According to the newspaper *El Satélite,* leftist COCEI was responsible for inciting the demonstrators to protest and was summoning a new march to demand that the will of the people be met. Two days later, when Oaxaca's governor Ruiz Jiménez went to quell the flare-up, an article in *Punto Cívico* described the event: "While attempting to convince representatives of Partido Popular Socialista to abandon city hall in Ixtepec, Governor Ruiz Jiménez was knocked to the ground and beaten by hundreds of women. He was able to break away from the women and reached his car only to be pelted with stones." The violence continued ten days later in Juchitán. Not to be outdone by the women of Ixtepec, the female vendors in Juchitán's market threw fish and vegetables at police when they attempted to detain a COCEI youth.

Two days prior to my visit to Ixtepec, I made an eleven o'clock appointment with mayor Vialba's secretary. On the appointed day, I took a bus to Ixtepec and hired a taxi to take me to Independencia #11, which I assumed would be city hall. The taxi driver soon found Independencia, but all along both sides of the street were middle-class homes painted white, some with red tile roofs and none that looked remotely like the kind of building that would house the mayor's offices. When the taximeter entered into three digits, I got out, let the taxi go and asked several people who were passing by where I might find #11. No one knew. Then I noticed a sticker on a white door held open by a rock. On the door, someone had posted a flyer in red, green, and white, the official colors of the PRI political party. At the top of the flyer was Vialba's name, and below, her post: Presidente Municipal, or mayor. It seemed like a public place, so I entered without knocking. The antechamber was small and very much resembled a typical Mexican office with metal desks and chairs, mechanical typewriters, and a trio of people behind a desk who looked as though they'd been stunned by the heat. They ignored me. A minute later, a door swung open, and a lively little man who spoke at the speed of light said:

"How can I help you?"

"I have an appointment with the mayor at 11:00."

"She's not here," he said without apology.

"I made an appointment with her secretary," I said.

"She's giving a progress report to her superiors at PRI headquarters," he said. "Maybe if you come back a little later she'll be here."

The man left, and my mind turned to coffee; I had yet to have my first cup that morning. On my way out, I passed by a desk I hadn't noticed at first. There a young woman stared into an old computer and an even older dot matrix printer from which a ream of pinstripe green computer paper flowed onto the concrete floor.

On the street, the little man I'd spoken to inside the office hurried past me.

"By the way," he said, "I'm the *sindico*."

"What's a *sindico*?"

"A *sindico* is a *sindico,* and what I do is make judgments inside the party."

"What party?"

"The only party worth belonging to, PRI."

"And where is city hall?"

"In the center of town," he said as he walked away. "For the moment, we've moved our offices to this site because there was a little problem downtown."

"So where can I get a decent cup of coffee around here?"

"At the grocery store on the corner," he said.

The "little problem downtown" that the *sindico* mentioned and the fact that Vialba was governing from a residential neighborhood could only mean one thing: There was a disagreement about who won the last municipal election, and one party had seized city hall, while the other, Vialba and PRI, had set up shop on the outskirts of town. This was an example of an Isthmus tradition called parallel government, and it was neither new nor unusual.

One of the first occurrences of parallel government came about in 1977 after PRI won Juchitán's mayoral election. COCEI termed the election a fraud and demonstrated peacefully at the PRI mayor's inaugural speech. But after troops shot and killed one COCEI demonstrator and wounded several others, the demonstrators looted nearby businesses, carrying away what they could. In the period that followed the protests and looting, they tried a new strategy. COCEI set up a parallel government that they hoped would bypass city hall and its newly elected mayor. Neighborhood committees resolved legal disputes, marital problems, labor conflicts, and difficulties that arose due to barrio rivalries. The committees also planned, organized, and ran COCEI's political undertakings. The party leadership made a point of not charging for appearance before a committee, which soon won them the devoted support of the poor.

At the grocery store, the owner said she served no coffee, and that I'd have to go to the center of town. Eventually, I found a café downtown not far from city hall. The coffee was as weak as tea, and a television blared a soap opera at a deafening volume. On the walk back to Vialba's office, anti-PRI graffiti was sprayed on abandoned buildings and government offices and many walls not belonging to anyone in particular. PRI, you must know, does not have a good reputation in the Isthmus political arena. Many Istmeños accuse PRI of defrauding elections, financing its campaigns with taxes, and winning elections with promises it never intended to keep. This would not be so insidious if PRI accepted a loss every now and then at the election box, as is the case with other political parties in Mexico. But the truth of the matter is that until the year 2000, PRI had won all of Mexico's presidential elections and the large majority of federal and local elections since it was founded in 1929. Few, if any, believe they have done so honestly.

By the time I returned to Vialba's office, it was noon, and she still hadn't arrived. I seated myself in a wooden folding chair whose backrest cut into my spine. After another half hour of waiting, the *sindico* ushered me into a large room where Vialba was seated at a desk in front of an empty wall. She was dressed in a velvet huipil and enagua and wore a gold bracelet on one wrist, a silver watch on the other. Around her neck was the traditional necklace with a single coin, probably a $20 piece. Chairs lined the other three walls that were filled with men and women in tattered clothing who looked as though they had come from the countryside to meet with the mayor. Many were old with dusty white hair, and all were skinny as pine needles. They were in a variety of states of alertness. Some were on the verge of sleep, others looked dazed.

"We have a meeting underway," Vialba said. "But if you like, I can spend a few minutes with you." I sat down in a lone chair at the middle of the room and asked Vialba about women's work in Ixtepec. "As with all Isthmus towns, Ixtepec is a place that has stood still in terms of costume, tradition, and culture." When the city was founded and the Isthmus represented one of the shortest routes between the Atlantic and Pacific, workers from all over the world came to labor in Ixtepec. "They even say that once," Vialba said, "a Russian resided here." The railway, which was the most modern and efficient means of transportation at the time, made Ixtepec competitive with other towns in the region. In addition to railway workers, many of Ixtepec's residents live by way of agriculture. "In most cases," Vialba said, "our women play a supportive role, working to help her partner achieve better living conditions through embroidery, cooking, weaving, and all other types of work available to them."

"Our women did not gain the right to vote until fifty years ago," Vialba said, "but women have always participated in politics in the sense that a woman represents a partner in a relationship." In recent years, however, women had made headway in terms of appointment or election to political posts. At the state level, five women held the post of mayor, and at the national level, eighty-nine. In the federal assembly, women represented 30 percent of the electorate. "In the past," Vialba said, "winning an election as a woman was difficult because Istmeños had not assimilated the idea that women should hold political posts." Still, there were women in the past who served as role models. One was a teacher named Juana Cata Romero, who distinguished herself by way of her intelligence. "Our grandmothers also speak to us about the Revolution in 1910," Vialba said. "The women weren't just bringing food to the front lines. They fought too, bringing encouragement and accompanying their men into battle."

In the most recent election for mayor in Ixtepec, Vialba insisted that PRI had won at the ballot box. "Despite the fact that we won the election, with a voter turnout of fifty percent, a coalition of COCEI and PRD (Partido de la Revolución Democrática) took over city hall." The reigning power, according to Vialba, was COCEI, who she accused of hiding in the skirts of PRD. "But now some of the opposition groups have taken up blackmail as a weapon, and I can only say that we are here and we will continue negotiating with the opposition." Then she paused and added, "The coalition always works in parallel, not integrated, because they work for their particular political interests. They aren't the kind who throw away the flag and say, 'We are the government, and let's govern for the red, the green, and the white and for everyone else, right? They always live in an eternal competition of political proselytism, and they are always feeding no one else except party members." Both PRI and the coalition funded themselves through their supporters. "Every parallel government has a director, and the director has people he feeds and encourages because fortunately, each one of us identifies with the people in his or her town."

The conversation then moved away from politics, and Vialba gave her opinion on the question of matriarchy. "I think that no one can live for themselves alone, they have to live in agreement with others. Even more so in the Isthmus where you must be in constant communication with your spouse. Here, the men and women make decisions together. I know, because I have four children and was married for twenty years to the same man. We always made decisions together."

Vialba spoke briefly about what she had accomplished for Isthmus women. "I have achieved many things. Most important, is that by being a woman mayor, I've made it possible for other women to aspire to political posts like mine and to feel useful serving the community." Vialba had also given support to the idea that women deserve a permanent pension. She had looked to other countries such as Canada, where more attention and care is taken with women because they are the source of life. "In Mexico, physical pain sometimes exceeds moral pain. Because when you get up and your children don't eat, this for you is an incurable illness. If you don't have the means to feed your children—and this is what happens in Mexico—the Isthmus woman works. She knows how to stew, to cook, and if not, she buys tamales and sells them. She also sells hammocks and embroiders. No, here in the Isthmus, you don't let your child die of hunger—you get to work."

The Princess

Born in Paris in 1932, outsider Elena Poniatowska was the child of two wealthy exiles, her mother Mexican, her father French. Early in her childhood, she learned that her father traced his ancestry to the last king of Poland. Elena saw little of her mother, Rosa. She liked to travel, and when World War II began, she was too busy driving an ambulance to attend to her daughter's needs. As a consequence, Elena and her sister were shipped to the French countryside where they were cared for by their grandmother and governesses. When Elena came of age, her mother enrolled her and her sister in a parochial school. "We got special treatment," Poniatowska said, "because we were considered princesses because of my father's family name." In fact, Poniatowska was destined to marry a European prince. Then the war worsened, and Poniatowska's mother brought both her daughters to Mexico, their new homeland.

Once they had settled in, Poniatowska developed a special relationship with her Indian maids and servants. Their lives fascinated her "because they didn't keep the distances that European maîtres d'hôtel and chefs do." She followed the maids as they shopped, made the beds, washed their hair, kissed their boyfriends on park benches. And although Poniatowska spoke French when she arrived, the maids taught her Spanish in a matter of months. "From that time on," Poniatowska writes, "I have always had very sympathetic feelings for the housemaids." But there were drawbacks from learning a language this way. "In fact, until recently," Poniatowska explains, "I still repeated certain expressions used by less educated people."

Elena completed her education in private schools, the last of which was the Sacred Heart Convent in Philadelphia. In 1953, when she was twenty, she used her connections to land a job as an interviewer with Mexico City's largest daily newspaper, *El Excelsior*. In the early years of her career as an interviewer, Poniatowska focused her work on politicians, artists, and celebrities. As time passed, however, she shifted her focus to the poor and came to be known as what critic Beth Jorgensen calls "a literary champion of the oppressed." She also became more vocal about her stand on feminism: "It would be absurd to say that I am not a feminist. I am completely on the side of women, I want women to progress." About Mexican men, she wrote: "The Mexican macho is always ready not only to dominate a woman, but also to squash her if he can; when he has squashed her and rubbed her into the floor, then he says, 'Now you need me.' Then he picks up that human garbage, that mop on the floor, and then she is his woman who will wait on him, bring him children, because he has taken all of her blood, all of her will and desire to do something in life other than serve him and be his property."

In 1963, Elena Poniatowska began *Here's To You, Jesusa,* a book that reveals much about the agenda she brought to the Isthmus and also about her approach to writing about women. As champion of the underclass, the author's stated goal for the book was to lend a voice to one of Mexico's disenfranchised women and also to reconnect with the Indian maids and servants in her childhood home. She began work on the book by searching out an appropriate narrator. She had to be female, but she could not have any of the so-called feminine characteristics: she could be neither self-sacrificing, submissive, or even a mother. Poniatowska found her ideal narrator in Josefina Borquez. She was a poor, illiterate washerwoman from the Isthmus of Tehuantepec who worked in the ritzy neighborhood where Poniatowska lived. "I met her in a laundromat when I heard her talking," Poniatowska told an interviewer. "I liked the way she talked, and I sought her out."

But from the beginning, Poniatowska and Borquez did not get along. They met every Wednesday for a year, during which Poniatowska attempted to record Borquez's turbulent life in and around the Mexican Revolution. "When I started out, it was extremely difficult to interview her. She'd say I was wasting her time. Then she wanted to talk about herself. She'd want to spend hours telling me that the pipes were stopped up and that the lady of the house didn't fix them." After *Here's To You, Jesusa* was completed, Poniatowska revealed in an interview that one of the most poignant scenes in the book, in which Emiliano Zapata dresses in Indian clothes to return Jesusa and other women to their troops, was invented. In other interviews, Poniatowska reports that in the course of editing the novel, she imposed her own ideological agenda, because, as she puts it, if she were to let her Josefina have her way, "The novel would have been only about spiritualism, high prices, and the dismal state of current affairs."

When Poniatowska presented the manuscript to Josefina, she was surprised by her reaction. In typical Istmeña style—strong language included—Josefina confronted the author. "No," she said, "you didn't understand anything." Josefina asked that she never be bothered with that "fucking thing" again and, above all, not to put her name in it. Poniatowska tried reading from the manuscript; Josephina wasn't interested. But somehow, the author interpreted Josephina's reaction in a positive light. "I felt she liked it," Poniatowska said, "but she didn't say anything to me."

Early in her career as a journalist, Poniatowska developed a passion for photography and photographers. In the 1980s, this passion led her to collaborate with a number of Mexico's leading photographers to produce three photographic essays for which she provided the text. First came *La casa en la tierra* (The House on the Land) in 1980, followed by *El último guajolote* (The Last Turkey) in 1982. Poniatowska's third collaboration came in the late 1980s when she and Graciela Iturbide produced a photographic essay devoted to Isthmus women. Given Poniatowska's fascination with indigenous causes and her devotion to women's issues, the project must have seemed ideal. The end product—*Juchitán de las mujeres*—was published in 1989.

Key to understanding the text that accompanies Iturbide's photos is this: The language Poniatowska has chosen to portray Isthmus women to the world is the language of poetry, rich with images yet loosely tied to reality. Rather than make the claim that Isthmus society is matriarchal, Poniatowska simply provides image after image of Isthmus women in which "man is a kitten between their legs." Here, for example, is the opening paragraph of *Juchitán de las mujeres:* "In Juchitán, Oaxaca, the men can't find a place to hide except in the women, the children hang from their breasts, the iguanas look to the world from on top of their heads. In Juchitán, the trees have hearts, the men, whistles sweet or salty, according to the appetite, and the women are very proud because they carry their redemption between their legs and they deliver to each one his own death. 'The little death' as the amorous act is called."

For those who know the history of the Isthmus, the book's opening image, in which men find refuge only in women, alludes not only to reentering the womb but also to a recurring theme of Isthmus women's involvement in political conflict. According to oral history, Isthmus men have literally hidden themselves in the billowing, full-length skirts of Isthmus women, as Porfirio Díaz is reported to have taken refuge in the skirts of Doña Cata. It is a powerful image, and the accompanying photos by Iturbide serve as a kind of visual confirmation of Poniatowska's writing. Many of the photographs were shot from below; we know this because the plump Istmeñas glare down at us from the photos. Most often the shots are posed with peripheral objects such as goats, chickens, or iguanas that cue us in about the grand proportions of the women Iturbide has chosen to photograph.

Although Poniatowska addresses the usual characteristics for which the women are best known—assertiveness and financial and social independence—the predominant theme in her rendition of Isthmus women is sex and the language of sex. At work in the market, Poniatowska writes, the women gossip and joke with each other, always speaking in erotic metaphors. Eggs suggest testicles, and salt, semen. "Zapotec women have always been openly erotic, and they wear their sensuality on their shirtsleeves. Sex is a little clay toy; they take it in their hands, mold it as they please."

Like all outsiders, Poniatowska compares the women of Juchitán with the image of women in other regions of Mexico. "The women of Juchitán are strong-willed, in contrast with other regions, where women shrink back and cry: in Jalisco, in the Bajío, in Mexico City. They have nothing to do with the self-sacrificing Mexican mothers drowned in tears." And how is it they are able to hold sway over their men? "Isthmus women impose themselves," writes Poniatowska, "with the white ruffles of their skirts, the tinkling of their jewelry, the golden lightning of their smiles."

Poniatowska never confronts the fact that there are few women in political posts in Juchitán. Instead, she attempts to use poetic language to sidestep the issue of women's role in Juchitán's politics, claiming that "women participate in marches, overpowering, with their iron calves" and that they "beat policemen." The women do participate in marches, but any evidence about them beating up policemen is lacking. But should we be surprised at the liberties Poniatowska has taken with the truth about Isthmus women? Probably not. Because as Beth Jorgensen reminds us: "For Elena Poniatowska photography, like print journalism, is both a documentary and a creative art with a unique power to interpret the world around us."

In a sense, Poniatowska is a modern-day Rabelais, and the Isthmus woman is her Gargantuan. Exaggeration is mixed with satire, insight, and occasionally wisdom. Take, for example, her treatment of the *totopo*, the Isthmus equivalent of the tortilla. "Right over there, the Isthmus *totopos*, those giant tortillas that are cooked underground, crunchy and rotund like the perimeter of a skirt over the earth. They are proof that life has no bitterness. *Totopos* laugh. They keep on laughing. They even laugh in the middle of a bite."

In interviews, Poniatowska defends this kind of exaggeration in her work as part of a literary strategy to make her point. This might be so. But whenever I read what she's written about Isthmus women, the word *hyperbole* comes to mind and a definition of it that I learned as a boy. "Hyperbole," I was taught, "is a lie told in service of truth." The question here is this: Just whose truth is Poniatowska telling, hers or Isthmus women's?

Purse Strings

NOVEMBER 1998. Juchitán's market is housed on the first floor of city hall, an imposing, two-story structure that occupies an entire block on the east side of the main plaza. The entrance to the market is flanked on either side by thirty-one broad arches that support a roofed corridor running the length of the first floor. The corridor is congested with women selling goods to a small army of customers who begin arriving at dawn and don't slack off until after dark, when the hot chocolate vendors arrive. At one end of this corridor are Zapotec hammock vendors, and at the other end, women hawking poultry and armadillos. In between are a variety of women selling bread, coconut candy, and regional dress, and jewelers offering gold necklaces *de fantasia* that poorer Istmeñas like to wear to fiestas.

Crossing this busy corridor and entering the market proper is a disappointment. Gray cement predominates, and the market's poor lighting and vaulted ceiling create the impression of an abandoned cathedral stripped of its pews and icons. Although the interior of the market houses butchers' shops, cut-flower stands, taquerias, and dozens of other businesses, some portion of the women who used to sell inside the market have fled and set up shop on the adjacent side streets. There, under multicolored canopies, are dozens of women selling fruit and vegetables from wooden crates and fish laid out in neat rows on rickety tables. Around the corner, elderly women call out invitations to sit down and enjoy Iguana cooked in tomato sauce or sliced into pieces and fried. Juchitán's marketplace seems to run on the principle that customers prefer shopping outdoors.

Other than to eat an occasional taco or to drink *licuado,* I had spent little time in Juchitán's market. But on this, my third trip to the Isthmus, I wanted one of the hand-woven hammocks sold at the northern end of the corridor. Color didn't matter, durability did. It would have to withstand several seasons of fog and occasional heat and, if possible, provide an antidote to my insomnia as it swung between the trees in my yard. Although the hammocks in Juchitán's market run between $15 and $25, they were considered big ticket items, so I knew there would be bartering involved. Rather than go unarmed, I enlisted the help of Rosa's mother, Elena. She had developed her bartering skills as owner of a ranch, a bus franchise, and an eatery in downtown Juchitán. If anyone could get me a good price on a hammock, it was Elena.

At two in the afternoon on a clear and windy Friday, Elena and I walked the five blocks from the mortuary to the market. While we were waiting for a stoplight to change, Elena turned and faced me. "Listen," she said. "I know a vendor named Manuela who sells hammocks at reasonable prices. She's seventy-one years old and has been selling in the marketplace since she was sixteen, so she's pretty crafty. Don't let on that you speak Spanish, and let me do the talking." I agreed, and we arrived at the market ten minutes later, sweating but ready to barter.

Much of the controversy concerning Isthmus women centers around the market, even though both sides agree that women dominate it and have done so for centuries. As long ago as 1580, Torres de Laguna wrote about women's key role in Isthmus markets, and in 1908, American naturalist Hans Gadow noted that "the whole of trade is in [women's] hands; so much so, indeed, that all commercial transactions are done by them, or at least require their sanction." Fifty years ago, Covarrubias's description of the market showed that across the centuries, little had changed. "It is evident that only women sell in the markets; the meek and rare men seen there come from elsewhere." A survey in 1991 counted 1,704 women and 87 men at work in Juchitán's marketplace. The men counted in the survey were foreigners or relatives of women vendors in need of temporary assistance during times of mourning or ill health.

Disagreement enters the picture when it comes to determining the significance of women's control of the market. Those who argue in favor of matriarchy tend to portray the market as central to the Isthmus's agrarian life, thus increasing the significance of this control. Covarrubias, for example, writes, "As in Tehuantepec, the heart and soul of [Juchitán] is the buzzing market, and its life and blood are its women." Poniatowska follows suit, depicting Juchitán as a rural community in which commerce begins and ends in the market. She describes the business cycle in Juchitán as follows: "[Men] leave home at dawn to work; they are iguana hunters, peasants, fisherman." When the men return, they hand over their harvest to the women, who carry it to the market. Because, as Poniatowska reminds us, "Only women sell." The business cycle is completed when the women return home with their earnings, which they dole out as they see fit. Women's control of the household purse strings is so broadly accepted that a phrase—*xhquie ni* (his penis)—is commonly use to refer to the pocket change a man keeps for himself after turning over his paycheck or the proceeds from his harvest or other cash-generating activities.

Some observers from the pro-matriarchy camp take women's control of the market one step further, arguing that by way of their dominance of Isthmus markets, women control the economy of the entire region. Insider Edaena Saynes-Vázquez disagrees, arguing that the picture painted by outsiders is dishonest. "It is true that women 'control the market,'" she writes, "but it is important to note that this commercial activity embodies a small trade compared to the large-scale commercial activity that takes place in the Isthmus region. This important issue is not expressed in Poniatowska's work. On the contrary, it seems to show that women dominate the entire economy, which is far from reality." Although Saynes-Vázquez presents no evidence to support her claim, one look at Juchitán's yellow pages is sufficient to be convinced that Poniatowska is not telling the whole truth in her depiction of Juchitán as a rural community. The list of businesses and commercial enterprises numbers more than three hundred, including video satellite retailers, sporting goods stores, travel agencies, appliance stores, auto dealerships, muffler shops, radio stations, credit unions, and so on.

Another cause of dissension is Isthmus Zapotecs' attitude toward market vendors. Many fault the tendency of the pro-matriarchy camp to glorify the vendors and their work. "It is the Juchitec woman who owns the market," writes Poniatowska. "She is the powerful one; the merchant; the bargainer; the generous, avaricious, greedy one." Others in the pro-matriarchy camp assert that money is secondary to the sense of community shared between women vendors and that they spend more time socializing than selling. The women exchange the latest news, they joke and laugh, and each transaction involves reciprocation of one kind or another. Howard Campbell sees women's activities in the market in a different light. "Although many external observers have celebrated Zapotec women's marketing role, vending is, in fact, hard work, which involves carrying baskets, standing or squatting in the fiery Isthmus sun, traveling on rickety buses for hours, and dealing with abusive tax collectors." Moreover, Campbell points out, competition in the marketplace is intense and volatile. Some women are even excluded from participating, and others must squat in uncomfortable positions in the grimy streets amid heavy foot and automobile traffic. As in Isthmus society generally, some vendors do much better than others, whereas the average market woman just struggles to make a living.

Manuela's booth in Juchitán's market had to be one of the most humble in the region. In truth, it wasn't a booth at all, but simply a cabinet on which Manuela had stacked dozens of hammocks in vivid, tropical colors. Unlike the other vendors who stood and called out to potential customers, Manuela was squatted on a low stool that was squeezed into a space no more than two feet wide. She had a dejected, world-weary face that was crisscrossed with lines from too much work and too many days exposed to the Isthmus sun. She wore a black and white skirt that was mismatched with a maroon, everyday huipil. Her white hair was pulled tight into a bun, and when she rose to shake my hand, her head did not reach to the top of my shoulders.

The space all around Manuela was tight. Behind her a young woman sold fruit from a stand, and, on either side of Manuela were women selling huipiles and enaguas. Across the corridor a vendor sold hats from a wire rack, and another plied holy cards, perfume, and candles. The lack of space in Juchitán's market is an old problem that city hall has tried to alleviate by constructing three smaller neighborhood markets that failed not long after they were opened. "Any attempt to relocate and decentralize commerce has met with fierce opposition of the vendors," writes anthropologist Marinella Miano Borruso, "and, in general, the people are accustomed to going to the city center to shop, which is the best place to meet and socialize with other women."

For several minutes, Elena and Manuela exchanged news and caught up on gossip. Then Elena suggested to Manuela that I might be interested in a hammock. Manuela's face rose, and she turned away from us to her cabinet where she had two dozen hammocks in a variety of colors stacked high. She reached for a yellow one, took it out of its transparent plastic bag and handed one end to Elena and walked three paces back. Elena was the first to speak:

"No, not this color." I hadn't mentioned a preference for one color or another but I assumed this was part of Elena's bargaining technique, so I kept quiet.

"What color do you want, then?" Manuela asked.

"Blue-green."

"I don't have anything in blue-green," Manuela said. Elena picked up a blue hammock from the table.

"How much are you asking for this one?"

"225 pesos." This was the equivalent of $22.50.

"If you had a blue-green hammock," Elena said, "I'd gladly give you the 225 pesos."

"It's 225 and not a *centavo* less," Manuela said.

"Since when did you get so expensive? That's too much for a hammock like this."

"No," Manuela said. "It's as cheap as they come. But because you're my friend, I'll let you have it for 200." Here Manuela held up two fingers as if Elena couldn't speak Spanish. Then she tried without success to put the hammock in Elena's arms.

"That's still too high," Elena said. "I remember paying a lot less the last time I bought one."

"Yes," Manuela said, "and at that time, the thread was also cheaper. Now that the thread's gone up, so has the hammock."

"But tell me seriously," Elena said, "how much do you really want?"

"I'll give it to you for 180," Manuela said.

"Too much," Elena countered. "My friend here wants to bring home a souvenir of the good times he's had here in the Isthmus. Let's not send him home empty-handed. I'll give you 150."

"You can take it with you for 170," said Manuela, "but not a peso less. My brother is sick, and I need the money for his medication." This sounded made up.

"What other colors do you have," asked Elena. Manuela pointed to yellow and red hammocks on the table near her stool. "I don't much like those colors," said Elena. "And isn't that a stain?" I looked at the hammock. There was no stain.

"You can take that out with Ariel laundry detergent," Manuela said. "It takes out the toughest stains. Grease, dirt, you name it." I still didn't see any stain. Then Elena looked at me and said to Manuela:

"We'll be back in a moment."

"I won't be here," Manuela said, but she didn't move. In fact, she followed us as we stepped out of the shade and into the Isthmus sun. "What do you think?" Elena asked me. "Buy it," I said. "Why kill yourself over 20 pesos?"

We returned to Manuela's table. The look of suffering on her face had returned. Before Elena could say anything, Manuela burst out: "I'll give it to you for 150, but only because you are my friend." Then she hit the hammock with her fist and repeated "because you are my friend." Several school children stopped to watch the drama, and I felt embarrassed.

"Give her the money," I said to Elena, who, for the first time in the afternoon, looked mildly entertained. Manuela's look of dejection had disappeared too. She handed Elena the hammock, and they smiled and hugged each other. Both knew it was a game, and only I, the outsider, had been fooled.

Before Elena and I left Manuela, I asked who made the hammocks she sold. In Isthmus society, the weaving of hammocks often falls to Isthmus men rather than women, and I had always been interested in meeting one of the male weavers. Once, on my first visit to the Isthmus, Rosa introduced me to a blind man who wove hammocks in his patio, but I didn't have the time to speak with him at any length. Manuela informed me that her husband wove the hammocks she sold. If I returned later in the afternoon, she said, I could walk her home and meet her husband.

I ate lunch with Elena at Casa Grande, and we walked back to the mortuary together. By the time I returned to the market, it was five in the evening, and Manuela was packing up her hammocks five at a time in large transparent bags. She left them with a trusted friend who also sold hammocks in a nearby booth. "I've got a nice white hammock here if you want to bring one home for someone in your family," Manuela said. "Maybe later," I said. This exchange was one of many to come. Manuela was always selling, no matter if we were eating together, discussing the tourist myth, or sitting next to each other in silence. In her, for the first time, I saw the kind of drive to sell for which Isthmus women are so well known.

When we began our walk to Manuela's house, she commented that Elena hadn't told the truth about my Spanish. In her estimation, she said, I spoke well enough to be understood. As we walked, I was struck by Manuela's size. In the market, driving a hard bargain over one of her hammocks, she seemed a taller, more formidable force. Now, when I looked down to make eye contact, she was so small that I only saw the silvery hair on the crown of her head. We must have appeared an odd pair as we walked slowly through market, lost in conversation, and we drew the attention of more than a couple of teenagers who had nothing better to do than to watch and smirk at the peculiar couple when we passed by. But I was not prepared for the attention we drew when Manuela grabbed hold of my hand and held it.

My first reaction was reflex. I gave a gentle tug on my hand, but she held on firmly, and I resigned myself to the snickering this brought on, tempted as I was to call out one of the few obscenities I knew in Spanish. And so we walked, hand in hand, and when we came to Belisario Dominguez, the street where Manuela lived, she let go of my hand to point in the direction of her house. I might have resisted holding hands with her had I not known that this sign of affection between friends, even a pair of male friends, is openly accepted in the Isthmus, as it is in other countries such as India. As we walked across the plaza, I thought of a photo I had seen in a book about the Isthmus. The photo was in black and white, depicting two Zapotec men holding hands by interlocking their pinky fingers as they walked beneath the arches at city hall.

When we reached Manuela's block, she pointed out a small adobe home with a red tile roof that stood out from the surrounding homes because the walls were covered with red bougainvillea in full bloom. At the front door, Manuela changed directions unexpectedly. Rather than entering her home, she crossed the street and entered a small adobe house—without knocking. By way of explanation, she said, "This is where my brother lives." The house consisted of a single room with concrete floors painted white. The room was large, and the ceiling was supported by twisted tree trunks that had been stripped of leaves and branches. The ceiling was twelve feet high and pitched. On the northern wall was a mural of angels and saints in a pastoral setting framed on either side with columns. Manuela left the room and then returned with a man she introduced as her brother, Felipe. Like Manuela, Felipe was small. White tufts of hair on either side of his scalp protruded past his ears, and on the top of his head he was completely bald. He had me sit down in a hammock, and began telling me jokes I couldn't understand. When he complained how hot it was, I offered to buy soft drinks. "I'd like a Coca-Cola," Felipe said. "And, if there isn't Coke, as they say in the commercial, then get me a Pepsi-Cola." *Cola* means "tail" in Spanish and was the source of many dirty jokes all over Latin America. Felipe shouted when he spoke as if increased volume would make it easier for me to understand his Spanish. Whenever Felipe had something to say to Manuela, he would switch to Zapotec, and Manuela did the same with him.

I bought the soft drinks in a small shop on the corner, and when I returned, I gave them to Manuela. Felipe took me by the elbow and steered me to the patio, where he kept a simple wooden loom. Stretched between the loom's vertical poles was a red and blue hammock in process, looking more like a volley ball net than something built for slumber. "This is a fifty-two-stitch hammock," Felipe said. "It's two and a half meters long." He demonstrated how he wove his wooden needle fifty-two times, in and out, from the head to the toe of the hammock. Then he brought out other hammocks he had made, one with eighty-four stitches that weighed four kilos. He was very proud of his work.

"What percent of hammocks are woven by men?" I said.

"I couldn't give you an exact number," Felipe said. "Men usually do the weaving, but not exclusively. My niece, for example, knows how to weave."

"How long does it take you to make a hammock?"

"To make a small hammock like the one in the loom, it takes two days—two long days."

Here Manuela returned with glasses for the soft drinks, and we took a moment to wash the dust and dryness out of our mouths. I asked Felipe about how he learned to weave.

"Let me tell it to you straight. My oldest brother, who died when he was nineteen, taught me how to weave when I was twelve years old. I'm sixty-five now, so I've been weaving hammocks for more than fifty years. My parents were peasants. They were poor. My mother kept house, and my father worked in the cornfields. To make our economic situation worse, our family was on the large side. There were nine of us, four boys and five girls. I never went to school. My parents couldn't spare what little money I brought in working odd jobs. Later, when I got married, I made hammocks full time."

"And your children," I said. "Have you taught them how to weave?"

"Every one of them."

When we had finished our soft drinks, Manuela and Felipe began belching at regular intervals. They didn't try to stifle the sound by closing their mouths, so it came out as a little roar that masked the words in our conversation, forcing me to ask them to repeat the words that were blotted out by the belching. When I commented on Manuela's talent for driving a hard bargain, Felipe spoke up:

"She's also very tricky. She'll show you a hammock big enough for an entire family, but when you go to pay, she'll switch the big one for another one much smaller in size."

"No," Manuela said. "Never. The real problem is that everyone who comes to buy anything in the market asks too much of a discount."

We talked for another fifteen minutes, and when the light began to fail, I said I had to return to my hotel. Manuela asked me to send a copy of the article I planned to write about her. When I asked for her address, she became quiet. Then she walked out the front door. A minute later she ushered in two young men, one with a red plastic flashlight and another with a pen. While one shone the flashlight on an empty page in my journal, the other wrote Manuela's address in florid capital letters. They returned my journal, and I rose to leave. Manuela said she would accompany me as far as the marketplace on my walk back to my hotel. "I need a drop," Manuela said. "They have my brand at Pharmacia 24 Horas." I was reading Checkhov at the time, and so I interpreted this to mean a little alcohol. Surely this was in order; Manuela had had a long day.

Shortly before we reached the pharmacy, I asked why she hadn't introduced me to her husband. "Because he lives two hours from here," she said. "We'll visit him another day." Tempted as I was to point out the contradictions in what she had told me about her husband, I let the matter go. I had doubts I'd ever see Manuela's husband, if she indeed had one to meet. The way in which she moved when Felipe was in the room and the way she murmured to him in Zapotec led me to believe Felipe was not her brother. More likely, Felipe was Manuela's common-law husband.

When Manuela and I arrived at Pharmacia 24 Horas and stepped into the glare of the pharmacy's neon lights, she quickly got the attention of a clerk. She pointed over his head at a small bottle that she then paid for with a handful of coins. We said good-bye, and I watched her fade into the darkness along the way to her house. Curious about what Manuela had bought, I again stepped inside of the pharmacy. "What was that you sold her?" I asked the pharmacist. "Eye drops," he said. "Manuela suffers from chronic eye infections."

The night I made my first trip to Casa Verde, the sky was moon-less, and the taxis pulled into the bare earth parking lot one after the other. The taxi I hired dropped me off shortly after nine, and as I got out, another taxi, full of teenage boys with close-cropped hair and gaping mouths, arrived. The boys piled out and strode past me onto Casa Ver-de's pink porch and then toward the entrance: a black metal threshold and a door that never closed. A bouncer, who had rolled back the sleeves of his T-shirt to advertise his strength, frisked us as we passed through the entrance and into the bar. Although there were at least twenty-five people milling around the dimly lit interior, Casa Verde's vaulted ceiling and spacious seating area made it appear almost empty. The walls were painted a shade of flat black, and posted at regular intervals were black lights that illuminated line drawings in day-glo orange of long-limbed women who had nothing in common with the short and portly Istmeñas the men interacted with all day long.

To the left of the entrance, eight chairs were lined up along the wall. Five or six were occupied by prostitutes. The others would be filled when the remaining prostitutes straggled in later that night. Few were pretty; most were dressed in short black night-shirts and negligees. The prostitutes' shoes had an orthopedic look. The soles were four-inches high, and the stiletto heels measured at least six, all in an effort to make themselves leggier like the blondes on the wall. Some of the prostitutes were slumped in their chairs, while others leaned their seats back against the wall behind them. All of them—except one—kept to this area unless a male customer invited them to his table. The exception to this rule was a sullen prostitute who had seated herself at an empty table in the middle of the bar. She had her feet up on a chair and groaned now and then but for the most part seemed to be enjoying a boxing match on an overhead, wide-screen television.

Adjacent to the row of seated prostitutes was a small bar from which Casa Verde's manager served bottles of beer, rum, brandy, and whiskey. He was a still-faced man whose roving eyes never left the circus unfolding in front of him, even when he was pouring a drink or answering the phone. Three feet away from his post at the bar was a door with a sign above it reading BATHROOM and EMERGENCY EXIT. This exit also served a function not mentioned by the sign. Every now and then a prostitute would stride from the bar through this dark doorway with a man following close behind.

As time passed and the customers stumbled in, the bar did a roaring trade. Waiters in white T-shirts crossed the room with bottles of rum and ice in tin buckets. At least 10 percent of the men were falling down drunk, and I remember one in particular. He was young and Zapotec, seated halfway between my table and the prostitutes. In front of him were three objects: a half-empty bottle of Bacardi, a glass of Coca-Cola, and a small tin containing ice. He made a fool of himself by hissing and clucking at the prostitutes and snapping his fingers at the waiters—none of whom paid him much attention. Then, when the bottle of Bacardi was near empty, he began to spit on the floor, much like any other drunk does in a bar in Latin America, leaving a glob of spit near his shoes. Later, he would fill his mouth with rum or coke and spit onto the floor in a way that sounded like someone was pouring liquid cleanser onto a concrete patio before laying into it with a mop.

After fifteen minutes of this, the sullen prostitute did something unexpected. She stood and threw her purse into the chair where she had been seated and walked to the spitter's table and sat down. Their marriage didn't last. His spitting had nothing to do with his lack of company. She got settled in her seat and the splattering of water began again, this time like a garden hose. None of the waiters who drifted over to check on the spitter every five to ten minutes threatened or admonished him, and the man continued filling the little puddle of rum around his feet. Meanwhile, we—the spitter, the sullen prostitute, and I—watched the fight on television. Then the spitter rose and pointed his chin at the men's bathroom, and I shared a look with a waiter that said we agreed he'd never make it without first slipping in his own muck. But the spitter surprised us with a kind of drunken shuffle, never lifting his feet from the ground. He'd obviously been through this before and had learned that even if the floor beneath him rocked like the deck of a ship, you could overcome the problem by keeping your feet in contact with the floor.

From the bathroom came the sound of a metal door slamming against a stall. The bouncer who had frisked us at the door trotted to the bathroom, and the rest of us waited for the yelling to begin. Then the spitter emerged, looking relieved, and once again took a seat at his table. For a time, he snapped his fingers to get the attention of the waiters until they served him more Bacardi, and then the spitting began again.

One of the last prostitutes to enter Casa Verde that night was a young woman I'll call Maria. She came with a friend, Sofi, the same friend who suggested she try prostitution as a means of income earlier in the week. Because all of the other eight seats on the other side of the room were taken, Maria and Sofi sat down in two chairs several feet away from my table. A close look at Sofi said she fit in fine with the other prostitutes. She had the hardened look and gaudy makeup you expect to see on a prostitute. Maria did not. Her pinstriped skirt and matching blouse looked as though they'd been purchased from a Midwestern mail-order catalog. Her hair and skin were dark, her eyes a deep chestnut, and her lips a soft red. Taken together, Maria had a decidedly wholesome look that made her stand out from the other prostitutes. When a man in a cowboy hat asked Sofi to dance, I sat in the seat Sofi had vacated. I introduced myself and asked Maria about how things were run at Casa Verde: what the prostitutes earned, where the private rooms were located, and so on. Because the music was unbearably loud, she had to scream in my ear, and I understood next to nothing. I waited until there was a break in the music, and said:

"Where can we sit and talk?"

"You can pay for a room in back," she said, motioning with her hand toward an area behind the bar. I asked her what a room cost. She mentioned a negligible amount of money.

"And for your time?" I asked.

"Mil pesos," she said. This was exorbitant—roughly $100—but it was also Latin America, where you shoot for the moon and settle for a street lamp.

"Four hundred," I said, and before I had pronounced the last syllable of my counteroffer, I was following her through the emergency exit and into a hall. At the end of the hall, she swung a door open, and we stepped down into a dirt patio. The patio was flanked on either side by a row of four rooms, much like the rooms in an American motel. The upper half of the doors had glass panes glowing with a warm yellow light. Later, I learned that the rooms served two purposes. First and foremost, they were a secluded spot where the prostitutes did their business. And at the end of the night, the rooms were a place where the prostitutes could sleep in peace.

Maria started across the patio, and though I hurried to keep up with her, I had to maneuver my way around a variety of objects blocking my path. A large white dog was drinking water from a red bucket, and a clothesline hung with negligees threatened to choke me. Then there was a row of eight mops, one for each of the rooms, leaning against a metal sawhorse, and I also remember trees: an almond tree, a palm, a saber leaf ficus, and there must have been an avocado tree because I remember kicking black seeds the size of avocado pits that rolled across the clay and gravel ground. Then Maria stepped up onto a cement porch and opened the door to a brightly lit room. I followed her inside and closed the door.

Years after my encounter with Maria, I returned to Espinal for a midday appointment with Casa Verde's manager, Mr. Reynolds. A watchman met me at the gate. "Mr. Reynold's still sleeping," he said. "He worked until five last night. When he is up late like that, it is better if I do not wake him till one in the afternoon." We negotiated, and at twelve-thirty, I followed the watchman behind Casa Verde to the patio lined with four rooms on either side. Wary that the watchman would incur Mr. Reynolds's wrath by waking him, I waited at the edge of the patio. The watchman proceeded to the fourth room at the farthest corner of the lot and rapped on the metal door. As we waited for Mr. Reynolds to respond, I wondered which of the prostitutes he was bedding down with. Fives minutes and several raps later, Mr. Reynolds emerged, and we walked to the bar and took seats at a table near the door. "I don't know if you are aware of this," he began, "but there is another, older Casa Verde in Juchitán. My grandmother, Doña Anastasia, started the business in a house like any other with white adobe walls and a red tile roof. This was more than seventy years ago when there weren't any political parties in Juchitán other than the liberal Greens and the conservative Reds. Because my grandmother was a big supporter of the Greens, she painted the adobe walls green and christened it Casa Verde."

A man who contributed to the early success of Doña Anastasia's new business was rebel and leader of the Green Party General Heliodoro Charis. A poor but ambitious Zapotec, Charis rose to prominence as a soldier during the Mexican Revolution and would often pay unannounced visits to Doña Anastasia, a crowd of soldiers in tow. "I was only five years old at the time," Mr. Reynolds said, "but whenever the general and his troops appeared, my grandmother would send me running out in the neighborhood to fetch women who had an arrangement with Casa Verde. I would go to one house, then the next, letting the women know there was business to be had, and they were invited to join the general and his men."

In 1972, when Doña Anastasia died, her daughter, Elbia, took control of Casa Verde. The best years came in the late 1980s, when there were many transient workers inundating the Isthmus. Some were *petroleros* from PEMEX who came from northeastern Mexico to work on the oil pipeline. Others were seasonal workers who traveled to the Isthmus after the federal government in Mexico City built a sugarcane factory outside of Espinal in 1980. These were Elbia's salad days. She employed as many as fifteen prostitutes, most of them friends in Juchitán. Business was so good that in 1994 Elbia built Casa Verde, Espinal. She installed her son, Mr. Reynolds, as manager, and the money rolled in. But as is the case with any lucrative business, competition entered the picture when copycat brothels opened up near the Pan-American Highway. To make matters more difficult, a law was passed requiring the prostitutes to have ID cards and regular health checks. Elbia's Juchitecan friends, fearing identification within the community, took flight. In their place came foreign women from all over Mexico and Central America. Howard Campbell describes this time in his *Mexican Memoir:* "One time I saw a towering Afro-Mexican woman from the Costa Chica region of Oaxaca (heavily populated by the descendants of slaves who mixed with indigenous Triques and Amuzgos) go off to one of Casa Verde's cribs with a short, elderly Zapotec man. The contrast between the young, powerfully built black prostitute and the diminutive brown peasant was startling."

Campbell also provides insight into Isthmus cantinas that are closely related in function to Isthmus brothels. In cantinas, sex for hire is always available, though not in the variety one might find at Casa Verde. And, unexpectedly, these bars were not always male owned. "Cantinas in the Isthmus, contrary to what I was told in graduate school, were often run by women *(cantineras)* and many made a tidy profit." The cantinas also provide a social outlet for men in much the same way that velas do for women. In the early afternoon, when Isthmus men begin congregating in cantinas, Campbell often sought and found male informants with tongues loosened by drink. Although much of the interaction consisted of jokes and satires of local politicians, Campbell also found time to learn about and discuss local politics, folklore, history, and customs. "Indeed, over time," Campbell writes, "I collected good ethnographic information in the bars."

Before leaving Mr. Reynolds, I asked him what motivated women to work at Casa Verde. "The large majority of the women are poor and work to feed themselves and their children." As a consequence, Mr. Reynolds said, he treated them with respect and felt that they fulfilled an important social need. "The women, who I like to think of as sexual service workers, prevent rape by addressing the sexual needs of our men." On some occasions, Reynolds permitted local women to enter Casa Verde and work. But in general, the women came from outside the region, and he accommodated their need for housing by allowing them to live in the rooms in which they work—hence the eight chairs, eight mops, and eight rooms.

For the first several seconds inside the room with Maria, nervousness overcame me, and I was silent. The floor in the room was carpeted, and there were two empty tin cans flung into a corner that still contained moist flecks of food, though I couldn't make out what. The only furniture was a single bed not much bigger than a cot. I sat down on the bed; Maria remained standing.

"Where are you from?" I asked.

"From here," she said. "North of Ixtepec on a ranch called Emiliano Zapata."

"That's a nice name," I said, and when she didn't answer I asked her age.

"Eighteen."

"And do you go to school?"

"Yes, I attend high school. I only work here between ten and eleven at night."

"Why is it that some of the women seat themselves at men's tables and others don't?"

"A man has to buy a two-liter bottle of rum or tequila before he can invite a woman to sit down with him. But once the man finishes the bottle, the woman must return to her chair against the wall."

"What does a bottle cost?"

"A two-liter bottle costs 200 pesos."

"What's it like working here?"

"In this business, all women run a risk. Many men here are brutes and don't treat us with respect."

"What made you decide to work here?"

"I live with my daughter at my aunt's house. I spent many months looking for traditional daytime work without any luck. I have to feed my daughter. What else could I do? The first time I had sex here was very difficult and very sad. Tonight is my eighth night."

When I returned to the bar, the sullen prostitute who refused to sit with the others stood up and walked out of Casa Verde through the main entrance. I let a minute pass and followed suit. But before I reached the entrance I spotted her on the porch, slumped in a white plastic lawn chair that faced the entrance. Her legs were spread, one on either armrest, and she was singing, song after song, in a voice so sad I could not go back to my seat and resume my voyeurism. Instead, I walked past her and then to the right where a young Istmeña named Juana sold food from a small shed. I asked for a coffee. She squatted over a bucket of cold water on the floor and washed out a Styrofoam cup and served me the black liquid piping hot. I chatted with her, and every now and then, one of the prostitutes emerged from Casa Verde or the motel-like rooms behind it. Juana took orders and began frying steak in a pan while the prostitutes made conversation.

"You're a bit chubbier than the last time I saw you," one prostitute said to another.

"We just met," said the second, "so how in the hell would you know?"

A taxi pulled into the parking lot, and the driver turned the lights out and sat motionless inside. Juana served the food to the prostitutes on oval shaped platters. When they paid, Juana made change from a wooden cigar box. For those who had no money, she wrote what they owed in a column under their name in a kind of credit ledger she kept in a notebook. Behind me, someone coughed. I turned to see the bouncer and a hefty waiter hauling the spitter by his arms out of the entrance to the club. His feet no longer shuffled; they dragged lifelessly behind him. The bouncer opened the back door of the taxi and dumped the spitter inside. Almost immediately, he slumped over sideways onto the seat. The waiter got into the front seat of the taxi. He didn't give the driver a destination, nor did the taxi driver ask for one, and when the taxi pulled out onto the highway, I realized they'd been through this a hundred times before.

The Blaseña

Insider Obdulia Ruiz was born in San Blas to a family of many children and little income. Her mother was a self-sacrificing, hard-working woman who could turn centavos into daily meals for her six brothers and sisters through ingenious administration. When she was not stretching money, she was making it by raising pigs and selling tortillas. Ruiz's father, a farm laborer, contributed only sporadically to the financial well-being of his family. During harvest, he brought home sweet potatoes, mangos, bananas, coconuts, and guavas. What the family didn't consume, Ruiz's mother brought to the market and sold.

Of all the accounts of the relationships between Isthmus men and women, Ruiz's is by far the darkest. "At an early age," Ruiz writes, "I realized that Zapotec women suffer from the temperament of their demanding, scolding, abusive, and drunken husbands." Isthmus men frequently beat their wives and children, Ruiz writes, and dole out punishments that verge on torture. Her father, for example, forced her and her siblings to kneel in the sun holding rocks on their hands and heads until they collapsed from exhaustion. "This punishment was my father's favorite." Her opinion of Isthmus men extended to both her grandfathers, whom she describes as adulterous men who mistreated their wives "until the day of their deaths."

In 1960, when Ruiz became an adolescent, *rapto* was still common in San Blas. Her girlfriends described the fear and pain as they were dragged away by their boyfriends to a room in their parents' house to be deflowered. Any sexual pleasure the young women might have felt was secondary to the embarrassment brought on by their boyfriends' families, who were waiting outside the room, eager to see blood on a sheet.

"At the same time," Ruiz writes, "they were afraid that the boyfriend might declare that they were not virgins (even though, in fact, they were) due to the boy's ignorance, inexperience or bad intentions." Ruiz's fear of *rapto* was heightened by accounts of female relatives who had endured it. Her mother, for example, was beaten on her legs so that she wouldn't resist as her future husband pulled her by her hands to his house. Whenever Ruiz's mother described her abduction, she would follow it with the refrain: "After the storm comes the calm."

That Ruiz and her sisters sought boyfriends outside San Blas is no surprise. "You see," Ruiz writes, "boys from our neighboring city (Tehuantepec) had already given up the custom of *rapto,* substituting for it the 'the marriage petition' *(la pedida de mano)* in which the sexual act occurs after the religious wedding as part of the famous *lunes* (Monday)." According to Zapotec tradition, church marriages in the Isthmus take place on Sunday mornings. The newlyweds then return to the groom's house to dance and celebrate. Near midnight, the couple is hustled into a bedroom where they are expected to have sex. The following morning, they present a bloody sheet as evidence of the bride's virginity. This evidence is cause for more celebration on Monday night. In this way, *lunes* has become synonymous with virginity.

When Ruiz turned twenty-one, her father and grandfather arranged a marriage for her to a man in his fifties. Her mother protested, but she had, as they say in the Isthmus, *ni voz ni voto* (neither voice nor vote). When Ruiz realized that neither her mother nor relatives could prevent the marriage, she moved to Mexico City. She found work as a secretary at the Department of Hydrological Services. Her government job paid well and brought a certain amount of satisfaction. Even more important, it was stable. But the Mexican men she met seemed always to want her to quit her job, bear children, and stay at home to take care of them. This she refused to do. And so it was that fourteen years after she moved to Mexico City, Ruiz was thirty-three and still unmarried.

In the 1970s, Ruiz took an interest in vegetarianism and meditation and even considered going with friends to India for the purpose of meeting a guru. To prepare for the trip, Ruiz took an English course that the twenty-four-year-old Howard Campbell happened to be teaching. In one of their first conversations after class, Campbell asked Ruiz if she was Indian. "I am," she replied. "But not from India, from

Mexico." They began dating and found they had much in common. Like Ruiz, Campbell meditated and espoused nonviolence, which was important to Ruiz given her family background. "He was handsome, kind, even soft," Ruiz said, "especially when compared to Mexican boys."

A couple of months after Campbell and Ruiz met, they went to swim in a *balneario* (spa) near a Nahua Indian village. They drank *pulque*—a milky, thick moonshine made from agave—until both were half-drunk. Then they swam in the hot springs, and the alcohol, warm water, and Ruiz's beauty inspired Campbell, who felt he was on a roll. "You need to come back with me so we can go live in the United States," he said. As much as she cared for Howard, this was not something a Mexican woman was willing to do, not without being married. "Yes," she said, and after a moment, "if we get married." Howard, who had always been impulsive, shot back, "Let's do it."

Within a matter of weeks, Ruiz and Campbell took an overnight bus to the Isthmus. Ruiz and Campbell were engaged, and the only remaining impediment was her parents' permission to marry. From the bus station, they took a taxi. Soon, the paved streets ended and they traveled along a maze of heavily rutted dirt roads to 25 Hidalgo Street, where the Ruiz family home sat peeling in the sun. Ruiz's parents were warm and welcoming, but Campbell's Spanish was weak and his Zapotec nonexistent, so when it came time to ask the question he felt inadequate. There was also a problem with the neighbors. The entry to the Ruiz home was always open, and a steady stream of neighbors, relatives, and curious onlookers came and went continuously. "Dozens of people came to see me," Campbell writes. "Not just to glimpse, but to stare and even to pull on the hair of my arms that were a golden color they found exotic." In the end, both Ruiz's parents agreed to the marriage.

In July of 1981, Campbell and Ruiz were married in a church in the dioceses of Tehuantepec. Immediately afterward, they went through the traditional rites of a Zapotec wedding party. First came the toast, then the *medio xiga* in which guests placed money in a half-gourd that Ruiz and Campbell held in their laps. In the jar-breaking dance, the young women present held ceramic jars on their heads in a circle around Ruiz and Campbell and then broke the jars on the ground in front of them. This was followed by the blind-chicken dance in which young women circled around the blindfolded Ruiz, who attempted to catch one of them. The woman Ruiz caught received the bridal wreath and was said to be the next to marry. Next came the tail dance. Campbell and Ruiz stood on chairs forming a small bridge with the train of her wedding dress. The young women formed a conga line until Campbell dropped the train of the dress onto one of the girls.

Until this point in the marriage ceremony, Campbell and Ruiz had followed the path described by Henestrosa as *la pedida de mano*. They had married in church, received the blessing from her parents, danced the traditional dances. The next step—in which the newlyweds are expected to retire to a bedroom and produce a bloody sheet—Campbell and Ruiz skipped altogether. At midnight, they climbed into the backseat of a Volkswagen chauffeured by friends from Mexico City and drove away. "We left behind my perplexed relatives because there would be no *pachanga* (wild party) on Monday," Ruiz wrote. "You see there is no *lunes* without the bride and groom."

More than a dozen years after their marriage, Ruiz wrote an essay titled "Representations of Isthmus Women: A Zapotec Woman's Point of View." In it, she describes the outsiders who observe the confidence with which women buy and sell in the market, and how astute the vendors are when bargaining with customers. "The hammock sellers are so insistent," Ruiz writes, "that their customers have no choice but to buy." She also notes the unique sales pitch of Isthmus women who lure their customers by complimenting them on the light color of their hair: "Lleva totopo, güero" (Take some *totopos*, blondie).

In addition to women at the market, outsiders also tend to see women's involvement in the religious and social arenas. They prepare for the masses offered for the souls of the dead nine days, one month, and one year after burial. The women also organize the celebration of the Day of the Dead. They bring marigolds to the graves of their relatives, weep on their tombs, and sell candy, beer, and soft drinks at the entrance to the cemetery. *Los vivos al gozo y los muertos al pozo* (The living to the party and the dead to the tomb) is a phrase that summarizes the attitude of the women as they perform this.

In the social arena, outsiders tend to see women at fiestas, where women give themselves over to risqué jokes followed by laughter and the clapping of hands. The women might seem to be sexually sophisticated, but much of this is wordplay. "At times," Ruiz writes, "male homosexuals *(muxe)* join them to 'raise hell,' and that is when the jokes get racier." Ruiz interprets this behavior as a kind of psychological relaxation or therapy for Isthmus women. She also points out that comic allusions to sex are more common among married women than for younger, unmarried women. The latter, Ruiz writes, must behave less boldly if they want to reach the altar with their boyfriends.

Having witnessed this public behavior—at the markets, cemeteries, and fiestas—outsiders leave with the mistaken impression that Isthmus society is matriarchal. They rarely see a woman in the private arena, where she must not only bear children but be responsible for educating and feeding them as well. "She must also be ready to meet the sexual needs of her husband when he requires it," Ruiz writes, "regardless of how tired she is from her many daily tasks." At times, Isthmus women must also control their husbands when they are able to or allowed to by their men. But if a woman actually does control her husband, she brags about it. "I want to make perfectly clear, however, that although one often hears the phrase 'te manda tu señora' ('your wife dominates you'), there are in reality few such cases." This lack of information about Isthmus women's private lives is compounded by the fact that outsiders seek only what interests them, what agrees with their sympathies, or what is new or most attractive. They romanticize what they find, exaggerating certain qualities, depending on their agenda. As an example, Ruiz cites the writers who exalt the powerful image of Zapotec women. "For feminists this is solid gold!" Ruiz writes. "One sociologist even wrote that all Juchitecas are lesbians."

Tirada de Frutas

JANUARY 1999. One of the great disappointments during the early years of my visits to the Isthmus concerned a curious ritual called *la tirada de frutas* (the throwing of the fruit). According to what I read, the ritual takes place when a religious procession reaches its destination at a church or cathedral. The girls who participated in the procession carry fruit in black bowls up through the belfry and onto to the roof of the church. At the same time, men and boys who watched the procession fight for position directly below the girls. And then the fun begins: the girls throw the fruit at the men and boys below.

In part, I found the ritual fascinating because it was unique to Isthmus Zapotecs, and like many of their rituals, it was divided along the lines of gender. I was also drawn to the *tirada* because those prone to labeling the Isthmus a matriarchy interpreted it as a means that women used to "assert their superiority as matriarchs." Though I doubted this interpretation, it was one of the few available in print, and if I were to develop my own explanation, I needed to witness the ritual in person.

Disappointment entered the picture when I set out to actually witness a *tirada*. Many Istmeños in Juchitán and Tehuantepec seemed sure that the *tirada* was still a popular part of one vela or another, but in the two years I spent looking, I must have followed more than a dozen processions to their end, and the roofs and bell towers remained empty. Afterward, when I confronted the person who sent me on a particular wild-goose chase, she would explain that although she had been mistaken about the *tirada* taking place in their barrio, she was absolutely sure I could witness it in the barrio next door. And so I went in circles.

When the third year of my visits to the Isthmus rolled around, I began to hunt up religious festivals that did not take place in Juchitán or Tehuantepec. I had time to spare in January, and a brochure published in Oaxaca informed me that the only festival of note in this time period was the festival of San Sebastian in a small town named Jalapa, thirty miles north of Tehuantepec.

Not an hour after my arrival at the Oasis, I caught a taxi, along with four other passengers, to Jalapa. On the highway, the heat was fierce. All of the windows were rolled down, and I felt that I had stuck my head into the hair-searing heat of an industrial blow furnace. The land on either side of the highway also showed signs of the heat. It was brown and parched, and to the north the mountains of the Sierra Madre were black as onyx. There was no vegetation, only the skeleton of a tree or two per mile.

When we neared Jalapa, which lay at the foot of the Sierra Madre, patches of blue began appearing between the mountains. This image made me question my senses until I remembered that the Benito Juárez Dam was very near Jalapa, and the blue that I was seeing was the color of the water backed up against the dam. The image was dazzling and surreal. The dry burnt mountains collided with the deep blue of the reservoir, and you knew something was wrong—nature hadn't made this image, man had, but it was striking in its beauty all the same.

One of the passengers the taxi driver picked up along the way to the festival was a native of Jalapa who provided my first head-on encounter with an Isthmus man. He was a skinny, nervous creature dressed entirely in white with a slinky gold bracelet on his left wrist and a belt with a flashy silver buckle. His name was Cesar, and the only belongings he carried were contained in a couple of black plastic bags. He spoke constantly, at a manic pace, and at times his speech seemed disjointed—though part of this had to do with the deafening roar of the trucks that drowned out all sound when passing by. Half of what he said concerned Mexico's corrupt political system; the other half were comments about religion that focused on Pope John Paul II's impending visit to Mexico later that month—an event that was very much on the minds of the profoundly religious, predominately Catholic Mexicans. In his most manic moments, Cesar quoted the Bible, and in the hours to come he repeated the same verse from the Psalms over and over: "They have mouths, but cannot speak, eyes, but they cannot see; they have ears, but cannot hear, noses, but they cannot smell—"

From the beginning of our drive north he begged for attention, and when he didn't get it, he began grilling the other passengers. From me he got my first name but little else. Other passengers weren't so lucky. After forcing the family name out of the woman from Jalapa who sat next to him, he set about comparing his family with hers: "My cousin just took office as mayor of Jalapa," he said. When we picked up another passenger, he repeated his questions and made the same comparisons. His speech was florid: "I am currently dwelling in a lovely neighborhood of our capital, Mexico City." Soon, a sign appeared on the highway that announced we had arrived in Jalapa. Mary Magdalene, the receptionist at the Oasis, suggested I get off at the first of Jalapa's three bus stops but warned me that the stops weren't marked. Then the taxi driver pulled to the side of the road, and Cesar, as if he were leading a troop of Boy Scouts, said, "We're all getting off here, right?"

Everyone said yes, so I did too. Cesar slammed the door of the taxi, and the driver screeched away onto the highway, happy to be rid of him. At first glance, it appeared Jalapa was just a collection of one-story homes and businesses that were randomly scattered along Highway 190 for several blocks. There were half a dozen roads that ran perpendicular to the highway. Only one of them, which ran through the center of town, was paved. In the distance, an elderly farmer in a cowboy hat rumbled along a dirt road in an oxcart, and beyond him two men rode horseback at a gallop. I turned away from the highway and followed Cesar and the other passengers into a brick and glass seafood restaurant named La Palapa. The restaurant was deserted, and a wide-screen television blared a soccer game. When no one from the restaurant came to attend to us, Cesar called out so loud that you could hear his voice over the screaming fans of the soccer game:

"Sopa de Camarones!" (Fish soup!) An odd way to get the attention of a waiter, I thought, but then came the answer from the kitchen:

"No hay" (There isn't any). A moment later a waitress emerged from the kitchen drying her hands on her apron, and at the same time, Cesar began rummaging through one of his black plastic bags. When he located what he was looking for he shouted:

"Look what I found!" Smiling broadly, as if he had changed water to wine, he pulled a large plate of shrimp, crab, and fresh-water lobster out of his plastic bag. No one seemed impressed, and Cesar's smile faded quickly. The waitress approached Cesar calmly. She took the plate of seafood, and Cesar touched her hand with his left pinky finger, as if to test the limit of the waitress. When she retreated to the kitchen, a second waitress in a blue-and-white-checkered apron appeared, pointing at an empty table in the center of the room. Cesar sat in the chair at the head of the table, and while the rest of us took up our places on either side of him, the waitress began taking orders. Everyone in our group was thirsty from the long, dry trip from Tehuantepec. Most ordered beer; I ordered a papaya *licuado*. When it was served to me before anyone else had their drinks, I couldn't resist the temptation and began sucking the milk and papaya and sugar through a straw with such force that my ears popped. Cesar didn't miss a beat.

"Tom," he said, from his place at the head of the table, "have you started without us?" Because of my many experiences in public humiliation with Rosa, my Isthmus skin had thickened. I took Cesar's comment in stride and continued drinking my *licuado*—to hell with what he thought.

The waitress served the fish soup, and we began eating. Cesar held forth on Raul Salinas, brother of the former president of Mexico, Carlos Salinas. Raul had been convicted of money laundering and murder and had begun serving a fifty-year sentence shortly before I arrived that year in the Isthmus. "What he deserves is a bullet," Cesar said. "They should shoot him on the spot, take his money, and divide it up." Then he looked at me and said, "The same goes for you if you ever double-cross me." After his third or fourth beer, Cesar began shouting and slapping the table when he wanted to emphasize what he considered an important point.

An elderly man accompanied by a reserved woman in her thirties entered the restaurant, and Cesar stood up to greet them. The man, Galaor, was one of Cesar's cousins. His height, which measured at least six feet, dwarfed the typically short Zapotecs who surrounded him.

This, together with his kind face and deep voice, gave him the air of a deposed nobleman. The woman accompanying Galaor was his daughter, Magda, who remained silent for the duration of our meal. Every now and then I caught Galaor looking in my direction, as though he had something important to tell me. But it wasn't until he had finished a beer or two that he gathered the courage to speak.

"Have you heard about our church?" I thought this an odd opening, but played along.

"No," I said. "No one's told me about your church."

"Our church, which was as old and beautiful as any in Mexico, is underwater."

I wasn't sure how to react to this, so I kept silent and let him continue.

"And have you heard about our town? Our town is also underwater. What you're seeing here is not the real Jalapa; it's the new Jalapa. The state forced us out of our homes in the old Jalapa, up to this rocky place where the soil is sandy and irrigating is an expensive waste of time. The old Jalapa, where we are really from, is one hundred feet underwater."

On hearing this, I made the connection. The water that Galaor referred to was the reservoir I had seen from the taxi, the same water that had flooded into the old Jalapa when the state finished the Benito Juárez Dam. Galaor saw the light in my eyes, and then came the deluge. "The old Jalapa was a fine place," he said. "The Spaniards founded it in 1537, between two rivers, and the people of our region liked to refer to it as little Mesopotamia or the bread basket of Mexico. Unlike the rest of the Isthmus, the land was fertile, the rivers nearby. Then, on the Cinco de Mayo of 1961, the government completed the dam and sacrificed our town to give water to the rest of the Isthmus." Here, Galaor paused and added a consoling note. "In dry years, you can see the cupolas of the church's towers though we haven't seen them in four years." His tone was apologetic, as if he didn't want me to get the wrong impression about the town, which, when I got to know it, was as barren and poor as any city I'd seen in Mexico. As if this weren't sad enough, Galaor handed me his business card. In gray and blue, the card identified Galaor Garrido Escobar as a distributor for Imagen Corporativa (Corporate Image). Though I was tempted to ask what it was that he distributed in a town that had exactly one paved road, I couldn't bring myself to do it. Galaor went silent, and Cesar embarked on a long, wandering monolog where Galaor left off.

"We can tell you this about the dam," Cesar said, "because we've lived it. Some, like myself, felt forced to leave Jalapa and live elsewhere. But let me tell you something deeper. Much of what we have suffered in Jalapa, including the dam, has to do with political interest. Many years ago, the people of Jalapa celebrated the festival of San Sebastian together. Everyone marched in the processions together, danced together, crowned the queen of the festival together, and so on. Now, politics has overtaken Jalapa, and the people have become divided. The conservatives in Jalapa have joined forces with PRI, the liberals with PRD. Because of this, the friction between the parties has become so intense that we cannot celebrate our festivals together. We now have separate dances, coronations, and processions, one for PRI, the other for PRD. Divide and conquer. That's the attitude of the federal government, and how are we going to progress if we divide?"

Despite his many detractions, Cesar spoke with such passion and clarity that we could not help but listen. He was an orator, a secular prophet whose speech was compelling even when failing to make sense: "What's worse is that the federal government and the decadent PRI that runs it are bringing Pope John Paul II to Mexico in an attempt to muster additional votes. But God says, 'I am your God and you shall not bring false images before me.' This includes the pope, and other idols like the Virgin of Guadalupe, Santo Domingo, and even San Sebastian. To further their personal interests, the fucking Spaniards and Catholic clergy have forced these idols upon us, taking advantage of our deeply held religious convictions. And I'll tell you what I think. The Virgin of Guadalupe, Santo Domingo, and San Sebastian do not exist." Cesar paused here. He looked around to make sure that everyone was paying attention. They were—now more than ever because he was blaspheming. Cesar ignored their stony looks, took a long drink of beer, and rambled onward. "God is very conscious of the fact that we Mexicans lack education and culture. Here, in this world, the big fish eats the little because he is better educated and better prepared." I remember that at this point, I stopped listening to Cesar because of the direction in which his sermon seemed to be headed. When he referred to bigger fish who were better educated and better prepared, I knew he was speaking about me and my countrymen from the north. I'd been cornered this way in third-world countries before. On a worldwide basis, my interrogator would ask, why was the playing field so unequal? And why did the United States always have the advantages, and third-world countries the disadvantages? No doubt about it, there were inequities in the world, extreme inequities when you considered America's wealth and Mexico's poverty, and I was ready to cede this point. But I was not ready to renounce my citizenship and follow Cesar into the desert.

"Look," Cesar said, and then tapped violently on his temple with his index finger, "with this mind I have long admired foreigners. But you have your own idols, your own San Sebastian, and you too are dragged down by your beliefs. How do I know? Because on your dollar bill, it says 'I Believe in God.' Isn't that what it says?" I didn't answer because I didn't want to correct him. Then he banged his fist on the table and repeated:

"Isn't that what it says?"

"Yes, something like that."

"So it's worldwide!" he shouted. Then he relaxed, and leaned back in his seat. "All of this is from my point of view, of course. And I'm not mad! I have a strong character, that's all. For me, for Mexico, for you, I simply want the best. Who knows? In a while, I might be the *mayordomo* of the festival of San Sebastian." Then he paused, looked me in the eyes, and said "And you, my dear, are coming with me." As in my confrontations with Rosa, I found myself swallowing the anxiety that rose in my throat at Cesar's brash mandate. In fact, I remember thinking that Cesar could very well turn out to be the male equivalent of Rosa. But before I could think up a way to circumvent Cesar and his plans for the two of us, he asked where I would be staying that night. I told him I had to return to Tehuantepec where I had left my luggage. He ignored this, and said that I could stay at home with him. I resisted this idea, but when he continued to insist that I at least have a look at his house, I followed him along a dirt road and into a residential district. On the way there, I said:

"How far away is your house from the center of town?"

"This *is* the center of town," Cesar said.

At the door of the house, a man named Armando appeared who handed Cesar the keys. How could the house be Cesar's if Armando had the keys? Inside, the heat was suffocating. The windows were sealed and the fans still. Other than the kitchen, there was only one room where there were three beds. Cesar unloaded clothes from one of his plastic bags and arranged them neatly in an empty chest of drawers. "Sleep here with us," Cesar said. "There'll be no women here, so you won't have to worry about that." Any doubts about Cesar's sexual orientation were cleared up later that day at the festival. When he thought I wasn't watching, he folded his tongue and inserted it into his bottle of beer while leering at a man in a cowboy suit complete with leather leggings.

When Cesar and I returned to La Palapa, I sat down next to Magda, who had begun a career in politics three weeks prior to my arrival in the Isthmus. "For the first time in thirty-seven years," Magda said, "two women have been appointed to Jalapa's thirteen-member town council. The post is voluntary. I represent PRD, and Juana Martínez Meléndez, PRI, which won the majority of votes in the last election. Juana will be responsible for culture and sports. Here in Jalapa, instead of having a Casa de Cultura we have what's called a Casa del Pueblo where historical and cultural artifacts relating to Jalapa are kept. Juana manages the Casa del Pueblo. She also promotes sports activities. This is important in Jalapa. We drink a lot of beer and seem to have more than our share of vice. Juana's looking for ways to get people involved in sports, which we hope will keep them away from their bad habits.

"The council post I hold is new, created in the current triennial. I plan to spend a lot of time convincing people about the importance of ecology. Here in Jalapa we eat a lot of deer, which, together with iguanas and lobster, have been hunted to the point of extinction. All of this is very serious, and so I'll have to look for a diplomatic way to say, 'Don't do it.' The problem here is that convincing people to stop eating something that is part of their way of life will be hard. I'll have to find a way to instill in people a kind of ecological conscience. I'll be spending the majority of my time with farmers, who are almost always men. The women here tend to devote themselves to their husbands and children. It's really unusual for a woman to leave Jalapa and study in order to prepare herself for a career."

"Why is it that some women wear huipiles and enaguas to the festivals, and others don't?" I said.

"The women who don't wear them are unmarried," she said. I knew this to be untrue. She was either joking with me or giving me a hint about her marital status. I then asked her opinion on matriarchy. "There is no matriarchy in this region. What might appear to be a matriarchy is really just women working in the market, selling the products that their men bring home."

When we finished eating, I walked Magda home. On the porch, we found Hortensia, Magda's mother, bent over a carbon grill similar to a hibachi. Set up next to the grill were two tables and half a dozen chairs. Hortensia was cooking and selling *tlayuda* to passersby, though she seemed to give more away to friends and neighbors than she sold. Magda asked if I'd like to eat *tlayuda* or *garnacha* and then served me both. When we began eating, a silent young woman with a knotted brow approached the area where we were seated. She was no older than thirty, and her eyes were as innocent as a child's. Without a word of greeting to anyone, the young woman approached Magda. They smiled at each other and began communicating silently with a kind of rudimentary sign language. Magda then guided the young woman in my direction and introduced her as Laura. We shook hands and then Laura left as silently as she had come.

Magda explained that she and Laura were nextdoor neighbors, and that since childhood they had been close friends. They developed their own sign language: fingers to the mouth indicated eating, arms cradled together meant baby, and so on. I asked Magda how Laura came to be deaf and mute. She looked away for a moment before she began to speak:

"Here in Mexico, when babies cry, mothers have the habit of rocking them in a hammock. According to Laura's mother, who was busy with her other nine children at the time of the accident, one of Laura's older sisters put her in a hammock to quiet her. After her sister left the room, Laura fell out of the hammock and onto the concrete floor, which left her both deaf and mute. This is what her mother says. But maybe it's not true. Laura got pregnant not too long ago, so I brought her to a gynecologist. While we were there, the gynecologist checked her to try and understand how she lost her hearing and speech. He said that problems like Laura's often originate at birth when a mother isn't taken care of properly and the baby's brain doesn't get enough oxygen. Here in

Jalapa, doctors aren't always around when a mother gives birth, and sometimes it's left to the midwives and then this kind of thing happens.

"If someone had taken Laura to the hospital as soon as they knew about her problem with speech and hearing, the doctors might have been able to find a remedy. Instead, they waited until she was six or seven years old and only then did they bring her to a specialist in Mexico City. But by that time it was too late. They couldn't adapt any kind of hearing apparatus for her because the time for that had already passed. In spite of being deaf-mute she's developed other abilities. Laura has a lot of initiative and does all kinds of handiwork."

"What was the sign language you were using?"

"Something we invented when we were children. She never learned any formal sign language."

"Can she read lips?"

"No, no one ever taught her, and I'm sorry to say she can neither read or write. Now she's pregnant, and the man responsible has disappeared."

Before parting ways with Magda, I asked her about the *tirada*. "Follow the procession tomorrow at five in the evening," she said, "and you will see women pitching things at the men from the roof of the chapel."

The procession was already making its way through the dirt roads of Jalapa when I began following it up a hill the next day. For an hour or more, the procession meandered through Jalapa's maze of dirt roads, picking up women and children as it went. Then we crossed the highway and entered an expansive dirt courtyard. At the far end was a tiny blue chapel with a bell tower. I checked the roof for women, but it was so steep that no one, woman or man, could stand on top of it. Once again, it seemed, I had been duped.

Rather than leave immediately, I decided it would be a good idea to enter the chapel, if only for a brief break from the relentless Isthmus sun. We crossed the dirt courtyard, and the women at the front of the procession stepped up onto a cement patio shaded by a thatched roof that stood directly in front of the chapel stairs. To the left of the patio a young Zapotec and his chestnut stallion stood idly by while a ragged group of fifty boys and a like number of men milled around in black pants and white shirts. The women paid them no attention. One by one, they marched past the men into the chapel and left yellow gladiolas and beeswax candles in front of a hand-carved statue of San Sebastian. The mood inside the church was solemn. I took a seat in a pew at the back of the chapel and fought the urge to doze off. Then I heard fireworks and then screams from outside.

I looked for signs of alarm on the faces around me, but they were either absorbed in prayer or vacant with boredom. I stood up, pushed my way past knees and feet and hurried outside. There, underneath the chapel's bell tower, the loosely knit group of men and boys had become a mob, packed so densely at the foot of the bell tower they moved as a single being. For a moment, I stood still and watched. All of them stood with their attention fixed on the bell tower, their arms over their heads, hands open, fingers splayed as though they were fielding fly balls in an imaginary baseball game. But from my position on the church stairs, I could not make out who or what in the bell tower held their gaze. So I waded into the crowd and turned toward the bell tower to see a blur of a woman in a bright red huipil and enagua throwing something over our heads toward the horse and rider, still standing idly near the patio. The mob moved quickly in that direction, laughing and shouting and grasping at the air with their fingers. When we neared the horse, he became agitated and rose up on his hind legs and whinnied. I pushed away from the animal but it did no good—I went where the crowd went. To make matters worse, the rider had begun to beat the horse with a switch in an irrational attempt to control him. The stallion, in turn, kicked violently against the cement floor of the patio. Then, another object flew from the tower, again toward the horse, and again he reared up. At the same second, the crowd swerved violently in his direction, and I came so close to the animal—still rearing back—that I saw the silver of his horseshoes.

When there was a lull in the objects hurtled from the tower, the crowd below relaxed, and I pushed myself free of it. From the sidelines, I took stock of what the women were throwing. As expected, they threw fruit, but it was a small part of many objects that rained down on us that day, which included jawbreakers, paper flags, plastic salad bowls, bottled water, suckers, cookies, matches, combs, Frisbees, and red plastic spatulas. You might think it unlikely that the men and boys should get so excited about so little. But imagine yourself living in Mexico's poorest state, where those lucky enough to have a job earn $3.50 a day. From this angle, the party favors represent charitable goods. To those who claim the women pelt the men with fruit to assert their authority over the men as matriarchs, I would say this: the men and boys were having too much fun to be bothered with assertions about anything—and so were the women. Still, I sensed a message as the women grabbed fruit and favors from the bowl with the crimson interior. Be reminded, the women seemed to say, that from the interior of this bowl comes all of life. It may appear that men have the upper hand in Jalapa, but without the crimson bowl, the world would come grinding to a halt. Let this serve as a reminder.

Covarrubias offers a more lighthearted explanation: "The women delighted in hurling heavy pineapples into the crowd, which fell back as the pineapples hit." The men, Covarrubias explains, "went home, proud of their prizes, not because of their intrinsic value, but because they were captured dangerously." Even in Jalapa the danger was real. Although I had not seen anything heavy hurled from the bell tower, an elderly Zapotec I met later in the day remembered attending a *tirada* in Jalapa when he was a boy. "I was hit in the head with a clay flower pot," he said, "and it hurt."

The Radical

Anthropologist Howard Campbell was born in Lansing, Michigan, to a middle-class family of academics. Every male member of his family—from his grandfather to his father and both of his brothers—pursued PhDs in math and the sciences as though they were one of life's necessities. And it was clear to Campbell from an early age that he would follow this example. But an interest in people and the Native American tribes who inhabited the remote region in northern Idaho where Campbell lived made him think that anthropology was more to his liking. Foreign cultures were also a factor shaping his career. The population of the town in which Campbell grew up was 15,000, so it was natural that he would travel after taking his bachelor's degree in anthropology. He began by touring Europe but felt as though he'd never left home. "I wanted Europe to be more radically other and different than it was. It wasn't different enough." He returned home, only to set out again, this time on a bike. He rode south along the Pacific, through California, still not finding what he wanted. On crossing the border into Mexico, however, he knew he had arrived. "The first time I walked into Mexico," Campbell said, "I felt like *this* is the place."

Eventually, Campbell hitchhiked his way to Mexico City, where he rented an apartment with a friend from the Netherlands he'd met on the road. "I was fascinated by what was, at that time, the largest city in the world, being a gringo and living completely with Mexicans with very little money. It was a romantic but difficult time in my life." Like many of the low-budget travelers in his generation, he took a job teaching English without the benefit of working papers, earning less than $400 a month. He made friends with the local people, and his life rolled along smoothly until a young woman named Obdulia Ruiz enrolled in his class. "She was a stunning woman," Campbell said, "a beauty queen in her own town." She was also demanding, intense, and willful, and in some sense, Campbell felt led by the nose. "Because there I was, a young man, living in Mexico City, trying to survive as a gringo. She'd already lived there for fifteen years, and she was very cosmopolitan and sophisticated in an urban way, yet Indian." Looking back on his experience as an anthropologist, Campbell admits that he had the mistaken tendency to view everything Ruiz said and did as somehow Zapotec—despite the fact that she had spent half her life in Mexico City.

Howard Campbell's first impression of Juchitán came the day after he was married. It was a time in which Juchitán was experiencing political revolt led by the ultra-left party COCEI. "Juchitán once again became a cause célébre in the 1980s when the radical COCEI's Ayuntamiento Popular (People's Government) was ousted from power and *coceista* political prisoners became poster boys for the Mexican left," Campbell writes. "Juchitán de las Flores, they called the town. The land of primitive communism where life was the color of fiestas and simple but sophisticated people carried on a millennial struggle against the mestizo oppression. Bohemia Shangri La, a place of outré fiestas, drunken orgies, and *toloache*. [Campbell explains *toloache* in a note at the end of chapter one: "Toloache is jimson weed, a narcotic plant used by Zapotec women to put men under spells and to control them sexually according to local folklore."] Hundreds of dissident anthropologists, curious journalists, gay activists, and thrill-seekers came to Juchitán in search of indigenous mystique and radical chic."

On his way out of Juchitán, Campbell and friends paid tribute to COCEI. "After we passed the bus station we were stopped by dissident students wearing scarlet bandannas and holding a rope across the street until we dropped a few pesos into their bucket." Campbell describes his first impression of Juchitán, which would become the focus of two of his books, as an interesting example of Indian culture, nothing more. "All I saw at the time was a big, dirty, Indian town with a market reeking of rotting seafood, moldy cheese, basil branches and *coyol* [a type of palm leaf]."

But when the young, leftist Campbell returned to Mexico City, he couldn't help but notice the attention Juchitán's unrest was getting in the press. "The stories and photos detailing huge COCEI political demonstrations and street fighting between *coceistas, priistas,* and soldiers ignited me." With the passage of time, Campbell saw the unrest develop into something Mexico had not experienced in decades. "As I read the Mexico City newspapers, I began to realize that something more significant was occurring: A full-blown Indian revolt was beginning in modern Mexico!" Between 1983 and 1984, Campbell gathered and read anything he could find about the revolt, including *Guchachi Reza* and leftist articles, books, and pamphlets describing COCEI's ongoing struggle against the federal government. "Exhilarated, I realized I had a dissertation topic!"

Four years later, Campbell completed his dissertation. In 1993, he served as coeditor and contributor for *Zapotec Struggles,* an anthology of essays, articles, poems, photographs, art, and stories drawn from the COCEI movement and *Guchachi' Reza.* The essay that Campbell contributed to the anthology focuses on politics but also includes a brief section in which he describes Isthmus women's role in COCEI. Although Isthmus women make up 50 percent of membership in COCEI, Campbell writes, they hold no leadership positions. Instead, they are the "shock troops" of the movement. "Women invariably comprise fifty percent or more of the participants in COCEI demonstrations, highway blockades, and sit-ins, and their vivid presence (COCEI women dress in their finest and most elegant apparel for important COCEI rallies), militancy, and emotion add zest to all COCEI events." But the women also suffer the consequences of their participation. "In fact," writes Campbell, "one of the key interests that sparked COCEI's expansion was the murder of Lorenza Santiago, a pregnant *Coceista,* during a march protesting vote fraud after the 1975 election."

On the question of matriarchy, Campbell joins the handful of deniers, placing the blame on outsiders with the same old saw: "Overwhelmed by women's seeming dominance of economic and ceremonial life, some outside observers came to the conclusion that Juchitán is a kind of pre-patriarchal, feminist paradise." One of the outsiders he singles out is Poniatowska, whom he cites at length in his 1994 book, *Zapotec Renaissance:* "You should see them arrive like walking towers, their windows open, their heart like a window, their nocturnal girth visited by the moon. You should see them arrive; they are already the government, they, the people, guardians of men, distributors of food, their children riding astride their hips or lying in the hammocks of their breasts, the wind in their skirts, flowered vessels, their sex a honeycomb spilling forth men. Here they come shaking their wombs, pulling the *machos* toward them, the *machos* who, in contrast with them, wear light-colored pants, shirts, leather sandals, and palm hats, which they lift high in the air as they shout, 'Long live the women of Juchitán!'"

Campbell's response to this passage is bristling: "While this makes for amusing reading and excellent literature," writes Campbell, "it does little to advance our ethnographic understanding of Juchitán life." But Campbell seems to miss Poniatowska's point. Her goal in writing *Juchitán de las Mujeres* was never to advance our ethnographic understanding of life in Juchitán. It was to call attention to Isthmus women by way of poetry and exaggeration and humor. Poniatowska's claim that Isthmus women shake their wombs at men is equivalent to Rivera's tale that Zapotec children are born white. To take either Poniatowska or Rivera seriously is to misunderstand them.

Later in *Zapotec Renaissance*, Campbell goes further than a simple denial of matriarchy. He questions Isthmus women's equality. "Although Chiñas states that Isthmus Zapotec gender relations are 'emphatically egalitarian,'" Campbell writes, "I have concluded that the balance of power and privilege in Isthmus Zapotec society is actually tipped towards the side of men." Women have had little choice when it came to occupations, writes Campbell, and when resources are limited, the Isthmus family tends to send the boys rather than the girls to school. As a consequence, white-collar work is predominately male. "Although a few especially talented Istmeñas such as Juana C. Romero, Aurea Procel, Guadalupe Pineda López Lena, and Neli Toledo have made names for themselves as doctors, merchants, judges, or civic leaders, the Isthmus public sphere is generally controlled by men."

For most Isthmus women, Campbell writes, day-to-day living is much more difficult, especially for women from the poorer sections of the Isthmus such as San Blas or Chegigo. These women must hustle to put food on the table, clean house, take care of members of their extended family, pay bills, and keep their worn-out huipil from disintegrating with age. The women must also put up with Isthmus men. Campbell cites high rates of male alcoholism, wife beating, kept women, sexual abuse, and irresponsible fatherhood as familiar realities for Isthmus women. One of Campbell's closest contacts, for example, had to leave town as a teenager to avoid a marriage her father arranged to an older man she hated. Alcoholism killed two of her uncles. Both her father and brother kept mistresses. Her thirty-year-old sister's sex life was still controlled by her father. "The women affected by these circumstances," Campbell writes, "complained bitterly to me about them." Despite this kind of abuse, Campbell shies away from homogenizing women as victims. "While, in some cases, these statements have some validity, there is obviously a great deal of variability among the large Isthmus Zapotec population. Furthermore, human relations are volatile and subject to change over time."

Day of the Dead

NOVEMBER 1999. When I attended the festival of San Sebastian in Jalapa earlier in the year, someone—I can't remember who—suggested I return there on October 31 for the Day of the Dead. Not only was the all-night ritual celebrated in new Jalapa's cemetery with brass bands and tequila, but there would also be a ritual to honor the dead in old Jalapa's cemetery. Near dawn on November first, I was told, those who had relatives buried in the old Jalapa would hire open motorboats called launches to take them to the spot on the reservoir above the old cemetery. Then, as the boats came to rest and the sun rose, they would scatter flowers on the water above the graves.

At ten thirty in the evening on a windy October 31, Julin and I boarded a second-class bus with a small entourage of Julin's friends and relatives that included Lluvia, one of Julin's closest friends; Memo and Coco, Julin's sons; and Christi, Memo's American girlfriend. The bus was crowded with Mexico's poor, and we were forced to spend the half-hour ride to Jalapa on our feet, clinging to the backs of the seats or anything else we could hang onto when the driver swerved or came to a sudden stop. The luggage racks were stuffed with cardboard boxes containing pungent marigolds that the Zapotecs use in the Day of the Dead ceremonies. Already it was late, and the passengers grew tense and silent as midnight approached. If they were not home by twelve, when the dead returned, it would be no small disgrace.

We got off the bus within walking distance of La Palapa, the seafood restaurant where I had met Magda earlier in the year. Everyone was thirsty, so we entered the restaurant, and all of us drank cold Coronas. Julin suggested that I call Magda and invite her to the festivities, but I explained that neither Magda nor anyone in her family had a telephone. Instead, we agreed to stop by her house on our way to the cemetery and ask her to come along.

Magda—who was eating dinner with her parents at the time we arrived—answered the door dressed in an orange T-shirt and white cutoffs. Despite the late hour, she seemed pleased to see us. From a far corner of the patio came the sound of a typewriter clacking against a sheet of paper. Magda's brother, an economist, was hunched over a photocopy of a census report, squinting to read the fine print in the dim light of the patio. He dictated and his wife typed cautiously at the antique machine. The following day, at eight in the morning, Pedro would give a formal presentation of his report in Tehuantepec before turning it over to the state government in Oaxaca, and I was reminded how hard Mexicans work.

Even though we insisted we were not hungry, Magda's mother, Hortensia, sent Magda to buy additional food. She reached for pots and pans that were stored under the patio's thatched roof and began cooking. Now and then, she shuffled over to a stack of banana leaves that Mexicans use to wrap tamales, counting them to make sure she had enough. A couple of minutes after Magda returned, her mother served the tamales, and everyone, including those who protested most loudly that they were not hungry, ate one tamale after another. Hortensia watched us eat, gauging the success of her powers as a cook. While we ate, Magda told us about her new post on the town council. In the nine months since she was appointed, she had been collecting data about who grew what in Jalapa but was forced to drop this because of flooding caused by El Niño. She had also hired a consultant to help her assess crop damage. Because of chronic corruption, it was difficult to convince state officials in Oaxaca that Jalapa's farmers did indeed need financial aid. At times, she felt isolated. Before the flooding, she had been educating Jalapa's farmers on how to use fertilizer. Noise pollution was something she had wanted to spend time on, but she placed it on a back burner while she solved the problem with crop damage. On Thursday she would take the four-hour bus trip to Oaxaca to push for additional funds. She would have to finance the trip herself.

Magda escorted me to a room off the patio lit by candles. "Today," Magda said when we had entered the room, "everyone in Jalapa spent the day resting, because tonight, no one will sleep. Are you afraid?" In front of a glass enclosure containing a life-size replica of baby Jesus, were three plates of freshly prepared food: chicken in chocolate sauce, tamales, and *pan de muertos* (bread for the dead). According to the faithful, the dead return to the holy table at midnight, drawn by their favorite foods. And though the food might look untouched the day after, those among the living who dared to eat it learn that the dead have robbed it of all flavor. To the left of the statue of the baby Jesus were photos of Magda's sister. They showed her to be a fine-boned woman with captivating eyes and inviting lips. When Magda saw that I had fixated on the photo, she explained that her sister was married. To prove her point, she drew my attention to another photo of her sister, this time posed with her husband and children. Magda did not understand that marriage, or anything else that made a woman unattainable, only made her more attractive to me. Since childhood, I have had a chronic case of wanting those I could not have.

When I asked Magda if I could use her bathroom, she didn't answer immediately. She fingered a silver bracelet she wore on her right hand and stared into the distance. Then she said, "Let me show you where it is." Inside the bathroom, I found that the toilet had no seat and no mechanism for flushing it. When I exited the bathroom, Magda was still there, again staring into the distance. "How do you flush it?" I said. She picked up a bucket and showed me how to use it to scoop water from a fifty-gallon steel drum that stood nearby. We returned to the toilet and she pitched the water into the toilet bowl so that it would flush. Not only did Magda's house lack a telephone, but it had no running water.

For a while, we lounged around on the patio where Magda's mother served us coffee the color of whiskey and, later, slices from a moist vanilla cake. At eleven thirty, I made motions to leave for the cemetery, and Magda expressed her fear of riding in a boat onto the reservoir.

"How far out is the old Jalapa?" I asked.

"Maybe one hundred meters," Magda said.

"That's not far," I said. Magda tried to convince her mother to go out onto the reservoir with us, but she refused.

"What would I do if there was a problem with the boat?" Magda's mother asked.

"They must have life jackets," I said.

"Oh no, they don't," Magda said.

"But you know how to swim," I said.

"No," Magda's mother said, "I don't."

"Shouldn't we leave?" I said. "It's almost midnight."

"There won't be anyone at the cemetery until one," Magda said.

"No problem," I said. "If no one's at the cemetery, we can return here and go again later." Everyone laughed at the anxious, nervy gringo, and then they rose to go. We paused in Magda's front room to look at the photos of her grandparents.

"My grandfather fought on the side of the rebels who overthrew Porfirio Díaz in the 1910 Revolution," Magda said. "He was a good marksman. He had five bullet wounds on different parts of his body. Much to his disappointment, the bullet wound in his leg forced him to sit out part of the revolution."

"How did they meet?" I said.

"My grandfather abducted my grandmother during the revolution. He was blue-eyed and tall, and she was a pure-blooded Indian. At the time my grandfather abducted her, she didn't speak any Spanish. She was barefoot, illiterate, and dressed in clothes she had made herself— none of which detracted from her beauty."

"Your grandfather actually abducted her?" Julin asked.

"Yes," Magda said. "My grandfather—who was fifteen years her senior—literally took her away by force when she was still a child." Abductions of this sort were common in the Mexican Revolution. Rebel or federal armies would enter a town, taking weapons, ammunition, food, and young women. In 1913, three years after the revolution began, the *Mexican Herald* reported on April 13 that more than forty women, "including all of the female population of a small village," had been abducted by the followers of Emiliano Zapata. Some women were forced to marry the men who abducted them, as was the case with the fifteen-year-old Istmeña Jesusa Palancares, the heroine of Poniatowska's *Here's To You, Jesusa*. Other women were pressed into service cooking, laundering, and carrying supplies. When soldiers came to town, families hid their young women in trunks, covered their heads with rags, or took them to the fields to spend the night while the rebels were in town. In her book *Soldaderas in the Mexican Military,* Elizabeth Salas describes several abductions, including one involving nuns. "Mother Elias de

Santa Sacto, a member of the Carmelite order, recalled that in one hospital forty or fifty nuns who had been taken by Carrancistas were 'about to become mothers.'"

"Years later," Magda said, "when my grandfather retired, his suffering began. His soul was weighed down from all of the lives he'd taken in the revolution, and there were many. So, my grandmother brought him to a psychiatric hospital where they told her that his suffering stemmed from his advanced age. The official diagnosis was senile dementia—but no one believed it. And my grandmother was still young and still beautiful when he died."

"She looks so intense and domineering," I said. "It's hard to believe anyone could drag her away."

"She had a very strong character," Magda said, "though I never had the chance to meet her. I only know her through photos and what my parents remember of her. But they've spoken so much about her that it's almost as if she still lives in old Jalapa. There was a time when the water in the reservoir dried up, and we had access to the church. My father took us to where he and my mother met, where they spent time when they were engaged, and where they used to live. But this was for a very brief period when the water level in the reservoir took a serious dip."

When we left Magda's house and began our walk north to the cemetery, Magda and Julin complained about the weather.

"It's going to be cold," Julin said. Magda handed her jacket to Julin.

"You're the one who'll be cold," Magda said. "You're wearing sandals."

The cold they spoke of was invented. Rings of sweat circled my armpits, and I took regular swipes at my forehead to keep the salty sweat out of my eyes. My cloth watchband stank of sweat to the degree that I was forced to wash it out in the sink every couple of days.

"In Tehuantepec," Julin said, "we celebrate Day of the Dead on Palm Sunday. Near midnight, when the festivities are about to begin, there are food stands set up along the way to the cemetery where you can buy tamales, bread, beer, sodas, and flowers. Inside the cemetery, there are an equal number of vendors who make a small fortune as the night goes on."

We walked in silence until I noticed the moon on the horizon. It was huge, full, and jaundiced; a moon that better fit the occasion did not exist. Then what sounded like a catfight crowded the air, and everyone but Magda turned their heads, looking for the source of the tumult.

"And the music?" Julin said. "Where's that coming from?"

"From the cemetery," Magda said. "They'll play all night. You'll see entire bands wandering around when we get there. They follow you like lost dogs offering to play songs that your dead relatives liked to hear."

Then we reached the cemetery, a vast, desolate expanse of land that occupied a corner lot at the intersection of two country roads. Magda stepped ahead of us to open the wrought iron gate, the only entry point in the waist-high concrete fence that surrounded the cemetery on all sides. We followed Magda inside and then down a dirt path to the rear of the cemetery. Wild grass grew on either side of the path, and the dirt underfoot was strewn with wilted marigolds. Beyond the path was darkness, and I kept close to the light of Magda's orange T-shirt.

We hadn't marched fifty feet into the cemetery when the dark yielded to a family of ten or twelve huddled around a grave, their faces lit by candlelight. The grave was nothing more than loose stones that delineated a small oval in the sun-hardened earth. Inside the oval the family had planted poor man's impatiens, and at one end of the grave was a weather-beaten wooden crucifix gone gray with age. The family smiled a ghoulish smile, and we walked past them, still deeper into the cemetery. A hundred feet further, we came upon a second family. They were dressed in Sunday clothes of pressed linen and leather shoes that shone in the light of slender white candles they held in their hands. At the center of this family's graves was the facade of a miniature cathedral carved in white granite with bell towers that rose over the shoulders of the gray-haired family patriarch, who looked more amused than bereaved in his white linen suit. In front of the facade was a tomb, and on the tomb lay a stone replica of an open book with an epitaph, part of which I was able to read:

> Frumencio Rodriguez Careño 1944-1996.
> Father, one day you said:
> When I die, give what remains of me to the children
> Hug anyone and give him what you need to give to me
> Look for me among the people I knew and loved
> Love doesn't die, people do

We marched on and did not stop until we were fifty feet short of the northern limit of the cemetery. Magda announced our arrival at the Garrido family gravesite, a small collection of graves surrounded on one side by two tree trunks lying in the dirt. All of us except Magda sat down on one of the logs with our backs to the cemetery. Julin lit a candle. "That's it, a candle," Magda said. "The only problem with candles is that they light up things that crawl, like toads. In the rainy season, Jalapa is full of frogs, and if one of them jumps out at me, I'll have a heart attack." Magda gave us a brief tour of the family graves. All were made of the same material, a ceramic tile the color of a blood orange. One of the tombs was particularly shiny. On closer inspection I saw that the tomb had been weatherproofed with a glossy bathroom tile. "Some time ago, my mother used to bring food to us which we would eat here where you are standing. Coffee, chocolate, bread, tamales, and sometimes, tequila." Magda reached into her bag, and brought out a spiral taper candle, which she lit. She turned the candle sideways, let a drop of wax fall onto one of the family tombs, and placed the candle on top of the melted wax. She repeated this process a dozen times, until each of the tombs had three or four lit candles standing on its surface and our area was no longer the cemetery's darkest corner.

"When your parents die," Magda began, "it's difficult, but when your child dies, the feeling is much worse."

"It's true," Julin said. "I believe my mother died from grief after my brother was killed in a car accident."

"Yes," Magda said, "the effects on a mother can be overwhelming. I feel that my mother still has an aftertaste of sadness ever since my brother died in the accident. She refuses to have his photo on our holy table because she says it would make her too sad."

"You can't erase it," Julin said.

"At times she smiles, and she appears happy, but no, the sadness in her face remains."

"How old would your brother be if he were still alive?" Julin said.

"Thirty-nine," Magda said. "He was a model son, a hard worker, and very studious."

"These are the grand questions of life," Julin said.

"And why is it always the good who die young?" Magda said.

"Some say that being good isn't the way. They say that it's better to be bad, though they say it with a certain amount of bitterness. When I think of my brother, who was so good, I often ask myself: Why have this debilitating experience of losing a child to a violent accident?"

Julin and Magda passed an hour in this way, exchanging ghost stories and laments for lost family members. At times, when the conversation lagged, I would hear a hiss followed by a pop overhead. Intrigued, I turned around to face the cemetery, and when the hiss came again, an arc of gray smoke divided the dark sky. Then came the pop, and a small fountain of fireworks spilled overhead. I asked Magda what the fireworks, called *triquitracas,* were about. "The people here tonight are demonstrating their happiness that their deceased family members are now here in the cemetery."

When I turned around and lowered my eyes to the horizon, I saw that half the cemetery was lit with candles, especially near the center where the concentration of graves was most dense. I told Magda and Julin I was going for a walk and started off along the path by which we came. I didn't get far. I found myself tripping over low-lying tombstones and, every now and then, sinking a foot into the soft earth of a fresh grave. I returned to our group, hoping I might talk Magda out of a candle or two, but I hadn't the heart to ask her to remove a candle from the family graves. Instead, I played with my camera until I discovered a way to fire the flash without taking a photo, and I started out once again. Every four or five seconds I fired the flash, took several steps, and repeated the process all over again. As I neared the center of the cemetery, I found that I no longer needed my camera. The candlelight had become increasingly strong until it appeared that the sun were about to rise, though it was not yet four in the morning. The mourners had pulled off this surreal feat not with magic but with the sheer number of candles. Every one of the 150 to 200 tombs and crypts crammed into the cemetery's center was covered with scores of candles. There were votive candles in glass jars with images of the Virgin on either side, short squat candles called *veladoras,* and dinner candles tapered gracefully to a point at the wick. There were fat spiral candles the color of beeswax, block candles with prayers inscribed in tiny Spanish lettering, and scented candles that released the thick sweet odor of jasmine into the air. And the scene the candles lit was equally surreal: hundreds of Zapotecs were crowded into an area the size of half a city block, moving through the flickering candlelight as though it were morning and they were at work in the fields. Some swung wildly with machetes at the grass and weeds that grew in and around the graves while others stuffed what was cut down into bags and sacks. Women on their knees stabbed at the earth with knives or twigs to make way for marigolds or zinnias that stood in terracotta pots all around them. Men carried wooden poles on their shoulders from which buckets of water hung on either end, and when they arrived at the family gravesite, women would snatch the buckets off and douse with water the flowers they had planted minutes before. Teenagers carried armfuls of cypress wreathes and cut flowers that the women arranged with flair over the marble or ceramic tombs where flowers could not be planted. Some of the women laid a single wreath on the graves, while others created a sea of flowers in which votive candles seemed to float. Children, when they were not pressed into duty by their parents, held still more candles while the better-dressed ones threw sparklers that spun in the dirt. Overhead, the fireworks continued to burst and flow—though only in blue or gold. "Blue is for PRI," a mourner explained, "gold for PRD."

As time passed, and the grave grooming wound down, many of the families spread out picnic blankets over the ground and stretched out to eat the traditional food for the occasion that Magda had mentioned earlier: bread, tamales, chocolate, coffee, tequila, and one ingredient Magda left off, mezcal, which plays an important part of the story I'm about to relate. On my way back to the Garrido family gravesite, I remember passing a woman sitting alone on a picnic blanket, food all around her, doling out mezcal to passersby from a plastic coke bottle with a screw-on top. She wore orange sweat pants and an orange blouse that were so heavily spotted with dirt and grease and food that in the half-light of the cemetery, she appeared to be wearing a leopard-skin jump suit. Her stomach swelled out of her clothes wherever it could, and her hair was matted on one side as though she had just rolled out of bed. I didn't take a second look; I passed by.

Soon, however, I realized that I was lost, so lost that I was traveling in circles, and once again I found myself in the presence of the leopard lady. Now she was listening to a trio of string musicians playing songs for a family nearby that was huddled around a plain headstone. The trio played impeccably, and the songs were so sad and enjoyable that I sat down on a tomb next to the leopard lady's blanket, but not before I had checked for flowers or candles or other signs that a relative had been there and would return. She asked where I was from and told me her name was Maria Guzman. We returned our attention to the music. When the song ended and the musicians went looking for their next customer, Maria offered me mezcal in a plastic cup the size of a shot glass. As soon as I had the cup in my hand, two of Maria's relatives materialized at my side: a woman with a faint trace of a mustache and a gaunt old man in a cowboy hat who I took to be Maria's husband. They stood so close to me I felt uncomfortable, and I could feel their eyes focus in on my face as I lifted the shot glass to my lips. They wanted to see me flinch from mezcal's sharp burn, and for a moment I was tempted to fake a cough and spray the three of them with their mezcal and my saliva.

"Why are you here in Jalapa?" the old man asked.

"I like it here," I said.

"And what do you like about it?"

"I like your traditions."

"And what is your line of work?"

"Journalist." I used the word *periodista*, Spanish for "journalist."

"No, a *periodista* is someone who sells newspapers. You are a *reportero* [a reporter]." I knew what he was saying was untrue, but I did not point this out to him. Mezcal, more than other kinds of alcohol, had the tendency to stir people to violence, and I sensed he was looking to pick a fight. Then he took another step toward me, pointed his chin at me with an accusing look, and said, "Aren't you a spy?"

I laughed, though I shouldn't have; it only made him more suspicious. He kept his face close to mine, so close that given enough time, I could have counted the bloody veins that coursed through the whites of his eyes. When I got a whiff of his breath, though, it didn't smell like mezcal, or any other kind of alcohol, and I knew then that he hadn't been drinking. His eyes were bloodshot for another reason. I took a step back, defusing the situation. I looked at the grave behind him, a humble cement block without so much as an epitaph or crucifix and remembered seeing him standing before it mumbling intently to himself or to whomever was contained in the tomb.

"And who have you come to honor tonight?" I said.

"My son," the old man said, "Ephraim Guzman. He died young." The long gray hair the old man had stuffed into the back of his cowboy hat was working its way out, falling into place behind his ears.

"How did he die?" I said.

"First write his name down in your notebook; then I'll tell you." I did so, and as if we hadn't been conversing in Spanish, he said in English:

"Boat . . . Explode . . . Navy."

"The boat he was on exploded?"

"Boat . . . Explode . . . Navy."

Then Maria nudged my arm and smiled. I looked down to see she was offering more mezcal. This time it went down smoother; the urge to gag was gone. I asked for another round, and another, and then I left them to mourn their son in peace.

By the time I was hoofing it down the road to the reservoir, it was five-thirty, and the moon had begun to set. I had gotten separated from the others when we were leaving the cemetery and decided to walk to the launches on my own. To make sure I was on the right road, I asked everyone I saw for directions to the launches. A hundred yards down the road, when the houses became sparse, a pair of parting lovers wandered out of an adobe home, and as one opened the door of a car to depart, I shouted out my question. "Las lanchas?" I asked. "Derechito, derechito" (Straight ahead) came the answer. I walked on, kicking stones to entertain myself as the adobe farmhouses were replaced by fields of tall grass. The stars looked as though I were viewing them through a zoom lens, close and bright and hot, and the moon set brown and crusty, bobbing up and down over the grass as I walked for a good five miles. "Around the next bend," I told myself. "You'll see the shore and then the launches." I walked on, sure that I had been sent down a path to nowhere to punish me for America's sins against Mexico. Then another road appeared out of the darkness that merged with the one I was on, and with that other road came the dark silhouette of a man who came within inches of colliding into me. I say silhouette for a reason. The moon was on the other side of him, so that for me, he was nothing more than a black figure whose only distinguishing characteristic was a machete that swung freely in his right hand. He immediately moved to the opposite side of the road, and we continued walking in this way for some time. Other than the initial scare, I did not find his presence frightening; in fact, I found it comforting. "Buenas noches," I said. He didn't respond; he kept on walking. This I passed off to confusion. I had learned at the cemetery that between midnight and dawn, Mexicans feel confused about these phrases. How can you say "buenos dias" when you're surrounded by darkness? Despite his refusal to speak, we fell into a kind of lockstep, and when I was sure he'd never reply to my initial greeting, I tried another tack.

"Is this the way to the launches?"

"Yes," he said. I never felt so uplifted by a one-word reply.

"And is there more than one place from which the launches leave?"

"No," he said, and he didn't speak another word to me in all our time together. This, I consoled myself, was a trait of good country people. They placed little stock in words, and what they did say could be trusted. It was an odd journey. At times, the irregularities in the road—the potholes, the way in which the road banked and turned—brought us together shoulder to shoulder in the middle of the road. Then we'd break our rhythmic pace and separate, though we eventually fell back into step. The reservoir began coming into view, at first only for seconds between two hills, and then almost constantly as we neared the shore. Then the lights of a truck coming up behind us lit our path and we separated to opposite sides of the road to let it pass. But when the truck pulled up between us, it slowed, and we took this as an invitation to jump aboard, and we leapt onto the back bumper and swung our legs over and into the bed of the truck. There were other men in back, and before I could identify my fellow traveler, he had blended in with the other men, and I knew it was no use trying to draw him out with questions. We rode in silence for another minute or two. Then the truck stopped, and we piled out onto the shore of the reservoir. Three launches, similar in construction to a rowboat but stretched out twice the size, sat in shallow water, buffeted now and then by ripples on the otherwise calm face of the water.

The sun rose at six, whitening the sky but deepening the color of the coal-black mountains that surrounded us on all sides. The groggy-eyed owners of the launches followed, and then came a crop of customers decidedly older than the crowd of cemetery-goers I had seen earlier in the night. I took this as a good sign. Only the elderly would have relatives buried under water in old Jalapa's cemetery. With them they brought dozens of marigolds in clear plastic bags with flower heads the size of Valencia oranges. At the same time that the elderly passengers climbed cautiously into the launches, Julin and Magda and the rest appeared at the shoreline, grinning widely when they saw the concern in my face. We followed Magda to a launch owned by one of her friends, a lean, leathery-faced man named Miguel who, despite his age, hadn't a single gray hair on his head. I stepped into the launch first and seated myself in the boat's midsection. After Magda and the others climbed in, I calculated I could best shoot photos of the flowers as they were dropped onto the water if I were seated at the front of the launch. I stood up and strode from seat to seat toward the front. The boat began to rock, very slightly from my perspective, but somehow more violently near the back of the boat. How did I know? Because a chorus of screams rose behind me, commanding me to sit down. I did, and then slowly I made my way to the front of the boat without standing. The rest of our group stayed at the back of the boat, eyeing me angrily. Meanwhile the midsection filled up with elderly passengers. Then Miguel yanked the motor's starter rope, and we were off, motoring our way across the reservoir.

Five minutes into our journey, I began to wonder where and when we were going to stop to allow the elderly to toss the marigolds onto the water. I remember Magda saying that the old Jalapa would be one hundred meters out—roughly the length of a football field. According to my estimate, we had traveled twice that distance. Now and then I would look behind me to see if anyone had tossed a flower on the water but nothing of the sort happened. Then an island appeared on the horizon. Unlike the barren mountains all around us, the island was green with ancient trees and wild grass that gave it a magical quality. Miguel steered directly toward it. He pulled the launch into a lagoon where the water was calm, and everyone on board waded out into the knee-deep water and headed for the shore. The group I was with avoided me, still fuming about the rocking, so I stayed behind and spoke with Miguel.

"I once heard about a ritual where mourners drop flowers onto the water over old Jalapa's cemetery. Have you heard of this?"

"No," Miguel said. Miguel wasn't the talkative type, and maybe he was new to the job.

"And how long have you been running launches on the reservoir?"

"Thirty-two years," he said.

"If no such ritual exists, then why have so many people come carrying marigolds?"

"The island is not really an island. It's a hill in one of old Jalapa's cemeteries. Some of the graves at the top of the hill are still exposed to the air, and the people have come to clean them up and leave flowers." With this, I lost all hope. I thanked Miguel for his time and headed uphill with the others. The rituals I witnessed were identical to those I had seen in the new Jalapa's cemetery, except that those who had come were older and therefore less energetic and thorough in attending to the graves.

An hour later, we climbed back into the launch, and Miguel steered us back to the opposite shore. Halfway there, I heard Julin shout from the front of the boat.

"Get your camera out," she yelled. Julin rarely ordered me to do anything. So I figured there must be something in it for me. I took hold of my camera and turned it on. Then I saw that she had two handfuls of marigolds, no doubt lifted from one of the graves on the hill, which she began throwing one-by-one onto the water. I raised my camera to my eyes and shot one photo after the other, until both her hands were empty.

The Italian

Social anthropologist Marinella Miano Borruso was born in 1948 to an upper-middle-class family in Napoli, Italy. Her father was a physician, and her mother was an ethnologist and writer, and there was little lacking in her upbringing in terms of comfort and attention. Despite this privileged childhood, Miano Borruso declared herself a communist when she was fifteen and a feminist not long after. Miano Borruso studied ethnographic anthropology in Rome and received her master and doctoral degrees in anthropology from Mexico's National University. In all, Miano Borruso spent four years and ten months in the Isthmus doing fieldwork, which lends her voice greater authority than any other outsider.

In her book *Hombre, mujer y muxe'* (Man, Woman and Muxe), which resulted from her doctoral thesis, Miano Borruso sketches the life of an Isthmus girl from the time she is born through adulthood and into old age. Her detailed, realistic portrait shows that even at birth, an Isthmus child's gender influences the attitude of his or her mother. "How nice that it's a girl," Miano Borruso quotes a midwife speaking to a mother at the birth of her daughter, "now you have someone to hold your hand, when you can't walk anymore." If, on the other hand, the child is a boy, the women present at birth sometimes express pity. "A bachelor is born," they say, "you're going to have to marry him." Marrying him, in this case, means funding the marriage of her son, which by tradition, falls to the family of the groom and can run to thousands of dollars and months of preparation. This joy at the birth of a girl is unusual, Miano Borruso tells us, because it contrasts sharply with the typical attitude of the Mexican mestizo family, where male children are preferred to females. But in the Isthmus, mothers know that male children are more prone toward crime and drugs and are less likely to look after them in old age, although they can and do provide economic support.

At baptism, boys are given a suit and a pair of shoes, girls are given a dress and jewelry of gold or coral, a potent amulet against the evil eye. Girls also receive more affection than boys from both the mother and father, and the circumference of their activities is always closer to their mother. As soon as the girl is perceived to be capable of helping out at home, she learns to make tortillas, take care of her younger brothers and sisters, add and subtract sums of money, and most important—she learns to sell. As early as seven or eight years of age, Miano Borruso explains, girls sell in the market or door to door offering fruits, tamales, or fish, all in an effort to contribute to the well-being of the family. Boys, on the other hand, often enjoy several years of infancy after baptism completely free of worry. At some point, however, if the father is fisherman, peasant, or craftsman, the son accompanies the father to work and learns his trade.

When the funds are available to further the education of a child, boys are given preference over girls. A typical mother will make great sacrifices so that her son will continue studying beyond grammar school. Miano Borruso assures us that a son is given preference over a daughter for a reason. A girl is perceived as being better able to fend for herself by way of commerce or marriage than her brother. But in the upper classes, where parents do not have economic constraints that force them to choose one child over another, both sexes are given equal opportunity to higher education.

"From an early age," writes Miano Borruso, "there is a complete separation of sexes between females and males that is developed and socialized in exclusive spaces." When a boy nears puberty, he spends the majority of his time outside the home, in the labyrinth of patios and alleys and streets, playing with his friends and chasing after animals and unwary girls. Girls, on the other hand, tend to accompany their mothers to work, where they learn a trade so that "they can develop as independent persons with their own economic base, allowing them to defend themselves in life without depending on anyone." It is also at this age that the family's control over a daughter becomes most rigid. Maintaining the family's honor depends on bringing the daughter to marriage as a virgin. "Between puberty and marriage the relations between mother and daughter grow bitter, because the girl resents the repression, while her brothers enjoy the maximum freedom." Unmarried daughters are subordinate to their brothers. They must wash and dry their brother's clothes, cook and even serve their food.

As a rule, Istmeñas marry young, after a long courtship and a short engagement. On reaching his late teens or early twenties, a young man will announce his interest in a particular girl to his brothers and, more importantly, to his mother. If the mother disapproves, however, the results can be devastating. "I've known several cases of men," writes Miano Borruso, "who have not been able to marry with the woman they love because of a negative response from their mother." Factors that might make a mother disapprove are many: opposing political affiliations, different economic classes, or even families who have long-standing conflicts.

Once married, the young couple settle in the house of the groom's parents. They remain there until the couple can build or buy a house of their own, under the supervision of the mother-in-law. According to many Istmeñas, early marriage years spent at the in-laws are heartbreaking. The mother-in-law inevitably works to drive a wedge between the bride and her mother. "Speaking with judges in family courts in Tehuantepec, Juchitán, and San Blas," writes Miano Borruso, "it turns out that many of the family conflicts that were vented in court originate in the fact that the groom's mother and female relatives meddle too much in the lives of the couple." Although an adult woman exercises a great deal of well-accepted authority over the organization of the home and children—thanks to their sizable economic contribution—Miano Borruso feels they do not reach the status of "head of family," a role of authority and power that corresponds to the man.

The celebration of a woman's fiftieth year has a connotation of special importance in the life of an Isthmus woman. She is free from the responsibility of her children and at the same time disassociated from sexuality. Within the context of her family, she acquires an authority and freedom never experienced in her earlier years. "It's the moment of 'enjoying life,'" Miano Borruso writes, "going to all of the fiestas she's invited to, taking charge of a *mayordomía*, traveling, participating in an electoral campaign of a relative or friend, dedicating herself to pleasurable activities, showing off her professional children, separating herself from an alcoholic husband, doing and undoing as she pleases." These elderly yet powerful women also help explain how—in Miano Borruso's mind—Juchitán developed a reputation as a matriarchy. "These women are the 'matriarchs' whose situation, extended arbitrarily to all Zapotec women, present themselves before the gaze of the naive observers as an expression of matriarchy." This interpretation agrees with my experience. Much of the market is controlled by mature women who are at the peak of their power, both economically and socially. An outsider who visited Juchitán's plaza or market was more likely than not to see these freewheeling, fifty-year-old women than any other. Still, Miano Borruso feels that these very women are not so privileged when compared to other women on a worldwide basis, drawing on her own experience to make the comparison. "Personally," Miano Borruso writes, "I don't find much difference with the condition of post-menopausal women of southern Italy."

Miano Borruso provides other clues as to how the idea of an Isthmus matriarchy might have taken shape in an outsider's mind. In addition to the market, the women of Juchitán dominate the system of community socialization that manifests itself in Isthmus festivals and velas. In this realm, women enjoy autonomy with respect to men because they hold a "monopoly" of *mayordomias* at festivals and velas. And—aside from the market—the next most likely point of contact for outsiders would be one of these festivals or velas where they would again be enveloped with the overwhelming presence of middle-aged women. According to Miano Borruso, women also dominate other contact points for outsiders, including the Catholic Church and, for the odd few, the cemetery.

Possibly the most outstanding feature of Miano Borruso's work is that she is one of the few observers who can live with the many contradictions of power and subjugation that are the facts of life for most Isthmus women. On one page she cites the apparent autonomy and dominant social presence of Istmeñas and on the next the subordination to which they are subjected to with respect to "their bodies and sexuality." Proof of virginity as a necessary condition for marriage, domestic violence, and a double moral standard in terms of sexuality are the most visible elements of sexual control by men. Other practices Miano Borruso cites even call into question an egalitarian relationship between the sexes. Men have better access to advanced degree programs, they frequently abandon their wives and children, and they exclude women from political, artistic and literary arenas.

Bloqueo

Several days after the Day of the Dead, I boarded a bus to Juchitán, where I hoped to rent a room from Zapotec linguist Florinda Luis. I sat at the front of the bus and amused myself with an article in the local paper, *El Sol Del Istmo*. On page sixteen, the headline read: TEMPERA-TURE IN JUCHITÁN DROPS. Below, the article lamented the weather: "On Sunday, the thermometer in Juchitán fell to sixty degrees. The people of the Isthmus resent this weather because they are used to temperatures in the eighties and nineties. Respiratory illnesses have begun to manifest themselves, causing a crisis in minors and adults." When I was halfway through the article, a collective groan went up from the other passengers, the kind of groan you often hear on Mexican busses when they run out of gas or a tire explodes. I pulled back the velvet curtain and looked out the window, but saw nothing other than the usual flatland with barren trees tormented by the Isthmus sun. Then the bus stopped, and we piled out onto the molten asphalt.

Directly in front of the bus was a long line of trucks, some big rigs, some flatbeds, all sitting motionless in the sun. The passengers formed a ragged line and marched toward Juchitán, parallel to the line of trucks. Minutes later, we reached the truck at the head of the line. A foot or two in front of it were a dozen roughly hewn boulders the size of bowling balls strewn in a line across the highway. These boulders, by themselves, wouldn't have stopped traffic. They were symbolic, because with a little help, any adult could have rolled the boulders out of the way. What was really blocking the road were two hundred women and children and a couple of dozen men milling about on a section of the highway half the size of a football field. But the passengers paid little attention to the crowd. They marched on toward Juchitán until they came to a row of boulders that blocked the highway on the other side of the demonstration. I took a seat on the curb, and the last I saw of my fellow passengers, they were boarding a flatbed pickup that would take them, at last, to Juchitán.

This march of passengers from one side of the demonstration to the other seemed to repeat itself every five minutes. Passengers would arrive by taxi, bus, or truck, climb out of the vehicle, and walk the fifty yards to the other end of the blockade, where they would board a like vehicle and continue on their way. But the trucks went nowhere, and every half hour, one of the drivers would begin to honk his horn in frustration, and the other drivers would join in until all other sound was drowned out. When no one at the blockade reacted to the sound of the horns, however, the truckers would cease the honking, and the sound of laughter and screaming children would return. What struck my gringo mind as somewhat unbelievable was the fact that this was not just any highway that the women had brought to a halt. This was the Pan-American Highway, the principle trade route between the Americas and the only continuous highway that stretches between Canada and Argentina.

Having nothing better to do, I stayed put in my seat on the curb and waited for the police to arrive. The demonstrators, as a group, were anything but criminal. They had the look of good country people, of the dirt-poor subsistence farmers the leftist COCEI called *campesinos* (peasants). The women demonstrators wore huipiles and enaguas, and some of them had fashioned makeshift turbans out of shawls to protect their heads from the murderous afternoon sun. They stood in circles of six or eight, shopping bags and purses hanging in the crooks of their arms, chatting and sucking on popsicles, or disciplining one of the children who ran mad throughout the area as they played tag and a Mexican version of hide-and-go-seek. The handful of men who had joined the demonstration stood in the middle of the highway—still and silent as always.

Also present were the entrepreneurs. They seemed to come from out of nowhere, wheeling their carts through the crowd selling cold drinks, oranges, sweet white corn, and popsicles, all of which made the event look more like a county fair than a demonstration. The most popular food by far was served from a taco stand mounted on a giant tricycle with a candy-cane canopy in red and white. Business was brisk; the stand was surrounded by hungry women squinting in the sun, who told stories and every now and then threw their heads back for a good laugh. In fact, laughter was the predominant sound at the blockade, and the atmosphere was so carnival-like that two men with faces made up like clowns—red rubber nose included—hardly drew the notice of the demonstrators as they passed from one end of the blockade to the other.

Time passed, and when the sun was directly overhead, everyone sought a place in the shade: under the ficus trees that lined the shoulder of the highway, behind a car stamped PRD, next to an empty cattle truck, or squatting in the shade cast by one of the entrepreneur's carts. And whenever the crowd sought shelter like this, and the highway was drained of demonstrators, a fat man with a bullhorn would squawk, "Get in the middle of the road. Everyone in the middle of the highway."

For the two hours I spent on the asphalt that afternoon, no vehicle passed around or through the blockade—although one trucker made an attempt. I was standing near a taco cart drinking a bottle of water when I heard someone shout, "He's getting through." A wave of nervous energy passed through the crowd. Everyone looked north to an open field where a speeding pickup truck followed by a cloud of dust bounced along a washboard road no more than two or three blocks in the distance. Almost immediately, twenty women and a couple of men set off running toward the truck. They moved across the field with surprising speed and positioned themselves directly in the path of the pickup. The driver had little choice. Either he ran the women over or he stopped, and, of course, he stopped. As soon as he got out of the truck, a heated discussion filled with violent gestures began, and ten minutes later the driver turned the truck around and drove back to search for a less guarded detour. When the demonstrators saw me shooting photos of the fleeing truck, they shouted things at me in Zapotec that I couldn't understand, but I got the idea. Why was I focusing on the sideshow rather than the demonstration? Why was I taking so many photos? But most of the women laughed and poked fun at me, and this made me feel at home.

Howard Campbell recorded the fate of another trucker who attempted to defy a 1991 blockade by COCEI. "At one point, an exasperated 18-wheeler driver pulled out of the left lane (facing Juchitán) of parked vehicles and headed down the right lane at a rapid rate of speed directly toward the *coceístas* who were blocking the road—immediately men and women picked up large rocks and poised themselves to throw them at the truck. . . . About thirty-five or forty feet from the barricade the truck came to a screeching halt and several more rocks were hurled in his direction. The driver got out of the truck nonchalantly amid jeers and insults and walked a short ways away. At that point the *coceístas* relaxed a bit and some put down their rocks; others hung on to theirs as they had before this incident, including many women."

When, after an hour or so, the arrests I was so certain of did not materialize, I began asking the demonstrators what the blockade was about. Either no one knew—which I found improbable—or they were doing something they weren't proud of. A girl of fifteen made an honest attempt to explain but got caught in the wording. She asked a man standing next to her if he would explain, but he turned away. I gave up on getting an answer from the demonstrators and asked about a ringleader. "Talk to Doctor Reina," most said, but when I asked for a description of him, they went mute. "He's right around here somewhere." Then, a lean-faced woman with a turban and no shoes brought me to Francisco López, who stood at the center of the demonstration with two other men. All had sly but intelligent faces and wore Levis and long-sleeved white shirts. Francisco, the tallest of the three, identified himself as a member of COCEI and answered my first question: "We are here demonstrating because the government has broken its promises to us. Both the federal and state governments swear they've paid out millions of pesos for reconstruction after the flood in July, but no one here has seen a cent. We'll be here until the government sits down with us to talk." With that, the conversation withered, and I understood that asking more questions would be a mistake.

Shortly before I left the blockade, a man with a bullhorn in one hand and a clipboard in the other climbed into the back of the cattle truck. He called out names, and the women would shout out their presence, which he would then record by checking off their names on his clipboard. Somehow, a roll call at a demonstration seemed incongruous, but there it was. After the roll call, I walked to the side of the blockade nearest Juchitán and hired a taxi to take me to Florinda's. She spoke with me briefly, and I rented a small but comfortable room on the roof of her house. Later, I ate dinner at Casa Grande and then took in a film at Juchitán's movie theater, the only one in the Isthmus.

At nine in the evening, not long after the movie let out, I boarded a bus to Tehuantepec. I planned to spend one more night at the Oasis before moving on to Florinda's with my luggage. Halfway there, the bus slowed to a crawl, and when I raised my head from the newspaper I was reading, I saw the same long line of diesel trucks that were there eight hours before, parked in exactly the same order. The bus pulled to a stop, and a collective groan went up, this time less audibly due to the scarcity of riders. The passengers exited the bus with caution, looking left and right before stepping out onto the pavement. I followed suit, and when I got a good look around me, the scene of the blockade appeared chancier, the mood more anxious, as if the crowd sensed something ugly were about to occur. A good portion of the women had taken their children and gone home; those who remained murmured to each other, and laughter came less frequently than in the afternoon. The men were silent and had taken off the cowboy hats and baseball caps they had used to protect themselves from the sun. Empty cola bottles and napkins and other litter were strewn about the highway as though a traveling circus had come and gone.

I took a seat on a curb and watched people arrive and cross the demilitarized zone between the two lines of diesel trucks. In addition to the usual crowd of impoverished souls who regularly ride the bus, middle-class car owners who the blockade had forced out of their vehicles and onto public transportation were also in evidence. Men in suits and ties carrying briefcases walked across the pavement in wingtips, rubbing shoulders with groups of women in huipiles and enaguas. Then the moon rose, and a man with a pigskin face climbed into the back of the cattle truck, now parked in the center of the highway. Slowly, a crowd began forming around it, and I stood up and pushed my way past the others until I was a foot or two from the truck. The man raised the bullhorn to his mouth and very literally screamed into it with such force that, for me, his message was distorted beyond recognition. But whatever he had to say, his words electrified the crowd. The once nebulous group of demonstrators formed into a marching army led by five women who locked arms at the front of the crowd. Without wanting to, I was swept up into the middle of the mob as they turned east and began a long-legged stride in the direction of Juchitán. Behind me, the demilitarized zone lay empty, and according to what Francisco said, this could only mean one thing: the mayor had agreed to meet with the demonstrators.

The marchers turned off the highway and into a residential district populated with adobe homes and cement sidewalks. Anger and determination marked the faces of the women around me, and though I wanted to free myself from them immediately, it took me several minutes to push my way out of the crowd and onto the sidewalk. Men carrying cans of spray paint ran alongside the marchers, spraying slogans in capital letters on the adobe homes. They wrote the slogans on the walls quickly and accurately, almost without breaking pace, as if they had had much practice. DEATH TO THE FASCIST GOVERNMENT was the most popular slogan; then came WE WANT PUBLIC WORKS — NOT BEATINGS and finally POLO OUT OF BARRIO 16 DE SEPTIEMBRE. The slogans agitated the crowd, which made them march yet faster, and in no time we had entered Juchitán proper and then the main plaza, where the marchers dispersed. A delegation from the demonstrators climbed the stairs to the second floor of the market where they met with the mayor.

"Which one is Doctor Reina?" I said to a man standing next to me.

"The one in the white sweatshirt," he said. The man he pointed out wore a new, baggy white sweatshirt and new blue jeans and white tennis shoes. His hair was matted against his head like a rodent that had been doused with oil. I was sorry I had not met and spoken with him at the blockade. I was sure he would have had interesting things to say.

The rest of us found seats on the curb or on the plaza opposite the market. As usual, separation of the sexes was in force, now more than ever because of the dark. The women formed groups of eight or ten and hugged themselves against the cool night air. All of them seemed to be wearing ribbons woven into their braids and skirts so long their sandals were invisible. Tall, skinny men with learned faces and Trotskyite beards strolled by as if on a promenade in Paris, and they wore a kind of uniform: white pants and khaki shirts and red bandanas around their necks, although one or two wore black T-shirts with Commandante Marcos printed across the front in red letters. A man in a wheelchair rested his face on one of the wooden tables where women like Manuela stacked and sold hammocks by day. He had wispy gray hair and terracotta skin, and his arm was extended across the table in a socialist salute.

I sat down with a group of old men on the cement benches that circle the trees on the plaza.

At eleven, a pair of men approached me. They were tall and skinny and bookish like the other men lounging around the plaza, but unlike the leaders I spoke with at the blockade, they had kind, honest faces. Both worked as teachers, and a couple of minutes into our conversation, I was able to coax out their monthly earnings: 200 pesos, or $20 per week. They were proud to say that they had participated in the demonstration, and when I asked them what the blockade was about, they cited several reasons. They first spoke about liberty for political prisoners, though they mentioned no names. They also wanted to see government grants called *becas* for those who would like to learn a trade such as hammock weaving. This, they were convinced, would improve the lot of the perennially poor. And though the federal government had already allocated the money for such grants, the teachers explained, it had disappeared in the hands of local politicians. This was the issue that angered them most, and I was reminded of a fourth slogan spray painted on the walls of the adobe homes: WE DEMAND CLEAR ACCOUNTING — COCEI. The culprit behind the corruption, the teachers said, was Polo. Better known as Leopoldo de Gyves Pineda, Polo was a longtime leader of COCEI and current mayor of Juchitán. "We are demanding transparency in the use of the people's resources," one of the teachers said. The teachers also explained that a group of Polo's men had harassed and beaten women in a barrio named 16 de Septiembre. Before leaving me, the teachers spoke about arming themselves if the federal government continued its repression of common people. "When the Zapatistas from Chiapas arrive in Juchitán," they said, "we will welcome them with open arms. We are also in touch with our brothers in El Salvador, the FMLN (Farabundo Marti for National Liberation)." Some of this was talk; it was difficult to imagine either one of them aiming a rifle at anyone.

Near midnight, officials began descending the stairs from the second floor of the market, and I crossed the street to get a better look. One of them was a woman in her late thirties with a thick head of black hair and an armful of pamphlets and papers. She looked at my camera and then at me.

"Are you a journalist?" she asked.

"Something like that," I said.

"Tomorrow, at seven in the evening, we'll be holding a press conference about today's events," she said as she handed me an invitation.

"I'd much prefer an interview with you."

"Can you come tomorrow at ten?"

"I'm moving from Tehuantepec to Juchitán tomorrow morning. Twelve would be much better."

"You'll find me in my office at noon."

The invitation identified her as Rogelia Gonzalez Luis, city labor leader. I folded the invitation up and tucked it into my journal and caught a taxi to Tehuantepec. On the Pan-American Highway, the driver asked what I'd been doing so late at night. I described the blockade. When I mentioned Doctor Reina, the driver spoke up. "The doctor is well known in these parts. He seizes land that is not his and offers it to the poor in return for votes and political support. Then he calls for his supporters to strike or block a highway and demands water and electrical power for the land he has seized. When the property owner finds out, the Doctor negotiates a price for the land he and his supporters have seized. All of this is a way of redistributing wealth *a la Zapoteca*."

On Wednesday, the day after the blockade, Julin and I caught a bus to Juchitán for the twelve o'clock meeting with Rogelia. Along the way, I described the demonstration and the land seizure to Julin. None of this was news to her. "They've seized every inch of the family land around El Cairo," she said. "I've considered putting a wall up, but I doubt it would stop them." We arrived in Juchitán with time to spare and took a taxi to city hall. In the antechamber to Rogelia's office, her secretary informed us that Rogelia would not make the meeting. Although this perturbed me more than Julin, the two of us left quietly. But in the hall outside Rogelia's office, Julin struck up a conversation with Jorge Magariño, secretary to the mayor. Jorge had the face of a man under siege. People stormed in and out of his dingy office, and the phone rang constantly. Despite all this, he agreed to field of a couple of my questions. I first asked him about the alleged harassment of women.

"Yesterday's demonstration involved two different factions of COCEI that are struggling for political control in one of Juchitán's barrios called 16 de Septiembre. Things have reached the point that there are confrontations, and immediately the trouble is attributed to the mayor. It appears that Rogelia wants to be the second mayor, so I have to be vigilant, not just with the accounting, deficits, expenditures, and properties; I also have to exercise an amount of justice."

"Justice?" I asked.

"I'll give you an example. Suppose one of the members of my family comes to me and asks authorization to close a street to make room for a fiesta. Even if I am the registrar of labor, I cannot say 'Authorized: Close the street.' No. What I must say is this: 'Go to the registrar of highway administration.' Here, people tend to think that all of us in city hall can do anything. It's not the case."

"Are there many registrars who act on requests outside their jurisdiction?" I said.

"No. We have sixteen registrars, and Rogelia is the only one who does."

Then the demands for José's attention became overwhelming, and he drew the interview to a close. But before we left, he let his guard down and asked if he could look at my camera. "I love photography," he said. "But with the job I have, there is no way I'll ever have time to devote to it."

It wasn't until several days after the blockade that I succeeded in catching Rogelia in her office. Like the vast majority of women who served as politicians in the Isthmus, Rogelia wore traditional dress. Her black huipil was marbleized with streaks of gray, and her enagua was made of a sheer, rose-colored cloth that touched the ground when she walked. Rogelia's thick black hair fell forward onto her forehead and cheeks, seeming to crowd her features into the center of her face. When we shook hands, she opened her mouth and flashed a row of even, impeccably white teeth. Unlike José's office, Rogelia's was spacious and freshly painted in a regal blue and gold. On all four walls were posters and paintings of women and children, many in traditional dress. One of the posters featured a bare-shouldered woman with long dark hair holding a white dove in the palm of her hand. When Rogelia saw me eyeing the poster, she said, "I made that," and then, a moment later, she added, "with some other women."

Before speaking about the blockade, Rogelia gave a brief preamble. "I'm not going to give you my opinion as a city authority, but rather as a citizen." Then she began speaking with a diction so formal I had the urge to look behind me for a crowd. "The act of blocking highways is a strategy for obtaining unfulfilled promises from the state and federal government." At times demonstrators used blockades to demand drinking water, drainage services, paving of roads, at other times the construction of schools, or even the struggle against some injustice or the detentions of a political nature. "In this instance," Rogelia said, "a group of Juchitán's women is contemplating a month of activities where women can learn new handicrafts and other helpful skills." The state promised the women funding for the workshops, but Rogelia had doubts it would ever arrive. "Today, the fifteenth of November, the budget the state uses to aid social demands will close. If the women do not mobilize with blockades or other similar demonstrations to demand funding for their activities, they will never get what they want."

The demonstrators also demanded information about city work projects. In 1999, Rogelia explained, the federal government delivered a little more than 12 million pesos to Juchitán. The city government had prioritized 137 projects to be funded from the 12 million pesos. Nonetheless, only 27 projects from this prioritized list were realized. "The mayor says that this amount got lost in the El Niño flooding," Rogelia said. "As the registrar of labor, I am responsible for reviewing the accounting of this lost money to see if what he is saying is true. But he will not give me the information required, and his supporters have this information. That's why the blockade came about. The state government says the money was sent. The mayor says it was never received."

Ironically, both the mayor and Rogelia belonged to the same party. When I pointed this out, she sat up in her seat and raised her voice. "Yes, we belong to the same party. But now there are two factions." Then she paused and took a breath. "Look," she said, "when COCEI emerged in 1974, it was a revolutionary organization of the masses with a tremendous amount of force brought by peasants, students, housewives, and everyone else." As time passed, and the party grew, COCEI's leaders were elected to the state assembly and federal senate. But according to Rogelia, they had forgotten both the cause and the people who elected them. And this was a travesty. "Because when COCEI began, many people died," Rogelia said. "And now, people continue in their poverty, workers continue dying, women continue dying, because there has not been any development in their lives."

"In 1981 COCEI won its first municipal election. This victory has been sustained through the force and strength of Juchitán's women. Women in Juchitán aren't afraid to confront the municipal or state police; they do it with great bravery. Between 1981 and 1983, when the government violently evicted COCEI from power, many women were picked up and imprisoned. One of these women was raped by the PRI-supported municipal police. After 1983, the Counsel of Civil Administration headed by a PRI president came to Juchitán and detained a lot of people, and many women were detained and thrown into jail. This experience is something that the women of the Isthmus and in particular the women of Juchitán have had. We've lived through the repression, and this has taught us to struggle, to struggle for the defense of our culture, to struggle to elevate our lot in life, to struggle to conquer the government, to struggle for better education, to struggle for support."

About COCEI's practice of seizing land belonging to others, Rogelia was dead honest. "Since its inception, COCEI has always struggled for the power to give people a piece of land on which to live. It's true there was a taking of land to support those who don't have a house to live in. Yes, this was done. But keep in mind that the owners of these lands don't work them. And that eventually they agree to the seizure provided the property is paid for because they know the people will keep the land anyway."

With that, the conversation wound down, and I found myself staring at a black-and-white photo of an elderly woman holding a photo of her son. "I'm going to put the woman you see in the photo into a poster I'm making. She is the mother of a political prisoner. The federal government took him away because he was the founder of COCEI. His name is Victor Yodo. He organized the workers and was seized on June 11, 1978. We still don't know what happened to him, only that he never returned."

The Journalist

Jocasta Shakespeare — the journalist who wrote the most controversial article ever published on Isthmus women — was born in the quiet of Wales, England. She was still a child, however, when her father accepted work at the foreign office in Lebanon, and the family lived in Basra, Baghdad, Ur of the Chaldees. Shakespeare speculates that these early years gave her a taste for exotic travel, and that her mother's success as a novelist made her consider writing as a career. She studied English literature at Cambridge and not long after began publishing in England's national journals — *The Observer, Telegraph,* and *Times,* and magazines such as *Marie Claire* and *Elle.*

An ongoing interest in gender has driven Shakespeare's focus on women's issues. "From the Ngomo women of Cameroon to Nike workers in Indonesia, the child sex trade in Thailand or female circumcision in Egypt," writes Shakespeare, "women are caught in the crossfire of political, economic and cultural shifts." In the early 1990s, Shakespeare began hearing of a modern-day matriarchy in southern Mexico. "I was fascinated by the idea of surviving matriarchies and a wish to get back to ancient, perhaps pagan roots." Shakespeare suggested the story idea to an editor and was sent to the Isthmus on assignment.

For all of the grief the *Elle* article brought Isthmus women, it opens with an innocuous image at what Shakespeare refers to as a seven day, seven night "velas (candles) fiesta in Juchitán." A young woman at the vela — whom I'll call Dolores — lifts her skirt "to expose underskirts and fat ankles." The music moves Dolores to swaying, "her face flushed and distracted like a somnambulist in an erotic dream." Shakespeare then pulls back from the scene to explain that what she is describing is a celebration of fertility rites in which full-figured women dance with each other to assert themselves as matriarchs. "Here it is the women who rule," writes Shakespeare. "Huge and sensual, their size is a status symbol and not a reason to feel ashamed."

Skinniness in men, and its opposite in women, are reoccurring themes in the article. Dolores, it turns out, has more than just fat ankles. She weighs fourteen stone, roughly two hundred pounds. "We like plenty of woman here," says Juan, her lover, who is half her size. He then adds: "Fatness is a sign of a woman's sexual energy and lack of inhibition in bed." Dolores's sister, Lucia, is also at the vela. She wears a gold necklace with medieval coins that swing between her "enormous breasts." The coins, Shakespeare tells us, in an interpretation that is entirely fresh, stand for Lucia's erotic achievement.

If the women in Shakespeare's rendition of Isthmus society are particularly strong, the men are extraordinarily weak. At velas, they wear sombreros, faded black pants, and white shirts. They do not "dare to penetrate the multicolored ghetto to ask for a dance." Likewise at the market. Nora, a coconut vendor, looks round her and declares what she sees as the dominion of women. "Men can't buy or sell—they don't have the mentality. They are soft and need the guardianship of women." In a spirit of generosity, Nora allows her husband small change to buy beer or to get a shave or maybe even a shoeshine. "Only women know how to look after money," Nora says. "Men have a different kind of brain. They are good for nothing but making babies."

And, lest she forget, babysitting. This we learn the following night, when Shakespeare and Juchitecan jeweler Delia Fuentes attend another vela, leaving Delia's children with her husband. At the vela, Shakespeare describes the sight of the women as "kitsch and gaudy." They wear fake flowers, costume jewelry, loud lipstick, sweaty huipiles, and dome-like enaguas. When Delia gets up to dance with another woman, she explains to Shakespeare, "Girls dance together. We don't care if no men turn up tonight. What's important is that the women turn up." As Shakespeare explains in the article, women come to velas to be seen in their latest huipil and enagua and also to dance and exchange gossip. She notes that for the fiesta she attends with Delia, the women spent much money on clothes and makeup, and there is vicious competition between them. The women even use dress as an indicator of financial well-being. Delia points out one woman who has worn the same dress for the last two years and concludes that her financial status "can't be that good."

Shakespeare closes the scene at the vela with a conversation between two women about their sexual practices. The first woman, who is visiting from Oaxaca, makes the claim that some women hire boy lovers. "Once you're married," she says, "you can do anything." Later, the second woman confides in Shakespeare: "A woman's got to be rich to keep a good boy. My Manuelito costs me about 60 pesos a month. But he's worth it. He's only 16 but he knows plenty of tricks in bed."

I am of two opinions whenever I read this passage. The naive part of me says that what's in black and white must be true—especially so in a long-established magazine such as *Elle*. The skeptical part, which knows Isthmus women's love of ribald humor and a tendency to exaggerate their sexual prowess, says that Shakespeare had been taken for a gullible foreigner. Poniatowska, who, unlike Shakespeare, was well acquainted with Isthmus women's love of erotic humor, once wrote, "A woman can say whatever she wants as long as she does not put her words into action. What men will not forgive is infidelity and Isthmus women are very faithful."

At the end of the article, Shakespeare returns to the theme of body size, this time in the context of Zapotec native healing. "Only the wisest women of Juchitán, the *curandero* witches who heal with the aid of elemental energies, are both thin and respected." Shakespeare pays a visit to Na Paula, one of Juchitán's most elderly and revered *curanderas*. Na Paula takes Shakespeare to the courtyard outside her house where a sacred tree grows. "This is a female tree," Na Paula says. She strokes the tree with one hand, and with the other, she touches Shakespeare's pulse points. Na Paula prescribes basil, lemon, and lime tea. Then she utters a charm and offers Shakespeare a bit of advice: "You need to be fatter."

Although everyone's rendition of Isthmus society is varied, certain details of Shakespeare's article did not ring true. Isthmus men do not wear sombreros. Not now. Not fifty years ago. The coins in women's necklaces are old, possibly from the last century, but in no way are they medieval—unless an unknown Viking expedition trooped four thousand miles to the Oaxaca coast after discovering Newfoundland in the eleventh century. And although there are a wide variety of festivals, fiestas, and velas in Juchitán, there is no such thing as a seven day, seven night Velas fiesta. Given these fabrications, I began to doubt other parts of the article. Was it true that once married, Isthmus women could do anything they wanted? Did women from Juchitán really have kept men? One way to verify these claims was to try to contact Delia Fuentes, the only person in the article identified by first and last name. Because she was present at the second vela, when the most outrageous claims were made, she might even be able to tell me whether the women were joking—in effect pulling the wool over the eyes of an outsider.

There were many means of contacting Delia, but at the time I first read the article, I was at home in San Francisco so that reaching her by phone would be by far the most convenient. Before attempting to call her, however, I reread the article and made a list of questions for every dubious claim I encountered. In all, there were more than a dozen. I then called directory assistance in Juchitán and got lucky. Delia was listed in the white pages.

My conversation with Delia was brief. I made small talk for a couple of minutes, but when I told her I was interested in learning more about the article in *Elle* magazine, she went silent—though only for a moment. She then explained that although she had never read the article, others had informed her what it had to say about her personally. I asked her to tell me what she could remember about Jocasta Shakespeare.

"I never met her," Delia said.

"But she wrote that she attended a vela with you, and that you left your children with your husband to babysit."

"In the first place, I don't really know who she is. And in the second place, I am not married. I don't even have any children."

I expressed disbelief; Delia persisted with her story. I looked at my list of questions. None of them could be answered if Delia had never met Shakespeare, least of all the question about kept men. Before giving up, I asked one more question that came to me on the spur of the moment.

"What was the reaction when the article came out?"

"There were a lot of people that didn't agree with what she wrote."

Here the conversation ended. I suspected Delia's estimation of the reaction to the piece in *Elle* was understated. But my suspicions wouldn't be confirmed until I saw the uproar over the article recorded in a documentary called *Blossoms of Fire.*

Marketplace Tehuantepec

JANUARY 2001. "Whether the men go to the fields or work in town," wrote Covarrubias in 1946, "from dawn till sunset Tehuantepec becomes a woman's world. Everywhere they are busy selling, gossiping." Although the single-story, brick and wood market of Covarrubias's day had given way to a much larger, two-story building of brick and cement, much remained the same. The predominant presence of hundreds of women buying and selling in and around the market was still in evidence, most in the same huipiles and enaguas seen in Covarrubias's black and white photos in *Mexico South*. Other than the market itself, the only visible change was transportation. Women, especially those carrying goods to or from the market, no longer came in oxcarts. Now they arrived in *moto-carros:* engine-driven tricycles with a platform mounted over the rear wheels for passengers. Standing upright on these platforms, the women would sail to the market, hair and full-length skirts blown by the wind. But at times the women paid a price for having abandoned the wooden carts of Covarrubias's era. Collisions between taxis and *moto-carros* were common; what the women saved in time with *moto-carros*, they sometimes paid for in broken bones.

Shortly after my arrival that year, I had two revealing experiences in Tehuantepec's market, the first involving a set of headphones. Because I did most of my shopping in Juchitán, and I knew that electronic goods were not sold in the market there, I assumed that this would also be the case in Tehuantepec. So, rather than looking in the market, I began my search for headphones at the record and stationery stores surrounding Tehuantepec's plaza, but with no success. Then I remembered I had once bought some cassettes from a vendor with a booth directly in front of the market. I paid him a visit and was given the runaround. "Speak to the lady in the locale behind me," he said. I did. She had headphones, but they were attached to a pocket radio, and the two could only be sold together. "Try inside the market," she said. "They'll have headphones for sure." I covered both downstairs and upstairs but came away empty-handed. I gave up, pulled the exact change out of my pocket, and presented it to the lady with the radio and headphones package. She gave me a sympathetic look and said, "Give me the money; I'll buy them for you." With this, she left her locale unattended. I followed her past the butchers, past the cheese, through the *totopos*. Then she made a hard right near the first-floor entrance to the market. She stopped in front of a booth like hers that sold a little of everything: perfume, toy cars, jewelry, watches, and barrettes. "I don't see any headphones," I said. She grabbed my shoulders from behind and positioned me in front of a hanging rack stuffed with a dozen headphones and then walked away. When I turned round to thank her, she was blending in with the crowd on her way back to her stand outside the market. I caught up with her and pressed a 10-peso coin in her hand. "For your time, Señora," I said. What I learned on this and many subsequent shopping trips in the area was that in Tehuantepec, 95 percent of the goods small enough to put in a bag or box are sold *only* in the market. Couple this with the fact that women control the market, and you'll soon come to the conclusion that if the Isthmus ever gave place to a City of Women, it would be Tehuantepec and not Juchitán. Spending time in Tehuantepec, at least in terms of commerce, was like taking a step backward in time. None of the department, electronics, clothing, jewelry, and other stores that were so common in Juchitán even existed in Tehuantepec.

A week later, I had a second experience that shed light on how women enforce the ban on men in Isthmus markets. I can't remember why I went to the market, only that as I was leaving I caught sight of an attractive brunette in a white apron surrounded by blocks of cheese that were wrapped in red and yellow foil. I brought my camera to my eyes and pointed in the direction of the young woman. And though I pressed down hard on the shutter release, the camera had trouble focusing in the market's dim light and refused to fire. While I waited patiently for the camera to focus, a chorus of catcalls rose from behind my back.

"Look at the size of that lens," one vendor said. "I wonder if there's any correlation between that and his you-know-what." This was followed by laughter, but before it died down, another call came from a vendor not two feet behind me. "What are you carrying in that backpack, gringo? It looks a little effeminate for a man like you to be carrying a bag that big." While I backed away without my photo, the laughter and derision snowballed, and I came to understand what it meant to be a man facing the wrath of Isthmus women.

If the derision stung—and it did—it was because Isthmus women had much practice insulting men, foreign and local alike. As long ago as 1859, European travelers remembered hearing marketplace women slinging taunts at their men, and Covarrubias concluded that through the use of this derision, Isthmus women kept the market clear of males. "Should a *tehuano* dare set a stand in the market," writes Covarrubias, "the sharp tongues of the women would quickly drive them away." Julin's father, Jorge Contreras, was more specific. "Fifty years ago, if a man showed his face in the market, the women around him would whistle at him or accuse him of being effeminate by yelling out the term 'Puto, Puto, Puto'—slang for a male whore." In the 1970s, women in the market relaxed the ban, so that now a small percentage of men work and sell in the Isthmus markets. Although no statistics are available on the degree of men's participation, most residents agreed that they constitute less than 5 percent of vendors.

Despite all of the foregoing evidence, the cynic in me still had difficulty believing women enforced the ban in this way. Part of my disbelief stemmed from the fact that I had never spoken to a woman about the ban; all of the accusations concerning the insults and taunts were made by men. To get a better balance of input, I sought out a female vendor in Tehuantepec's market who had been around before the ban was relaxed. After several false starts, I came across an elderly vendor selling cloth on the second floor. Her name was Alicia. Like most Zapotec women, she had a small frame, so that the countertop on which she unfurled bolts of material rose near the level of her shoulders. I first asked her how long she had been working in her locale.

"More than fifty years. I started as a young woman, or more accurately, a young girl."

"So you own this booth?" I said.

"We hold the title, but pay a small trust."

"When did the city build the brick and cement market?"

"In 1970, they moved us to the park while they constructed the new market. Many vendors sold their booths for as much as 30 thousand pesos. Others have ceded them on a payment plan. The mayor built this market not for vendors but for the people of Tehuantepec. The trust was set up so that with this money city hall could continue with public work projects."

"What's your opinion on the matriarchy question?"

"Maybe fifty years ago, you could say there was a matriarchy, but not any more. The Isthmus has become Mexicanized like all other parts of Mexico."

"Was there ever a time when men did not enter the market?"

"Yes. Because before, men spent their time in the fields, in other types of work. But not anymore."

"Why weren't men allowed in the market?"

"Because selling in the market was considered exclusively for women. 'Men to the fields, women to the market' was the saying. That's just how it was."

"Jorge, the man who owns the Oasis Hotel, once told me that thirty-five years ago, whenever a man entered the market, they called him *puto*. Is this true?"

"Yes, when a man came to shop, he was made fun of. That's why many men needed a woman to do their shopping for them."

"And if the man wasn't married?"

"He would ask a woman who was his neighbor."

"To me, this sounds like the women were defending their power any way they could."

"Not at all. It was just the custom during those times."

Later in the week, I spoke with several other elderly Istmeñas on this topic. All insisted that the ban on men was a Zapotec tradition that had nothing to do with conserving their own power. But wasn't this the answer I should have expected? Those in power rarely have a ready rationale for subjugating their victims—other than trumped up arguments such as divine right or royal prerogative. It is the oppressed who are most keenly aware of power structures. And though you could argue that the ban on men was benign, the effects on the disenfranchised are usually subtle. Isthmus men could not show scars or bruises that were the result of their exclusion from the market. But it wouldn't be difficult to argue that, in some way, the ban had contributed to their meek nature.

When I returned from the market, I ate lunch in the Oasis restaurant. Halfway through an order of chicken enchiladas, Julin pushed her way through the restaurant doors, swinging bags in either hand that banged into the tables as she made her way to me. She laid a bag of mango halves marinated in their own juice on the table. "Do you want to try some?" she said. She wiped off my spoon with a napkin and then turned to call out to the waitress who had been hiding in the kitchen for the last half hour, but she could not remember her name. She paused to think. "Nilidia," she shouted, and then softer to me, "What a ridiculous name, eh?" Julin asked Nilidia for a plate, and when it arrived, she laid half a mango onto the plate and spooned a little juice on top. The mango had a green chili embedded in the fruit, which I knew would burn a hole in my tongue, but I ate it anyway. Slowly, and with glass after glass of water.

"You should have been with me," she said. This is what Julin often said on seeing me after a brief separation. "I did some pretty fierce bargaining with the Tehuana selling the mangoes," she said. "You should have been there." We talked, and I told her what Alicia had to say about the unwritten rule that prohibited men from entering the market, and Julin provided another interesting detail: "When the women in the market began to relax this rule in the seventies and eighties, a man wouldn't carry a straw basket or a bag to hold what he bought in the market because of the abuse women would unleash in his direction. Instead, he was forced to carry his tortillas and onions and goat's cheese in his arms. I was reminded of this tradition when I went to the market this morning without a bag. The woman who sold me the mangos accused me of shopping like a man."

On Friday, two days after speaking with Alicia, I packed my suitcase and prepared to leave Tehuantepec. Lugging my suitcase down the stairs made the tendons in my neck stand out, and I was listing slightly to the left by the time I reached the receptionist's desk. I paid Mary Magdalene my overdue rent, and when I turned to go, advice Julin had given me earlier in the week about arriving unannounced came to mind. So I took a detour to a public telephone and called Pablo. Sonia answered, her voice singing with surprise.

"Pablo is delivering a box," she said. "He'll be back at three." As always, she was reticent, and as always, it stirred in me a desire to make her laugh.

"Had any babies lately?" I asked. She was silent for a moment.

"As a matter of fact," she said, "I did. Five months ago I had a baby boy."

In Juchitán, I found Sonia seated in the kitchen feeding Ramona and Flora a red broth from a porcelain bowl. Sonia had a smudge of soup on her cheek. The girls stared at me and mumbled between spoonfuls of broth, occasionally reaching for chopped onions and lime slices that lay in the saucer of a coffee cup. "How's your girlfriend?" Sonia asked. Whenever Sonia and I were alone, she would begin our conversation with this query. She wanted to know about my love life, but her question was also a subtle reminder that both she and I were spoken for, and there would be no funny business between us—alone or in a crowd. "She's fine," I said. "Happy to be rid of me, I imagine."

"You're going to stay with us this time, aren't you?" This had been a bone of contention over the years. Pablo wanted me in the spare bedroom above the mortuary; I preferred the air-conditioned rooms at the Fortress or Oasis. None of my explanations about my insomnia nor odd working hours satisfied him.

"I can't stay here," I said. "I've already taken a room at the Fortress." Then the conversation lagged, and I asked to see her most recent arrival. Sonia padded through the apartment to the master bedroom. The baby was fast asleep, but he woke without complaint. In the kitchen, she bounced him, fat and placid, on her knee. "Is he walking?" I said. He seemed to be the right size for this. "Not yet," Sonia said. Then she reminded me gently: "He's only five months old." His name was Francisco, given him in honor of Francisco López, who, fifteen years before, had taught Pablo his trade.

To keep the conversation alive, I tried to think of questions that weren't too personal or too demanding.

"Will you ever wear a huipil and enagua?" I asked. Last time we spoke, the answer had been no.

"When I go to fiestas," she said, "I wear traditional clothes."

"Where did you buy them?"

"From Manuela in the marketplace."

"What made you change your mind?"

"They attend to you better at the fiestas if you wear huipil and enagua."

"You probably feel more of a solidarity with the other women, too."

"Exactly. If you're not in huipil and enagua, you sit apart from the rest."

At three thirty, Pablo called to say he wouldn't be back until six. I told Sonia I had business to take care of and would return later. She looked for a way to keep me in the apartment, as Pablo had instructed her to do. At first, she plied me with questions, and when she ran out, the struggle to find something interesting to say made her fidget in her chair. Then the children began making noise about playing in the lobby, and we followed them downstairs. Six-year-old Flora looked around for something to do until her eyes lit on an empty one-gallon paint can. She picked it up and made for the door. "I'm going out to sell a little," she said. She went outside, ignoring the pleas of her mother to return. Meanwhile, Ramona closed the front door. "Leave it open Ramona," Sonia said. "Your sister is out there. And what are we going to do if someone comes and wants to buy a box?"

At four, Pablo pulled up in front of the mortuary in a new Ford pickup. I got in, and we drove north along Highway 49 toward Ixtepec—though Pablo did not say where we were headed. Shortly after we crossed the Pan-American Highway, the buildings thinned out, and yellow fields of burnt grass began opening up. In the distance, Casa Verde came into view, squatting like a frog in the dusty parking lot that surrounded it. Pablo slowed the truck and pointed out a construction crew that was busy building a structure identical to the original Casa Verde on the lot next to it. "I owned that lot," he said, "and I sold it to Casa Verde's owner for a substantial profit."

Pablo pulled into a lot where a brick building was under construction. At the time, the building looked flimsy. "This will be my crematorium," Pablo said. "I had to build it here, because the people at city hall would not let me construct it within Juchitán's city limits. They were too worried about the smell. So I bought the land here and began construction several months ago. We still don't have any water service, but we will try to arrange something with the aqueduct that runs through here from the Benito Juárez Dam. For now, I bring water and store it here in steel drums."

On our way back to the mortuary, Pablo spoke about Sonia and how he met her in Ixtaltepec. "This is a great place to find a wife," he said. I told him about an experience earlier in the afternoon in which Ramona showed me her ability to write upside down.

"Ramona is exceptionally bright," I said. "Will you send her to a university?"

"Yes," he said. "Absolutely."

When we crossed the Pan-American Highway, Pablo honked his horn. I looked up to see Rosa standing in front of a taqueria she had recently opened. It was packed wall to wall with people. When she spotted me in the truck, she shot her hand in the air and screamed my name. Who was I to these people? Before parting with Pablo, he invited me to dinner the next day at three. Elena and all of Pablo's family would be there. The women were cooking up something special.

I woke the following morning thinking of Victoria, the elderly Istmeña whose corpse I had helped Pablo lift into a coffin four years previously in May. The rituals that marked Victoria's death represented my first memorable experience in Juchitán, and my thoughts often returned to her frail figure wrapped in a white felt blanket. I felt as though I had not yet heard all of Victoria's story. I wanted to know who she was, how she spent her time, and more about her family and friends. It might have been a writer's need to get the complete story, or possibly to tell it in the best manner possible. In either case I had the ending; the beginning and middle would require a return to the scene of Victoria's last days.

After half-a-day's procrastination, I hailed a taxi in front of the Fortress hotel at two in the afternoon—one hour before the dinner at Pablo's. When the driver, a furry headed man with two-day's beard growth, asked where I was going, I hesitated. I did not know Benita's address or, for that matter, the street on which she lived. I knew we had to cross the River of the Dogs. I knew we had to make a hard left once we crossed the river. And I knew we would be close when there were chicken feathers in the air. Rather than giving the taxi driver these vague directions, I asked him to drive south until we crossed the river. He groaned at the uncertainty of my instructions but gave in, and we drove off in the direction of Victoria's old house.

Everything about the trip to Victoria's—except for the chicken feathers—went so smoothly that we arrived within minutes. Victoria's cinderblock house was exactly where I expected it to be, squat and gaunt, like an empty cardboard shoebox. Pablo had warned me repeatedly not to come to this side of the river, so I asked the taxi driver to wait. He agreed, and I crossed the lot to the front of the house. I stepped into Victoria's patio and saw that after four years it still lacked a door. Inside, someone was sleeping in a hammock who, from the look of him, had to be the two-hundred-pound Eulalio.

"Buenas tardes," I said. No answer. I crossed the patio and stood at the door. "Buenas tardes," I said. He didn't move. I stuck my head into the room. Eulalio had pulled the excess material of the hammock over himself, possibly to ward off mosquitoes from the river. The holy table was in the same spot, still featuring the lone snapshot of a pale, distracted young man in a straw hat, spit curls hanging on his forehead. I turned to leave, and then Eulalio sat up, rocking in the hammock. "Would you happen to know where I can find Benita?" I said. He looked at me as though he were still dreaming. Then a glimmer of recognition shone in his eyes. He closed his fist and extended his thumb and used it to point behind him.

I left Eulalio and walked behind Victoria's house. There, exactly where Eulalio had indicated, was another cinderblock structure twice the size of Victoria's. I stepped into the patio. As if on cue, a young woman walked out of the house. I said:

"I'm looking for a woman named Benita whose mother died some years ago."

"I'm her sister, and she's not here."

"When will she be back?" I asked. Her eyes said: Who in the hell are you?

"She'll be back at four," the young woman said.

"And so will I." It was with great relief that I found the taxi parked in the same place. I got in and ten minutes later he dropped me off in front of the mortuary. I arrived with time to spare for the three o'clock dinner.

In the kitchen, Elena and Sonia were still preparing the meal. Because the kitchen table seated three, we had to eat in shifts. I was part of the first shift with Pablo sitting opposite me and with Elena at my right. We drank from a bottle of mescal labeled Jamidor. "My mother and her friend drank half the bottle on New Year's Eve," Pablo said, pouring himself another shot. "Two big gulps of this stuff, and I fall asleep."

Sonia served the first course, a *consomé de pescado* (fish consommé). The second course was shrimp the size of small lobsters. Pablo and I ate in silence, but Elena felt compelled to talk.

"The shrimp were caught yesterday," she said.

"They were probably caught this morning," Pablo said.

"They were probably caught this morning," Elena said to me as if I were deaf to everyone's Spanish but hers. The third course was *huevos de lisa.*

"Baby fish eggs," Elena said in English, "the caviar of Juchitán."

"Why are you speaking to him in English?" Pablo said. He squinted at his mother as if he couldn't recognize her, as if she had tossed a handful of salt into his soup, not enough to make it unpalatable yet sufficient to take any savor or pleasure from the act of eating. I ate to the brink of nausea, and they continued to pile shrimp on my plate. Then the phone rang, and Sonia brought it to Pablo. Something, a door or a coffin lid, wouldn't shut like it should. "I've got to go," Pablo said. This was a blessing. The call opened up the possibility of returning to Benita's. Before I could leave, however, the topic of travel came up.

"Pablo says he's going to Spain in May," I said.

"Right," his mother said, "he's always saying that. Last year it was as soon as he bought the ranch. This year it's as soon as he finishes the crematorium. He's been saying the same thing for years."

"I've got to leave for half an hour," I said. There was another course of dinner still to be served and no doubt dessert after that. But if Pablo could leave for business, then why couldn't I?

"Why are you leaving?" Pablo's mother said. Her face registered hurt.

"I've got something I need to attend to."

It was ten minutes before I was able to flag down a taxi. Halfway to Benita's, a parade materialized, blocking our way. Girls in huipiles and enaguas were climbing onto the backs of flatbed trucks that were decorated with crepe paper flags and hundreds of flowers. The taxi driver pulled over to the side of the road and waited for the parade to pass. Fifteen minutes went by in this way. Then the driver made a U-turn and headed in the opposite direction.

"Where are we going?" I said.

"You don't expect me to drive through the parade, do you?"

We arrived at Benita's after a long, circuitous route. It was already four thirty—thanks to Juchitán's constant parades—and I knew that I would never make it back to Pablo's in time to avoid upsetting him and his family. I should have gotten back into the taxi, returned to the dinner and eaten more shrimp, and been more responsible. But who wanted to return to Pablo's and Elena's bickering? I knew the Laroche family well enough that they fought openly in front of me, but not well enough to ask them to stop. And so I waved the taxi away and crossed the lot in front of Benita's house. I stepped into her patio. The house looked deserted. I walked to one side of the house where a young man with his back turned to me poked branches into an adobe oven the size and shape of a large igloo. Smoke was escaping from the oven's rectangular door; there was no chimney.

When the young man failed to notice me, I coughed, and he turned around. He introduced himself as Benita's brother and entered the house. A minute later, he returned with Benita and her sister. Benita wore Western dress: a short black skirt, a light cotton blouse, and heels. Her lips were red with lipstick, her hair pulled back into a knot at the nape of her neck. I did my best to explain who I was. Benita seemed to recognize me, but kept quiet. Her sister and brother eyed me suspiciously. I rummaged in my backpack for a magazine with my name on it, which I carried with me as a kind of writer's identity card in tricky situations like these. This took time, and when I couldn't find it among all the other rubbish in my backpack, I went down on one knee and considered emptying the contents onto the patio. Then I found it, dog-eared and frayed. I held it in front of me and pointed to my name above the article I had written and smiled. Benita's brother took the magazine from me and studied what I'd written. He looked impressed, and I was pleased. Then he said, "Do you mean to say that you wrote all of this in English?"

This was an odd comment, I thought, until I realized he had mistaken me for a native Spanish speaker. Given my accent, this was difficult to believe. But the more I heard him speak, the more it was clear that Zapotec was his first language, and he had his own share of problems with Spanish. Still, I didn't know how to respond to his question without insulting him, so I began asking questions. Answers, when they occurred at all, came one or two words at a time. I looked at Benita and said:

"What did your mother do for a living?"

"Housewife," Benita said.

"What was she like?" Silence.

"Did she have any hobbies?" Silence.

"Look," I said, "let's do it this way. I'll ask a question, and then you can ask me one." I felt as though I was trying to melt an iceberg with a pack of matches. A seven-year-old boy rode up on a bike and smiled. Progress, I thought, this might be progress.

"Was there anything she liked to do?"

"Sewing."

"Ah! She like to sew. Did she sew her own clothes?" Silence.

"Go ahead and ask me a question." Silence.

"She sewed our clothes, too."

"What exactly was her last name?"

A pause, then: "De la Cruz."

"What else can you tell me?"

"She liked cleaning."

"What else?"

"She didn't like festivals." This was truly unusual, and she must have suffered greatly, because the *fiestas* are nonstop in Juchitán. Then, unasked, came this:

"Her favorite holiday was September 8, La Natividad. She invited all our relatives and fed them tamales and chocolate she had made herself."

"How many children did your mother have?"

"Victoria had seven children, not counting the two she adopted. But Victoria wasn't my mother," Benita said. "She was my grandmother." I felt like an idiot. But if Victoria had seven children, why had Benita, her granddaughter, gone to purchase the coffin? And why hadn't any of Victoria's children, save Eulalio, been present for the rituals I witnessed when Pablo delivered the coffin?

"I understand," I said. "She was your grandmother. Why did I think—"

"Yes, she was my grandmother. She had seven children, not counting the two that she adopted."

"Nine children?"

"Counting the ones she adopted."

"Is her husband still alive?"

"He was killed."

"Who killed him?"

"Assassins. A band of assassins and robbers."

"Why?"

"They just killed him. They were robbers." A glass of orange Fanta materialized in my right hand. More children appeared from inside the house, leaning into Benita and her sister like kittens in search of affection.

"What work did Victoria's husband do?"

"He made things with bricks. Then he was a night watchman, but they separated after all her babies were born. This was at the old house, the one she had to leave."

Our one-sided conversation went on in this way for a good fifteen minutes. I would ask a question, and Benita or her sister would toss out a scrap or two, and then I would ask another question and so on. In the end, what I was able to piece together about Victoria was this: After her separation from her husband, she sold door-to-door. Her earnings were never enough to buy her children new clothes, so she took up sewing. When these two sources of income grew, and Victoria was sure her children would not go hungry, she adopted two more. Their names were Eulalio and José.

Zapotec mothers, you must know, are no different from mothers around the world. They aim to treat all of their children equally, but in the end, the lastborn is a magnet, a lodestone. In the mind of the Zapotec mother, the last child, on leaving, takes motherhood with him, and Victoria was unprepared for this. El Xhunko she had called him, not because it was his name, but because this is how all Zapotec mothers referred to the lastborn, a role so significant in Zapotec culture it needed a word to itself: El Xhunko.

When all but the last of her children had married and left home, Victoria hatched a plan. El Xhunko would not leave home, would he, if the home and the land were his? She drew up a will, bequeathing to him, and only him, the house and the land and everything she owned. Her plan worked. He stayed. Years passed, and Victoria became truly old and was diagnosed with diabetes. Her drinking aggravated the problem, and soon she could not walk. Then El Xhunko drew a line through the middle of the house and insisted that she not enter his half. He seemed to have lost his hearing, too. In the last months of her life, El Xhunko turned away when Victoria spoke to him, and her appeals for a doctor went unheard.

When it was clear that El Xhunko would not call a doctor, Victoria turned to her natural-born children. One by one, she learned that their hearts had calcified over their exclusion from her will, and in the end they had disowned her. Only as a last resort had Victoria sent a messenger to Eulalio. And though he had no home, he vowed to build one and did. You could fit neither ox nor oxcart in it, but it kept the rain out in June, and Eulalio and Victoria slept there side-by-side on cots until the day Benita rapped on Pablo's door.

There was one piece in the puzzle that didn't fit. If her husband, and all of her children had abandoned her, then who was the pale, distracted man in the photo with the spit curls? He must have been someone close to Victoria if he was the only person to grace her holy table. I asked Benita who he was.

"El Xhunko," Benita said. "Her favorite." Then Benita left me and entered the house. A moment later, she returned with a chair. She sat down so that she was facing me. I took this to mean she'd warmed to me, so I asked her the more probing questions I had about her.

"How old are you?" I asked.

"Thirty-three," she said.

"You look ten years younger. Are you married?"

"Yes, and I have three children."

"What does your husband do?"

"Three years ago, my husband went to Los Angeles. We haven't heard from him since."

This saddened me. I looked at Benita's brother. "You Isthmus men are terrible," I said. He laughed. I didn't know how to feel. He began to talk about Isthmus men, their reputation, and the lie of matriarchy in Juchitán. He invited me to take a closer look at his new oven, and I followed him around the side of the house. He explained that he had paid $100 to have it made. On the average salary of $3.50 a day, the oven represented a month of work. He directed my attention to the oven's domed roof. "Not everyone can build an oven like this and have the roof hold up," he said. "A chimney would have cost me another $100. I didn't have it. So I have to be careful the smoke doesn't taint the taste of the sweet breads I bake. Later I'll buy a chimney." As I spoke with Benita's brother, I felt for the first time that things were right with my presence in the patio. In the Isthmus, men must commune with men, women with women. And if a man has a question for a woman, he should direct it to a male in her family, who will in turn relay it to the woman. This was why Benita refused to ride with me in the front of the truck when we delivered the coffin for Victoria, and it explains, in part, my troubles with Rosa at the vela. Had I respected local customs regarding separation of the sexes at the vela, I might have avoided some part of the fiasco that followed. All the same, I would have liked to speak to Benita directly, but it seemed my opportunity had come and gone.

Benita and her brother offered me food, and though I was still gagging on shrimp, I said yes, I'd love to eat. Benita handed me a porcelain bowl of chicken soup. Drops of amber fat floated freely in the reddish broth. I could not bring myself to eat the chicken, though it looked fine. I handed Benita my almost empty bowl. Then it was on to sweet bread striped with sugar made in the new oven. The bread had no smoky flavor. When I finished the sweet bread, I checked my watch. Five thirty. Pablo and family would be pissed. I told Benita I had to leave. She offered to walk me to the bridge, where, with a little luck, I could catch a taxi. I said goodbye to the others, and we began walking. Not fifty feet from the house, we encountered a pig walking in the opposite direction, nose to the dirt road. "Is it dangerous here?" I said. "Not yet," she said, referring, I thought, to the disappearing light. As we neared the bridge where I knew we would part ways, I remembered Pablo's warning. In the distance, a taxi passed by. "Caray" (what luck), she said. The dirt road ended and the pavement began, and we were six giant steps from the bridge. She gave me her hand. I shook it and turned away toward the bridge.

I did not like the idea of standing still in that neighborhood, so I crossed the bridge with several long strides and felt the nervous tension begin to dissipate when I reached the other side. I had walked half a block toward town when, at my feet, I began to see drops, then patches, of blood. I followed the trail of crimson until I came upon a man laying still in the gutter, eyes closed, nose pointing into the wind. A clean blue sling from an earlier battle, probably the day before, cradled his right arm. Dots of blood, the size of tiny centavos, marked a line on his shirt that crossed his chest near his heart. I examined his features, and it was clear: his was not the face of a criminal. A liar, perhaps, or an alcoholic who was hostile when drunk. It was easy to imagine him bumbling down the sidewalk, two days into a binge, colliding into someone's mother. Then the fight and the fall. I paused long enough to see his chest was still. I moved on.

At the end of the block a parade dense with brightly clothed children had stalled, blocking the direct route to town. For a moment, I considered wading through the parade but discarded the idea just as quickly. The man in the gutter had renewed my anxiety about the neighborhood. So I waited, because there is safety in crowds, and particularly in this one, because everyone present was focused on a float with a towering gazebo. The gazebo had three roofs, stacked one on top the other pagoda style. All three were painted Chinese red and gold, calling up images of the Forbidden City. The gazebo's builder, in a rush to construct the parade's tallest float, had miscalculated. The third roof had cleared the telephone wires, but a golden figurine of the Virgin who crowned it had not. Now the gazebo leaned sharply toward the back of the truck. Men in dark suits ushered a girl wearing a silver tiara and gold dress outside the gazebo. She sulked while men carrying wooden poles climbed onto the truck that carried the float. They pushed the telephone wires higher, and the gazebo passed by. But the damage had been done. The three roofs had been crushed together like an accordion squeezed at one end.

I looked back at the bridge. It was empty. I returned to the man in the gutter. I stared at him, then at the people passing by. The man in the gutter was invisible to them; he did not merit a second look. They had come to see the parade. And the more I stared at him, the more the man in the gutter reminded me of a photo by Graciela Iturbide, published in Howard Campbell's *Zapotec Struggles*. I bought the book before I made my first trip to Juchitán. I was so impressed with the photo that I cut it out and carried it with me in my wallet. When friends asked where I planned to spend my next vacation, I would take out the photo and say, "This is where I'm going." The photo was posed; I liked it anyway. A woman, moon faced and full-figured in an enagua and huipil, stood next to a life-size cross with flowers where the body of Christ should have been. She was straight-lipped, and behind her, a man was laying face up on the sidewalk in clothes three sizes too large. To me, the photo implied that the man had passed out on the sidewalk from drink, and also suggested a relationship between men and women that might not be all that healthy.

A mean-looking Istmeño emerged from the house across the street and watched me stare at the fallen man. I did not like the look he gave me. I walked back to the parade, where two men in scruffy clothes were mounted on the same burro, no saddle, their legs dangling in the air. One of the men, his jaw slack, gawked at me. In a gesture reminiscent of Mr. King, he turned his palms skyward and shrugged, a kind of "what's up?" gesture that was more of a challenge than a question. I looked away, and a taxi pulled up. I got inside and felt safer, but we went nowhere because of the parade. I asked the driver what the parade was about. "It's the feast day of the Black Christ of Esquipulas," he said, "patron saint of the seventh ward." When the parade passed, and the driver started his taxi, I looked back. The man was still in the gutter. But as we pulled away, he reached between his legs with his good arm and scratched.

At six, an hour and a half after I promised to return, I rang the bell at the mortuary. Sonia came to the balcony drying her hands with a towel. Her face was unusually stony.

"What do you want?" she said. I was in trouble. Sonia did not speak this way.

"Can I talk to Pablo?" I said.

"He's at the ranch," she said, "he'll be back at seven thirty." I returned to my room at the Fortress. At seven thirty on the dot, I parted the curtains. Pablo's pickup truck was parked in front of the mortuary. I called. Sonia answered. "He's not here," she said. "And don't worry about calling him. He'll call you."

As if I were being punished for my misdeeds, I discovered at breakfast that I had lost my debit card. I had no traveler's checks; my debit card represented the only direct access to my bank account. Although I did have a credit card, I knew from experience that getting a cash advance was difficult if not impossible in rural Mexico. Everyone paid in little ways for Mexico's chronic corruption, travelers included. Rather than going out and confronting the problem, I moped about in my hotel room and distracted myself with writing. In the afternoon, I remembered that I last used the card at Banco Bital, two doors down from the Oasis. I called Julin. "When are you coming back home?" she said. I described my predicament, and sweetheart that she is, Julin promised to check for my card at Bital, but she came up empty-handed. In the meantime, I went to Banamex in Juchitán. I tried and failed to get a cash advance using my credit card. They suggested I use their ATM, but I couldn't remember my PIN number. "Call your bank for the PIN number," they said. I did. My bank refused to give me my PIN number because I could not remember how to spell my mother's maiden name. Was it *McCarthy* or *MaCarthy*? I guessed and got it wrong. I retreated to my bed and fell asleep.

The following day, I counted my cash. I had $50. I returned to Banamex, where a manager explained that his bank would advance me cash on my credit card, but only in Oaxaca—a five-hour ride by bus, one way. On the way back to the Fortress, I discovered a couple of restaurants that accepted my credit card. I ate at one of them. I returned to my hotel and packed an overnight bag.

By the time I arrived at the bus station, it was seven thirty. I spoke with the first ticket-seller I could find.

"Do you accept credit cards?" I said.

"Where are you going?" he said.

"Oaxaca."

"When are you leaving?"

"The sooner the better."

"I'm sorry, but we only accept cash."

"Why didn't you say so at the beginning of our conversation?"

He shrugged.

I bought a ticket, which left me with $25. I boarded the bus. Two hours into the trip across the Sierra Madre a movie featuring a martial arts comedian rolled on the overhead television screens. Near midnight, I looked around and learned that of the fifty overhead lights only mine was lit and stayed lit until we arrived. I remember thinking: the same drive that pushes me to be awake and accomplishing something would give me a heart attack in the end. At one fifteen, the bus pulled in front of the bus station in Oaxaca, and I had a scary realization. I did not know if the Hotel Vera Cruz, where I usually stay in Oaxaca, accepted credit cards. If not, I had little choice. Sleep in the street or stay awake at the always crowded Oaxacan bus station. My worries dissolved ten minutes later when Hotel Vera Cruz honored my credit card and put me in a room with five beds, four bars of soap, and two miniature bottles of shampoo. In the morning, I skipped breakfast. I caught a cab to Banamex, where they advanced me $500 — no questions asked. At the bus station, I splurged on a first-class ticket that left the same day at three in the afternoon. Then I crossed the street to Café Colibri, where I gorged on chicken with chocolate sauce and caramel crepes. The ride back to Juchitán was splendidly uneventful.

The Filmmaker

Maureen Gosling couldn't have picked a worse time to begin filming *Blossoms of Fire,* her feature-length documentary on Juchitán's women. In February of 1994, several days before she arrived in the Isthmus, *Elle* magazine delivered its premier Spanish edition to the news racks surrounding Juchitán's market. On the front cover of the magazine, in large block letters, was the headline "Juchitán, The Place Where the Women Give the Orders." This alone would have been enough to enrage the Isthmus population, men and women alike, turning them off to anyone with a camera or microphone in hand. But inside the magazine, Jocasta Shakespeare's article was accompanied by a photo of two Juchitecans in blazing gold huipiles seated at a vela. Caught at an off moment, both have their mouths open, and the woman on the left holds a bottle of beer upright on her leg. The caption below the photo identified one of the women by name and claimed she kept a sixteen-year-old lover. Adjacent to the photo, in bold red letters, is the article's lead. "The women prohibit the men from buying and selling. They leave the men at home to baby-sit while they go have fun, and they pay young lovers. Juchitán (Mexico), where fatness and sensuality are the same thing, lives under their command. It is the singular empire of the Zapotec Women."

Rather than avoiding the scandal provoked by the article, Gosling had the good sense to embrace it. She opened her film with footage of a car that has a loudspeaker attached to its roof, blaring a recorded message, street by street, to all of Juchitán. "The French magazine *Elle* has been sued by the State of Oaxaca for moral damages caused to two Juchitecán women. A caption below a photograph of the two merchants provoked outrage among the families and the community. Their case was taken on by the Oaxaca Professional and Technical Association. More than two hundred signatures supported their case." The camera then shifts to an unhappy group of women marching four abreast on a side street, much like they march at political demonstrations. "There were some people who didn't like article," one woman told the camera. "They went to buy a copy of the magazine. But the man couldn't sell it to them because he was prohibited from doing so. Some ladies told him to stop selling it or they'd beat him up." We next see an elderly woman at the market whose expression is somewhere between sorrow and anger. "Dear Jesus, protect me," she says. "I come here to sell, but to sell myself? No! I ask God all the time to bless me. But whoring? God forbid." According to Gosling, the women were disturbed about the allegations involving their sexual habits, but they were even more enraged by the portrayal of their men. In an interview with the *Austin Chronicle,* Gosling remembered a man, near tears, who ran up to her while she was filming. "Are you with *Elle* magazine?" he said. "Tell me the truth!"

In the time immediately following Gosling's arrival in Juchitán, the women who she had come to film wanted nothing to do with her. "We're also part of the foreign media," the film's narrator says. "So a lot of people are just as worried that our portrayal of them will be just as distorted as the magazine's. They're suspicious of us, so they cancel interviews and avoid our camera crew." The documentary proves this with footage of two women descending from a truck behind Juchitán's market. When they see the camera, their faces fall, and they turn their backs and walk away in the opposite direction. But as time passes, Gosling makes contacts with key figures in Juchitán, principally Florinda Luis, who assures interviewees that Gosling's untimely arrival has nothing to do with the inflammatory article in *Elle* magazine.

Before the film gets fully underway, the narrator reads overblown quotes in which Covarrubias compares Juchitán's women to South Sea maidens and Eisenstein describes the Isthmus as the true Garden of Eden. We even hear from NPR's Katie Davis. "The women of Juchitán work, drink beer, dance, and make love all in a day. Then they get up at dawn and do it again, and do it again, and again. That's the way things have always been in Juchitán, Oaxaca." At first we think the film will only add to this kind of glamorization, but Gosling is sharper than that. "For centuries," the narrator says, "Mexicans and non-Mexicans have built story upon story about Isthmus Zapotec women. We realize we need to get past these fantastical notions about a matriarchal utopia. More than ever, we need to listen." And Gosling does, beginning with a pair of men drinking Coronas in a patio. The first repeats the question asked, which at best, is leading. "Why does a matriarchy exist here? Because the mother gives the orders." The second man, who wears a pair of sunglasses pulled up on top of his head, laughs at his friend's response and then adds, "Because the woman dominates. She has the last word. That's a matriarchy."

We next hear from Gosling's ally Florinda Luis. "Matriarchy doesn't exist here," she says, and then points into the distance to indicate foreign influence. "Outsiders come here and they think the men don't work." Luis goes on to recite the tourist myth, and the film shows men fishing at daybreak, and a farm laborer placing a wooden yoke over a pair of oxen. As Gosling continues her interviews, we come across Istmeños who at times seem to contradict themselves. But the fact that Gosling leaves the contradictions in the film makes you trust her rendition of Juchitán's women. A good example is a dark-haired, articulate young woman who speaks with such force that her gold-hooped earrings wave wildly in the air. "What I can say is that patriarchy didn't totally take hold here, like the majority of other societies that have been dominated by industrialization." Juchitán's women have the weight to direct their own lives toward a secure existence. They feel supported and valued for what they do, including bearing children. "And if they want to call that a matriarchy, then it's a matriarchy. But for us, it doesn't have that name."

Like its predecessor *Que Viva Mexico,* the film focuses on the market as the cornerstone of Isthmus women's independence, but it does a much better job showing just how hard the women work. A fruit vendor explains how she begins her day so early that it is still dark outside, and how other vendors do the same. "Florencia and Irma, at four on the dot, they're already here. Anastasia too. She comes from Chegigo at four. At seven PM , I leave here. I get home and there's housework. All of us here are *compañeras* and sisters at the market." A woman selling pineapples explains that in other parts of Mexico—where women don't work so hard—they aren't as financially independent as in Juchitán. "The man takes money out of his own pocket when his wife asks for a sweet. 'Buy this, buy that, she says.' They don't help the man work." Another vendor with silver-capped teeth adds her opinion, "All those women do is paint their faces." What's better than that, the movie's narrator asks? The vendor responds, "Work, work, work."

Household finance is another theme that the film covers, and many of the women interviewed explained why they so often are in charge of this task. "*We* know how to manage the money, not the men. The custom here is the man works and hands it over to his wife." Even some of the men see it this way. "Our salaries, those of us who've had salaries, we deposit in our wives' hands. They administrate, do the financial planning, so that the money will bear fruit." His wife expands on this theme, explaining that "When men run around with money in their pockets, they get ideas, or they meet up with friends. They waste money. That's why we women are in charge of the money."

Motherhood, the often overlooked relationship that is one of the most powerful motivating forces in an Isthmus woman's life, is given special attention by Gosling. Throughout the film, mothers most often cite children as the reason they work so hard. "I failed my first marriage at twenty-two with four children," an elderly Juchiteca says. She then explains how she got herself back on her economic feet selling plums on the main plaza. "When [an Isthmus woman] starts to guide her own destiny, to support the household, look after her family, her kids, if a woman has her wits about her, even a little bit, she wants to get ahead. I chop seven or eight thousand plums [per year], all by myself. My children went all the way through school and now they're in Mexico City. They've got their own destiny, their work, thanks to my efforts." Another vendor, who'd been selling in the market for twenty-eight years, explains how she brought her first child with her to the market everyday when he was one year old. "That's how we got by. [My children] took their naps in a big basket under the table. I raised them all here." Even the women who have a man contributing financially to the family's well-being are forced to work because his paycheck is not enough. "That's why we help our husbands support the children."

Gosling also explores the relationship between a mother and her offspring from the perspective of her children. "It's through our mothers that we acquire all the flavor of our native dishes," a man on the plaza explains. "And the taste on our palate gathers from all the wisdom they possess. It's through our mothers that the Zapotec language is transmitted. It's through our mothers that we learn to value our own culture."

Even in old age, Isthmus children's attitude toward their mother remains strong. Gosling interviews an eighty-year-old hammock vendor at home. In a corner, we see a holy table thick with flowers and votive candles, and at the center of it all, a photo of her mother. "Two years ago today, we buried her in the afternoon. Thursdays and Sundays I go to the cemetery. If I don't go, I can't eat. I just lay down in my hammock feeling sad. She was very old. She'd sit in her hammock and talk to me. We can't forget our mothers, since we live so closely with them."

Inventing Santa Inés

The bus from Oaxaca did not arrive in Juchitán until after dark. Despite the distance from the terminal and the cash that I carried in my wallet, I walked from the bus station to the Fortress. By eight fifteen I was inside the lobby and headed back to my room when a woman in Western dress stopped me to ask a favor. She introduced herself as Cristina Dominguez. She was beautiful, easily as beautiful as Rosa, though she hid some part of this under a layer of gloss. Her gold earrings and bracelets, her lips and teeth, and even her skin glistened in the fluorescent light of the lobby. I told her my name, and she was quick to explain her problem. Her two sons attended university abroad, she said, and she could not make sense of a message in English that played whenever she dialed her sons' phone number. She was anxious and determined, and she spoke in a high-pitched, nasal tone. She seemed particularly worried about her youngest son. "He's giving me problems," she said, "lots of problems." I dialed the number four or five times, but in the end, I too failed to understand the message. I apologized and turned to leave, but I hadn't put one foot in front of the other before she began asking questions. Who was I? What brought me to the Isthmus? What was I writing about? As I answered her questions, I realized that her last name—Dominguez—was part of the Fortress's full name: Hotel Dominguez Fortress.

"Do your parents own this hotel?" I asked.

"No," she said, "I do."

"And managing hotels is your chosen career?"

"I was once a judge—" she said, but before Cristina could tell me more, a call came in for her, and the receptionist handed her the phone.

When she began speaking, I waved goodbye and returned to my room on the second floor.

The following morning, I was on my way to visit Juchitán's new office of tourism when I passed Cristina in the hotel lobby. I expressed an interest in meeting with her to get her views on Isthmus women. We agreed to meet in the hotel restaurant that night.

Juchitán's office of tourism sits on the ground floor of city hall, directly opposite the northern side of the main plaza where the women sell freshly cut flowers. Inside, black masks with hairy foreheads, fake gold-coin necklaces, and armadillo shells were posted along the walls. A clerk selling souvenirs said that the armadillo shells were from Ixtepec—though she gave the impression she did not know what she was talking about. On the wall facing the plaza were two posters that quote from *El concepto de la muerte entre los Zapotecas* (The Concept of Death among the Zapotecs). Pablo and I had been searching for this book for years. Although the posters were only an excerpt from the book, I was sure they would please him. I bought two and caught a taxi to Pablo's. He stood in front of the mortuary talking with a handful of friends. Without saying anything, I approached him and held out one of the posters. To my great relief, he accepted it and thanked me. I might have damaged our friendship, but I had not destroyed it.

Although Cristina did not specify a time for our meeting, I began checking the restaurant and the lobby at seven thirty. At eight, I grew tired of waiting. I took a table near the bar and ordered chicken with chocolate sauce. At eight thirty, when I had finished my meal, Cristina arrived and sat down next to me. At first, we talked about her transition from law into business. "When I married and became pregnant," she said, "I took time off to help my mother with one of the family's thirty businesses." In the process, Cristina discovered an affinity with commerce so strong she never returned to court. When her parents died, the three children divided their inheritance equally—except for the gold. "Isthmus men don't wear gold, so my sister and I divided it up between the two of us."

"Tell me about your family," I said.

"First, you must know that my mother was from the lower class and my father from the upper, and as a consequence, he was head of the family."

"So you feel that class determines power in Isthmus families?"

"To some degree," Cristina said. "But even more crucial is a couple's economic situation, which has a primordial importance from the moment they are united in marriage." Like many before her, Cristina described Isthmus women as hard workers, explaining that this trait was constant across class and level of education. This attitude toward work earns them money, and money means they take part in decisions made at home. "You'll find the rare occurrence where a poor woman dominates a wealthy man," Cristina said, "but this is not the norm." Cristina's perspective—that money is power—shed new light on Isthmus relations and held my interest. But I would soon learn that Cristina analyzed almost everything from an economic perspective.

"Did your parents speak Zapotec?"

"Yes, and so do I."

"And do you consider yourself Zapotec?"

"Yes, and so did my parents."

"Were you ever married?"

"Yes, but my husband died of a heart attack when he was forty-one years old, also a lawyer, and a very hard worker."

"When did he die?"

"Five years ago."

Then I asked Cristina a series of questions about Zapotec culture. In my experience, Istmeños at the top of the economic hierarchy seem to be the first to abandon Isthmus culture.

"Do your children speak Zapotec?"

"No, because you learn Zapotec through business when people arrive and want to buy this or that. The Zapotec spoken here is a dialect. You learn as you go."

"But you never prohibited Zapotec at home?"

"Never. Just the opposite. My parents, for example, always spoke Spanish at home. But whenever someone arrived speaking Zapotec, they would answer in Zapotec. Time passed. We learned. But in homes where parents speak only Zapotec to their children, it becomes more difficult for them to learn Spanish, and they speak it poorly. That's why people say, "First Spanish, then Zapotec."

"Do you wear a huipil and enagua when you attend a festival?"

"Of course. One curiosity you'll see in the Isthmus has to do with our fiestas. If, for example, you've attended a wedding or a birthday party or a vela, you'll witness something unthinkable in other parts of Mexico: our women come to fiestas alone. She arrives, perfectly natural, without her husband, carrying a bottle of liquor or a case of beer as her contribution to the fiesta. This is one of the differences between our culture and others. Isthmus women are very, very independent."

"Another curiosity concerns the way our women dress. We are the only women in Mexico who wear our native dress with pride across all social and economic levels. Also important is the fact that inside our market, you'll find people from all economic classes and several different cultures."

"What's your opinion of Isthmus men?"

"My father was a very hard worker, and so is my brother and both of my boys. What happens is that there is a constant struggle between men and women in terms of economic support for the family, and also a struggle about who gives the orders." Cristina and I talked together for another fifteen or twenty minutes. I paid for the bill, but before leaving, I asked Cristina if she had any questions for me.

"No," she said. "Not me." Then she paused and looked at me in the eyes. A moment later, she picked up the questioning she had begun when we met in the lobby.

"Do you drink?"

"A glass of wine now and then."

"What about drugs?"

"Too expensive where I come from."

"What do you do for fun?"

"I have a garden. I like movies and books that tell stories. What about you?"

"I work a lot. I work too much."

"Are you a workaholic?"

"Work is a way of avoiding problems. I also have a ranch that I like to visit."

"Where?"

"Nearby. I also like being in my garden. But now that my sons are away, our house seems big and solitary, so I prefer living here in the hotel."

"How old are your children?"

"One is seventeen, the other twenty. They've both passed through the difficult stage, I hope."

"Are you going to be here for several days more?" Cristina said.

"Three days."

"My sister-in-law lives on a ranch called Los Mangos, one hour south of Juchitán. On Sunday, there will be a vigil honoring Santa Inés, the patron saint of the ranch. Would you like to go?"

"Sure. As long as it's not too early."

"It's not. We're leaving here at seven in the morning, and we won't be back until late."

When I first met Manuela the hammock vendor in November of 1998, she described her mother as a *viajera*. A *viajera* spends the majority of her time on the road, selling *totopos*, dry shrimp and fish, hammocks, and the traditional gold necklaces worn at velas. In part, the reputation of Isthmus women in other regions of Mexico is due to the *viajeras*. They wear the same enaguas and huipiles they do at home and have been known to travel as far north as the border with the United States and as far south as Central America. I decided to visit Manuela in hopes that she could provide me with specifics about her mother the *viajera*.

At noon on Saturday I walked to the northwestern corner of Juchitán's market where Manuela had worked for the last fifty years. A dark-haired woman selling hammocks from Manuela's old locale informed me that Manuela had retired. "Manuela's niece Lupe will know how to contact her," she said. "Look for a woman with a black scarf who sells hammocks on the plaza." Almost immediately, I found her. She had Manuela's features and her assertive style of selling. "Manuela is living with her daughter," Lupe said. "I'll take you there, but you should know that not all of the women who sell hammocks would leave their posts to do this kind of favor. You could buy a hammock from me. I sell the very best." We boarded a cab that took us up Avenida Juárez and into Juchitán's fourth ward. We passed the Social Security offices and the Taqueria Fogata. Then we stopped in front of a middle-class dwelling, and

I was relieved to see that Manuela was living in a comfortable looking home. "You never would have gotten here on your own," Lupe said. "Never." I paid the taxi and headed for the front door. Then Lupe grabbed my arm and guided me around the side of the house and through a gate. We crossed a patio to a tiny, two-room shed at the far end of the property. Lupe entered without knocking. The first room was a storage space for an odd collection of broken tools and worn out hammocks. The second room, at the back of the shed, was no larger than a bathroom. One of the walls was covered with images of the Virgin of Guadalupe. Some of the images were on holy cards, others cut from magazines. The other walls were bare. Manuela was folded up into a fetal position on a canvas cot. Her legs below the knee were red and swollen. Two dark crevices ran from the bridge of Manuela's nose downward and across her cheeks.

"I'm sick, papa," she said. "I had to stop selling. I haven't sold anything for a year."

"What's wrong?" I said. Dogs barked while Manuela formulated an answer.

"My legs burn. It feels like someone ground chilies into my calves."

"Are you taking any medicine?" I asked. Manuela nodded toward a desk. Lupe gathered Manuela's medications: three bottles of pills and a small cardboard box that contained a hypodermic needle. She handed them to me. I read the labels. From what I was able to discern, none of the medications had anything remotely to do with Manuela's problem with her skin.

"Have you ever tried using a cream?" I said.

"No," she said, "never. I'm seventy-three years old, and I feel bad, papa." Manuela's Spanish seemed to have deteriorated. At times, when I couldn't understand her, I looked toward Lupe, and she would explain to me in Spanish what Manuela was trying to say. I told Manuela that I also had a skin problem called psoriasis and that I used hydrocortisone to control it. I suggested Lupe and I buy a tube at the local pharmacy. Lupe agreed, and we left.

On our return, Manuela was still in her cot. I handed her the cortisone, hoping she'd try it immediately to see if it would help. "I'll put this on later," she said. I told Manuela that I admired the images of the Virgin in her room. She reached for the cardboard covering of a book about the Virgin of Guadalupe whose pages had somehow vanished. The front and back covers featured paintings of the Virgin in vivid colors. "Take this," she said and handed me the cover. I thanked her, and she said, "Have you eaten?" I told her I hadn't, and she sent Nelson, her nephew, to buy tamales.

We moved outside to the patio. Manuela sat in an old white chair leaned against a blue door that was losing a battle to a swarm of termites. She called out to Felipe, the man I had met three years ago who wove Manuela's hammocks. He brought her a footstool to prop up her aching legs. "You've come to buy a hammock, right?" Manuela said. It never took her long. In fact, when I realized that I'd been with her for twenty minutes, I wondered why she hadn't started sooner. Illness, I thought. Or maybe the illness was part of her pitch.

"I might be interested in a hammock," I said. I remembered that my girlfriend in San Francisco had asked for one.

"Felipe," she shouted. "Tom wants a hammock." Then the sorrow went out of her face, and Felipe bolted out of the house with a hammock so large he needed both arms to carry it. The color was striking, a deep indigo that I often saw in huipiles and enaguas. Manuela stood and grabbed one end of the hammock, Felipe the other. Then they separated across the patio. Three paces later, the hammock was still unfolding.

"I can give you a good price for this one," Manuela said.

"Don't you have anything smaller?" I said. The hammock was ridiculously large, made for Goliath and family, not for my girlfriend in San Francisco. She would have to knock out a wall or two to stretch it out completely.

"No," she said, "this is all we have. Isn't it a wonderful color?" I agreed and then changed the subject. I asked Manuela about her best day ever selling hammocks, or her worst, but these kinds of questions have always been beyond her.

"You once told me your mother was a *viajera*. What else can you tell me about her?"

"I was twelve years old when I began selling hammocks with my mother. I was little, so I kept close to her. At times, she would travel to other cities to sell hammocks, and I stayed home and made tortillas and cooked. If it was a one-day trip, she would take me with her. She went to Playa Vicente, Tres Valles, Loma Bonita, Isla, Tonola, Chagüite, Tapana, Tapachula, Sochiate."

"Did she stay in hotels when she traveled?" I asked. Her mood was letting up. She began twiddling her thumbs as she spoke.

"No. She stayed with her *paisanas* that had houses near the market. She died eight years ago when she was ninety-two. My father lived until he was ninety-eight, and until the day of his death, he spoke and heard just fine."

"Do you get Social Security," I said.

"No," she said. "And neither does my husband. You have to work a regular job for that, so we'll get nothing. But I still sell hammocks from home now and then. The other day, Elena stopped by with two gringas, and both of them bought one."

"You're life in San Francisco must be good," she said.

"It is very good," I said.

"Here, we are very poor, papa. You've been visiting us for years, and you already know how hard it is for an Isthmus woman. She makes tortillas, pozol [maize drink], beans, and rice that she sells in the market. Meanwhile, her husband goes out and looks for work. Sometimes he finds work, sometimes not. If not, he goes around drinking, sucking alcohol from the first bottle he finds."

Nelson returned swinging a purple plastic bucket full of tamales. Manuela stood and shuffled across the patio to the main house. "I can walk," she said, "as long as I take it a little at a time." Inside the house, a plate and a fork were set in front of me. Manuela fetched a tamale out of the bucket and laid it on my plate. Though most tamales are rectangular, the one on my plate formed a perfect square, a glossy green against the white porcelain. The tamale was tied and knotted with straw, in the same fashion that boxes were at the beginning of the century. I could not untie the knot, and when Manuela noticed, she drew the string around one of the corners and unfolded the banana leaves. I ate with gusto until I uncovered a piece of scaly black skin at the bottom of my tamale.

"What is this?" I asked Manuela.

"That," she said, "is iguana flesh, and what we've been eating are iguana tamales."

When we finished the tamales, I stepped outside and began to wish Manuela good-bye. "What about the hammock for your friend?"

Manuela said, as if she were looking out for the good of my friend and not her own.

"It's so big," I said.

"Felipe," she shouted. "Fold the hammock up nicely. Tom is worried about it fitting in his suitcase."

I gave in, moaned, and asked how much.

"This hammock is easily worth 400 pesos. But for you, papa, we'll make it 300." I counted out 300 pesos, and when I turned to her, her eyes were more watery than usual. Had she worked up these tears as part of her sales pitch? Or were these tears of joy? I only know that as I walked toward the gate to leave, I turned back to wave a final goodbye, and Manuela was whispering something in her daughter's ear. The daughter smiled the smile of a pirate on boarding a captured ship full of gold, a smile of adventure and conquest, and I came to understand why Isthmus women live so long.

On Sunday, at seven in the morning, I took a seat in the lobby. Cristina arrived five minutes later in a full-length dress fashioned from a cotton print with showy flowers in pink and blue. Although she had assured me two days earlier that she always wore a huipil and enagua to Isthmus festivals, the only thing traditional about her dress was its full length. I let this go, and we drove in her new, gold-colored Chrysler to pick up her sister and her sister's husband. Shortly after we crossed the Pan American Highway, Cristina turned left onto a side street lined with two-story mansions. "This area is called the Riviera," Cristina said. "It is the most exclusive area in Juchitán." She pulled the car to a stop and pointed out her mansion. She looked at me, searching my face for a reaction. I stared straight ahead.

Cristina's sister and brother-in-law were waiting for us at their house, directly across the street from Cristina's. Ivan, her brother-in-law, was good-natured and kind, and like most Isthmus men, he rarely spoke. Gabriela was Cristina's older sister and had none of Cristina's effervescence. Her manner was dour, her expression nun-like. When Cristina introduced us, she had to repeat Gabriela's name twice; I simply couldn't grasp the sound of it. Rather than asking Cristina to repeat it a third time, I offered Gabriela my pen and asked her to write her name in my journal. She drew her hands away from the notebook as though it were diseased. But in one graceful movement, that won me to her completely, Cristina reached between us and wrote her sister's name. I thanked Cristina and resolved to maintain my distance from Gabriela.

After a brief discussion between the two sisters, Ivan was chosen to drive. When he reached the Pan-American Highway and turned south toward the border with Guatemala, I asked Cristina how her parents had accumulated their wealth. "My parents lived near Matias Romero," Cristina said, "in a village name Mogna. They began their first business by making use of the train system to transport large quantities of fruit. Then they moved to Matias Romero, selling enaguas. Business died off when the highway across the Isthmus was built in the fifties. Because of this, they moved to Juchitán, where they established a department store in which they sold a little bit of everything. This was not common at the time. As children, we lived in the same building."

We drove in silence until we came to a section of the Pan-American Highway bordered on either side by a shantytown. Cristina sat upright and began gesturing at the uneven grouping of ramshackle houses. "Do you see that land?" she said. "That land was—that land *is* ours. Some years ago, a group of squatters invaded and settled in. They are called *paracaístas* or parachuters because they drop from out of nowhere onto the land. The government won't evict them. In fact, they refuse to do anything at all. There are even politicians who used our land to buy votes." What made matters worse was that the land seized had real value because of its proximity to the intersection of Juchitán's main artery with the Pan-American Highway, which only added to Cristina's furor. When we had passed through the town, Cristina leaned forward in her seat so that her head was almost touching mine.

"Are people allowed to do such things in the United States?" she said.

"No," I said. "Not that I know of." I understood Cristina's indignation at the illegal acquisition of her land while the government looked the other way. Still, what percent of wealth did this strip of roadside dirt represent to one of the richest women in the Isthmus? I checked Gabriela's and Ivan's face for signs of bitterness, but they were blank.

We drove another forty-five minutes south before Ivan turned right onto a country road. The land was greener than any I'd seen in the Isthmus, or even Oaxaca. It was as though we'd entered another climate zone or that we were on the edge of a tropical forest; the burnt grass and stunted trees of the Isthmus gave way to green hills and mango trees the size of hot air balloons. The sight of all of the greenery moved the silent Ivan to speak: "This is Tapanatepec," he said. "Capital of the mangos." In the back seat, Cristina paid little attention to the pastoral setting. The prolonged company of her older sister and brother-in-law had transformed Cristina into a younger version of herself. The articulate judge I interviewed in the Fortress restaurant became the youngest in her family, and she laughed pleasantly in the back seat with her older sister.

Ivan drove for another five miles through mango orchards and open fields. Every now and then we crossed depressions in the road where creeks had washed away the pavement. Then we reached Los Mangos, and Ivan turned and drove along a dirt road until we came to a circle of mango trees. Within the circle a small crowd of houses was grouped around a bare-earth plaza. Ivan pulled over and parked on one side of the plaza, and a small group of family members greeted us with waves and smiles. The sun roared at us when we got out of the car, and we did a quick march to the plaza where an overhead tarp provided relief. We took seats at an empty table, and Cristina introduced me to an array of relatives and friends whose names and relations I soon confused.

The exception to this confusion was Angela, Cristina's mother-in-law and sponsor for the vigil. She was warm, bright, cultured, and like most of the landowners in the Isthmus, she was of European descent. As soon as Angela seated us at a table on the plaza, a cook served each one of us breakfast: a bowl full of a regional delicacy called *sangre de toro* (bull's blood). I stirred the soup to see what it might contain, and a variety of bovine body parts with varying degrees of fat and gristle floated to the surface and sank. Cristina watched as I spooned the stuff into my mouth while doing my best to hide my displeasure. When I wasn't picking at my soup, tiny flies attacked it in pairs. "We killed two bulls yesterday," a man at the head of the table said. "And before the day is over, we'll kill another. It was terrible," he said with a smile. "First they tied each one of his legs and then drew a machete across his throat like this." Here, he slid his finger across his neck and, once again, smiled.

"So how did you two meet?" He wasn't asking me, he had directed his question to Cristina.

"I was having trouble understanding a recorded message I got in English when I was calling my boys," she said. "So I asked Tom to help."

"Sounds like a flimsy pretext if I ever heard one," he said.

"Exactly what I thought," I said. Cristina laughed, and my estimation of her grew. She was not only beautiful; she was mentally and emotionally fit, able to handle a joke at her own expense. Her look was healthy, and unlike me, she had no tics, no obsessions, no skittishness. You could look at her straight in the eyes.

After we had eaten, Cristina explained why Angela was sponsoring the vigil for Santa Inés. "Five years go," Cristina said, "Angela made a promise to Santa Inés."

"And what was the promise?" I said to Angela.

"I took a vow that if my son succeeded in graduating from law school in Monterey, I would sponsor a vigil in honor of Santa Inés. My son succeeded with flying colors, and here we are." Then Angela gave us a tour of her house. "It's the only house on the ranch that doesn't have dirt floors," she said. "This is Santa Inés." The statue looked like every other female saint I'd ever seen, except for her long, fiery red hair and a look of rigid determination.

Shortly before noon, Ivan drove us to the site of the vigil. Like everything else at Los Mangos, the vigil for Santa Inés unfolded in the middle of a mango orchard. A butter-colored chapel stood next to a clear creek, and near the chapel an old woman scooped broth from a cauldron that rose from the red clay at her feet to the sash she wore round her waist. On the opposite side of the chapel, a thatched roof shaded a dance floor and a crowd of empty chairs. A stoop-shouldered woman with graying hair sprinkled water over the dirt dance floor, leaving black pockmarks in the brown dust. Her purpose was clear: to dampen the flow of dust that would soon be kicked up by the thrusting feet and flat-footed stomp of Isthmus dance.

After a brief good-bye, Ivan crossed a field of burnt grass to the shade of a mango tree where several dozen men stood drinking beer and liquor from plastic cups. Cristina draped her shawl over a pair of seats adjacent to the dance floor, and Gabriela led the way to the chapel, though to call it a chapel is an exaggeration. Where there should have been a wall at the entrance to the chapel there was none, and if you were to use it as a garage, it would have been a tight fit for all but the smallest cars. There were no pews, and the women of Los Mangos had so overwhelmed the altar and tile floor of the chapel with votive candles and bouquets of hibiscus, tulips, lilies, and gladiolas that there was no room for the women to sit or for the priest to say mass. To circumvent the problem, the women had set up eight wooden benches in front of the chapel, where thirty women in huipiles and enaguas waited for mass to begin. For an altar, they had improvised a folding card table covered with a yellow plastic tablecloth. Then they had moved some of the flowers aside and placed the table a good two feet inside the chapel, lest someone think they were sinning by attending an open-air mass.

When the three of us arrived there were no empty seats; Cristina and Gabriela stood near the altar, and I retreated to a position behind the last row of benches.

For a while, this arrangement of altar and seating suited everyone. Then Father Ben, as the women called him, arrived carrying a green nylon handbag, the wind blowing against him as if to warn him away. He was taller and broader and more confident than most Isthmus men, but as he approached the provisional altar a perturbed look overcame his dark, Zapotec face. Nonetheless, women approached him, seeking advice and asking if he would be willing to bless some of their belongings with holy water after mass. Soon the women returned to their seats.

Father Ben swung a white, one-piece cassock over his head, and when he had it on, it brushed the floor of the chapel. He began mass, but not before he settled a score with the women. "Unless we lend our attention to the sacred rituals of our faith, we will continue to lose ground to the evangelists from the north who have invaded our parishes one after the other." His fervor and confidence were impressive, his diction inflated. "Now," he began again, "if any of you had respect for the holy sacrament I am about to perform, you would have known that Catholic ritual demands the altar be covered with a white linen cloth. You have failed me and our holy mother the church, and I resent it deeply."

This said, he dug into one of the pockets of his pants and opened a white linen handkerchief, which he laid at the center of the table. He took a marble chalice out of his handbag, along with two plastic bottles with screw-on caps that held water and wine. The chalice he placed on the handkerchief, the water and wine and a small plastic vat containing unconsecrated hosts he positioned on the yellow tablecloth.

"We will begin the mass with a hymn," he said. He sang openly. The women followed, and by the end of the first verse, they had engulfed that part of the melody he carried, and I could no longer single out his voice. Cristina and Gabriela sang along fervently with the other women, and I envied the comfort their belief must have brought them. Every now and then the wind would blow the smell of the beef cooking in the cauldron in our direction. It reminded me of the soup I had eaten earlier and had a sickening effect on me.

When it came time for the sermon, Father Ben did something decidedly un-Catholic. He abandoned his card-table altar and wandered into the crowd as if he were a televangelist with a cordless microphone.

"Who amongst you," he said, "can tell me about the martyrdom of Santa Inés."

He waited, and a woman in Western dress spoke, albeit quietly.

"She was a virgin," she said. "They killed her."

"Is that all?" he said to the crowd. "Is that all?" It then became clear that some of his anger about the altar cloth had lingered. When no one answered, he wandered into the crowd and began asking the women one by one if they knew the story of Santa Inés. Some reddened, others laughed nervously, and he continued his inquiry woman by woman until he reached the last row of the benches. The first woman in the last row professed her ignorance and turned her head away to hide her shame. But then Father Ben met resistance. "Father," one of the women said, "let's drop this. Let's have a little talk about Santa Inés so that we'll know for next year's festival." She spoke with a kind, solicitous calm, but when he moved on to embarrass the next woman, her tone changed. "Talk to us, Father," she said. "This is going nowhere. Why embarrass us like this?" He ignored her and moved to the next woman. Then, from the other side of the crowd, a woman whose head rose above all others bellowed at him. "Enough," she said. "If we don't know the story of Santa Inés, it's your fault, not ours. You failed to teach us. How can you expect us to know the lives of twenty saints when we are busy feeding and praying for our families?" Silence intervened, and then the wind blew so hard that the plastic vat containing the hosts slid to the edge of the provisional altar. When Father Ben saw this, he paused, considering his options. Then he moved away from the last row and returned to the altar. Almost immediately, he told the story of Santa Inés. Some of the confidence in his voice waned, and I grasped only fragments of the story. But Cristina and Gabriela were in the front row, I told myself, so I'd get the replay from them.

After the sermon, a swarm of men and women numbering at least 100 crowded around the benches. They had come to fulfill the letter of the church law requiring attendance at Sunday mass. As a bare minimum the faithful were required to be present for transubstantiation, when, according to church belief, the bread and wine became the body and blood of Christ. At communion, only a handful of the 130 believers—all of them women—came forward to receive the host from Father Ben. Gabriela, but not Cristina, was one of them. Once communion was over, the crowd dissipated, and only the women on the benches waited to leave until mass was formally over.

After mass, I joined Cristina and Gabriela in the wooden chairs near the dance floor. The band kicked off the dance with a rousing version of "No me molesta mosquito" (Don't Bother Me, Mosquito). The song brought many of the women to their feet. Soon they were in each other's arms, their bodies bobbing up and down as though they were riding a horse in circles around an empty pasture. Only women wearing huipiles and enaguas danced, and very few of the women present wore traditional dress. This might have been due to poverty, or the distance from the Zapotec capitals, Juchitán and Tehuantepec.

When the song ended, the women returned to their seats, and I turned to Cristina and said, "So tell me Father Ben's version of the story of Santa Inés." Then I did something rash. When Cristina didn't respond immediately, I began telling her what I remembered of the story, filling in the gaps of what I didn't hear with guesswork. I hated people who answered their own questions, and there I was doing just that. "Santa Inés," I began, "was a Spanish martyr. When she was fifteen, a man tried to take advantage of her . . ." And that was as far as I got because Cristina stiffened in her seat and barked, "No inventes" (Don't invent). I felt insulted. Had she wanted, she could have waited until I finished my rendition of the story and then pointed out that I had some of my facts wrong—in a gentle tone of voice. But instead she barked. Rather than bark back, I counted the hours I had spent with Cristina: an hour at the hotel on Thursday night, another hour on the drive, and slightly more than three at Los Mangos. This added up to a grand total of five hours, and already she was directing my behavior. *One minute they deny being matriarchs, I thought, and the next minute they're telling you what to do.* All the same, I kept my mouth shut. Cristina kept quiet, too, letting the tension die down, and then, in a calm voice, she began, "Santa Inés was a Spanish princess in the last century. Not long after she was born, her father and mother arranged a marriage for her. Fifteen years later, on the day of the wedding, Santa Inés refused to marry not only her betrothed, but any man at all. The king became enraged. He ordered his servants to strip her of clothes and march her through town on a horse. The servants carried out his order, but God had mercy on her. He made her red hair grow so long that it covered her completely, and she rode through town without shame."

Before long, we put the Santa Inés business behind us and moved on to the next source of tension: food. Some of the women feasted on pork tripe tacos with chunky red salsa and goat's cheese. Others ate the delicacy of the day: meat stripped from a cow's head that was stewing in the cauldron and a side dish of potato salad or macaroni and cheese. Most of the women held a bottle of beer in their hand or were reaching for a fresh one, although a small minority sucked *horchata* (rice milk) from clear plastic baggies tied in a knot around yellow straws. The children seemed to have their own menu. A solitary boy shoveled beans into his mouth with a pink spoon. Little girls nursed each other with baby bottles shaped like Teddy bears filled with a drink like Kool-Aid.

Cristina said she was hungry and suggested I go with her to the area around the cauldron where people waited in line for food. I begged off, even though I wanted to join her. My digestive track refuses to process food until the late afternoon. Until then, food to me is an annoyance. And so it was that when Cristina reappeared and began eating alone, the tension between us grew. An hour later, she left to fill her plate once again, and when she returned, she sat on the other side of Gabriela. Later, Gabriela read my face and concluded I was bored. She approached me and said, "If you like, Ivan can introduce you to some of the men out back." I had been wrong about Gabriela. She was a lot sweeter than she looked. I thanked her and took her up on her offer.

Ivan walked me to the area where the men stood smoking and drinking under a mango tree. He introduced me to a half-dozen men who stood in a circle talking. Within minutes, all but one disappeared. His name was Abel Trejo Gonzalez. He was the congressional representative for the Isthmus at the federal level in Mexico City. He wore small rectangular glasses, and because of his profuse sweating, his glasses slid down his nose faster than he pushed them up. His complexion was unusual, a grayish purple, almost liver colored. Because Abel belonged to PRI— famed for corruption and thrown elections—I felt as though I were standing next to a Mexican mafia boss. But make no mistake, Abel was proud of his political affiliation. "We are the only party that understands the Mexican people," he said. Men stopped by to shake Abel's hand, get their backs slapped, and then merge into the crowd. I asked Abel what he thought of Mexico's president, Vicente Fox, and it was as though I'd ruptured a sewer line. "The fucking press," he said, "they're in love with the bastard." There are television programs devoted to the color and style of his suits (he has twenty) and his ties (he owns forty). "Who gives a shit what he wears?" Abel said. The question, according to Abel, was this: Can he govern? "He can't," Abel said. "He can't govern because he has no experience, except as a manager of corporations. Mexico is not a corporation, and he'll learn that soon enough because the Mexican people have a tradition of revolting against incompetent leaders, including presidents. My advice to Fox is this: Be careful with the Mexican people, they'll drag you out of office and kill you! They did it to Madero and they'll do it to Fox. I predict—and I want you to remember this—Fox will not finish his term. The Mexican people will have their revenge."

When I returned to Cristina, I found her tossing the pit of a prune she had been eating onto the dirt in front of her, where a dozen more were collected. "Try one," she said. I did. The taste of the prune was masked by the brandy in which it had been soaked. Cristina had a beer in her hand, which she drank between prunes. I followed suit, and both of us were soon drunk. But who could accuse us of drinking to excess? We'd only eaten some prunes.

We left Los Mangos at seven, and when we arrived in Juchitán, we dropped Ivan and Gabriela at home. Cristina drove on to the Fortress, and when she pulled up in front of the lobby, it was near nine in the evening. She turned the engine off and said:

"Do you feel like doing something else, or are you tired?"

"I'm okay," I said. "What do you feel like doing?"

Though it was unintentional, my comment must have cut through her skin and nicked a nerve, because she responded with intensity, squeezing the steering wheel and raising her voice to a shout. "Wherever *you* want." she said. "Wherever *you* want." There wasn't any kindness in this phrase; she said it so forcefully that I feared what might happen if I didn't express my wishes exactly. I often got the sense that some part of the problems I've encountered with the opposite sex were not my problems at all. They were my predecessor's, and the women were carrying on unsettled arguments with their former husbands or lovers, wrestling, in a way, with their ghosts. Possibly, Cristina's husband had been indecisive, and when she saw this in me, it disturbed her. Or maybe when he was alive, she didn't let him decide as much as she would have, given a second chance with him. The more time I spent with Cristina, the easier it became to imagine her as a judge.

"Do you know anyone who's been a victim of *robo*?" I asked. *Robo* (robbery) is synonymous with *rapto*, the sometimes violent marriage ritual described by Henestrosa in his essay "The Forms of Sexual Life in Juchitán." Cristina thought for a minute and then spoke.

"Yes, I know of a couple who married in this way," she said. "Their names are José and Rita, and we can pay them a visit." Arriving unannounced at nine in the evening to ask questions about abduction and sex seemed presumptuous to me. But who was I to say? Cristina started the car and drove north along 16 de Septiembre to Juchitán's first ward where José and Rita lived.

The Grad Student

In a paper she published while studying for her doctorate in anthropology, insider Edaena Saynes-Vázquez writes about an experience many Isthmus women endure when they travel outside the Isthmus. "So you are Zapotec!" the conversation begins, "You know how to control men!" Saynes-Vázquez decided to write her paper because of her concern and frustration about the way outsiders interpreted women's role in Isthmus society and the way she experienced it as a Zapotec woman. According to Saynes-Vázquez, the gap between the two is so vast that she likens outsiders' portrayal of Istmeñas to magical realism.

From the very start of her paper, Saynes-Vázquez engages you with her honesty. Unlike most insiders, she does not lay the blame entirely on outsiders for exaggerated representations of Isthmus women. As early as the middle 1930s, Saynes-Vázquez found literature written by Istmeños who glorified Zapotec identity, some of which she believes contributed to the current stereotype of Isthmus women. "Women's dress—where homage is paid to color—is the smile of the street," wrote one Istmeño. "In the mornings these women are Zapotec canephoros (women carrying baskets on their heads). I still see them passing in front of my eyes: with their upright bodies, they carry on their heads huge baskets or beautiful gourds full of flowers." Saynes-Vázquez explains that much prose such as this originated from young Istmeños studying in Mexico city who were experiencing their first prolonged separation from home. This separation had the natural effect of increasing the appreciation of their own culture, the most potent symbol of which was often their own women. Further evidence of this trend came in the 1940s when the valorization of Isthmus women reached its peak, and the Mexican mint began searching for someone who would best represent the country's many indigenous peoples. After much deliberation, they chose an Isthmus woman and printed an image of her on every 10-peso note.

But it does not take long before Saynes-Vázquez turns her attention to outsiders, and once she does, she never looks back. "When outsiders," Saynes-Vázquez writes, "such as social scientists, arrive for the first time in the Isthmus of Tehuantepec, they are impressed by the 'differences' in the area compared to other indigenous regions." The physical environment is unattractive, the weather inclement, the architecture anything but charming. As a result, outsiders tend to focus on people, and in particular women. Saynes-Vázquez finds this perfectly natural. She only finds fault when outsiders fail to take in a wide panorama of Istmeñas, choosing instead to concentrate on market women, their traditional dress, and their way of reciprocal trading rather than paying fixed prices. The problem worsens when outsiders take the market and its women as the norm and extend what they find to all Isthmus women. Saynes-Vázquez provides evidence of this skewed perspective in what she describes as a growing literature by anthropologists, sociologists, and feminists. "These works base their interpretations only on that part of the female population that still practices traditional activities, without mentioning those women who do work in other economic spheres and without mentioning the gender discrimination that takes place in their lives." In this way, outsiders exclude the majority of Isthmus women. "Most women in Juchitán are not market women, and most of the economic activity in the city is not included in the open air market where one class of woman predominates."

If, as Saynes-Vázquez tells us, the women of the market no longer represent a broad array of Isthmus women, who then are they? She does not answer this question directly but provides a clue from a study done by Beverly Chiñas in 1992: "She found that marketing activities are viewed as low-income activities, that people devoted to such activities have a low status, and that they are stigmatized as persons with no competence for other productive activities." Lamentably, this agrees with my experience. The market women I spoke to were among the poorest in the Isthmus. Add to this the fact that women—especially poor women—are last in a culture to let go of tradition, and it begins to make sense that women in traditional dress should be concentrated in the market.

What Saynes-Vázquez leaves unsaid about market women is that there was a time when women of the market *did* represent the majority of Isthmus women. As recently as one hundred years ago, economic activity was conducted exclusively in the market, women wore huipiles and enaguas to a fault, and trading was carried on solely through bartering and reciprocation. We see this in the documentaries of Eisenstein and Covarrubias and read about it in the documents produced by Bourbourg and Von Tempsky. This line of thought has interesting implications. Although it might not be true now, the possibility of a matriarchy at some time in the past certainly exists. Many of the women I interviewed in the market suggested the possibility when they said, "Matriarchy? Maybe before, long ago, but not anymore—no way."

Another general pattern that Saynes-Vázquez notes in outsiders' renditions of Isthmus women is that they tend to focus on the favorable aspects of traditional women, emphasizing the positive and ignoring the negative. One example she notes is women's sexuality. Outsiders focus on the freedom with which market women discuss and joke about sexuality but fail to report on the sexual assaults they suffer at the hands of their husbands. "It is unfair," writes Saynes-Vázquez, "to ignore such dimensions of such sexual life and highlight only partial attitudes." Saynes-Vázquez also points out that women's outspokenness on the topic of sex is not a unique Zapotec feature. Other Native American cultures share this feature, as in the case of the Hopi of Arizona and the Indians of Alto Xingú from Central Brazil.

Although Saynes-Vázquez cedes the point that women's strong participation in Isthmus politics is seen as unusual in other parts of Mexico, she calls into question just what "participation" means. Men and children are also present at rallies and demonstrations, yet their presence is not interpreted as political participation. "I wonder why women's presence, on the one hand," writes Saynes-Vázquez, "has been the center of attention and why children's attendance in the rallies and marches, on the other hand, is not a big issue."

Saynes-Vázquez summarizes what she feels is Isthmus women's opinion of themselves and their relations with men in a way that is funny and poignant. While many outsiders claim women enjoy egalitarian relations, and some even claim they are matriarchs, the women themselves say otherwise: "Galán pa dxani" (That would be great if it were true). Saynes-Vázquez then adds, "I think that this phrase expresses the personal feelings of Zapotec women, which have been ignored."

Green Mangos

José and Rita's house was shuttered and dark when we arrived, but Cristina knocked anyway. A clever-looking woman with fast eyes and black hair answered the door. Her husband, whose glasses had slid halfway down his nose, stood behind her, peering over her shoulder at the late-night intruders. Cristina introduced us, and we followed Rita into a sparsely furnished dining room and sat down at what appeared to be José's end of the dinner table. Cristina explained what I was after, and Rita left for the kitchen to make coffee. In her absence, we sat in silence until I turned to José and asked to hear the story of his marriage with Rita.

"I met my wife while visiting with friends in Mexico City," José said, "and from that meeting, our love at first sight was born." José spoke in flowery, halting Spanish, and by the time he'd finished this first sentence, I began to doubt he had abducted anyone. He was a bookish man with a weak chin and a kind heart whose prize possession was a bookcase that read like a who's who of Western philosophy. *The Fundamental's of Marxist-Leninist Philosophy* leaned against Kant's *Critique of Pure Reason,* and next to it was Pico's *Modernity and Post-Modernity.* But José was more than a collector of books. He planned to write them, too. His first would be about Juchitán's gunfighters, his second a history of Juchitán's leading homosexuals. And under the glass that protected the table, José had inserted an article by French philosopher Michel Foucault, no doubt to keep his mind busy while he ate.

"We didn't dawdle with our romance," José continued. "Within fifteen days we proposed marriage."

"Seriously?" Cristina said. "I didn't know about this." Then she turned her head toward the kitchen and called out, half jokingly, "You'd better get out here Rita, your husband has been trying to deceive us." José paused, and we waited for his wife to return.

At Rita's end of the table was a cupboard with glass doors roughly the same width and height as José's bookshelf. Everything feminine about the room seemed to congregate in and around this cupboard. On the shelves inside were crystal goblets and champagne flutes and porcelain dinnerware and a handful of photos of Rita and her two daughters hugging each other in the vivid colors of traditional Zapotec dress. On the third shelf, leaned up against the legs of a doll from Rita's childhood, was the only image of José in the room: a three-by-five, black-and-white photo of a younger, skinnier José, handsome for the last time in his life. Directly to the left of the cupboard, and above all else in the room, was a life-size portrait of Rita as reigning queen of Vela San Vicente. The portrait depicted a teenage Rita wearing a cut-glass tiara and matching choker. The stiff white collar of her cape extended six inches in front of her chin and an inch or two over her ears. She was not smiling but looked contented as she surveyed the contents of the room.

When Rita returned with the coffee and took a seat next to Cristina, José continued telling the story, now more cautiously and in a voice so low I had to lean forward to hear him. "It's true that my wife and I have known each other since we were children. But we didn't begin our love life until we crossed paths as adults." At the time, José was a thirty-three-year-old unemployed university student. Rita was thirty, making a decent living selling jewelry, still hopeful she would marry and have children.

Not long after their chance meeting in Mexico City, José and Rita returned to Juchitán for a vacation with their families. José wanted to buy Rita a gift but lacked money. So, one morning, he climbed his mother's mango tree and cut off a large cluster of mangos with a machete. He put on his best clothes and tied a red handkerchief around his neck, which was the fashion in those days with the leftwing political party he favored. The mangos were still green, but he delivered them to Rita anyway. Later that night, José and Rita attended a festival. They saw each other the next night as well. But inside Rita's house, a dispute between mother and daughter was brewing. Rita's mother, Juana, had grown suspicious.

"You are no longer a señorita," she said to her daughter. Juana explained that as everyone in Oaxaca knows, pregnant women have strange cravings. And among the most common of these cravings was an uncontrollable urge to eat green mangos with chilies and lemon. Juana's last words in the confrontation were these: José was not the man for Rita.

At the end of his vacation, José visited Rita at her mother's house to say that he was returning to Mexico City. Rita described the dispute that had arisen over the green mangos and that her mother had prohibited her from returning to Mexico with him. José said a final goodbye and returned to his mother's home.

In the morning, José packed his belongings and walked to the second-class bus station to purchase his ticket to Mexico City. To his surprise, Rita was there waiting for him. She explained how she had suffered in the dispute with her mother, and José sympathized. But when her tears had dried up and her calm was restored, she announced a plan. "The truth is," Rita said, "we'd be better off if we just ran away." They boarded the bus together, and when it was out on the highway, Rita turned to José and said: "You know what? We are going to get married on the fourteenth of February." As the bus neared Mexico City, José came to feel as though he had won this match against Juana. But later on Rita made things clear. "I soon came to the conclusion," José said, "that it wasn't going to be easy to go—" José searched for the right word, and Cristina said:

"To go where?"

"To go where my male mind wanted to go."

"No, José," Cristina said. "If you set the date of the marriage beforehand, then you did not really rob Rita." Then the three of them argued about the finer points of the courtship. What struck me as I listened to them speak was their use of the term *robo*. Because of culture and language, only José could be the robber, and only Rita could be robbed. Somehow, they couldn't hear themselves speak. If anyone had been robbed, it was José, who Rita had led by his libido halfway across the country and back.

And though I did not realize it at the time José related the story of his marriage to Rita, I see now as I write this story that no mention of Rita's or José's father was ever made. Their father's approval or disapproval didn't seem to be a factor, and I had become so used to the fact that

Isthmus mothers dominate at home that I did not miss the voice of a father figure. It never even occurred to me to ask, "But José, what did your father have to say about the marriage?" or "Rita, did your father agree that José was an unsuitable husband?" Although Istmeños blame outsiders for jumping to conclusions when they see women dominating the market, I believe that any outsider listening to a conversation on family matters might think the same. It might suit Istmeños to listen to what these casual observers have to say and, in the process, learn about who they are when compared to the outsider's culture.

After a long discussion, Cristina, José, and Rita agreed that by fleeing from Juchitán, the couple had broken with the traditional form of *robo*. Usually when a bride flees with a groom, they go to the groom's house, where he seeks proof of her virginity. Some say the couple has sex, others, including sociologist Marina Meneses and anthropologist Marinella Miano Borruso, say the groom breaks the woman's hymen with his finger. In either case, the blood of the bride on a handkerchief or sheet or underwear are considered legitimate proof of virginity. If the bride turns out a virgin, a delegation is sent to the mother's house with the blood-stained cloth, no matter the time of day or night. Only then—when the bride proves to be a virgin—is a date for the wedding set.

In his essay "The Forms of Sexual Life in Juchitán," Andrés Henestrosa explains that the underlying motivation for this ritual is male mistrust. *Robo* occurs when the groom, for some reason, doubts that his bride-to-be is a virgin. Henestrosa describes the ritual as a "search for virginity, the results of which determine whether or not there will be a marriage." Even more to the point, he explains that the Zapotecs, "like all primitive men, have an absolutely fanatical concern with virginity." Later in the essay, however, he defends the men's fanaticism, calling it a kind of kind of retrospective jealously.

Sociologist Marina Meneses offers a different explanation. On one hand, the deflowering of the bride and the proof of virginity with a blood-stained cloth is a way of putting the facts before the bride's family so that they will accept the wedding. "On the other hand," writes Meneses, "[*robo*] implies a resource for protecting the woman since the man who fled with her is obliged to marry her or pay an indemnification if the woman or her family does not agree with the marriage."

Meneses also recounts a telling anecdote about a traditional wedding she attended. When the bride's mother—who is always first to view the blood-stained cloth—sees the proof of virginity, she said, "Look, this is what counts for a woman."

When Rita and José arrived in Mexico City, José did not want to return to his student housing. He wanted to live with Rita in the apartment she shared with her cousin. Rita said, "I want to make my mother proud and at the same time shut her up. I am a señorita, and we will marry. But you are going to respect me in the meantime."

"And you didn't insist on eating the cake?" Cristina said.

"No," José said.

"You respected her, that's fine."

A few days before the civil marriage on February 14, José called his mother and informed her of his plans to marry in Mexico City. She approved of the marriage, asking only that the wedding take place in Juchitán rather than Mexico City.

"And did your mother approve of Rita?" Cristina said.

"Always," José said. "But how could she disapprove if she'd never met her?"

José's mother added that he should not worry about the cost of the wedding party. She would take care of this. Nonetheless, José felt that this would be an imposition because he had never contributed a cent to his family's economic well-being.

"You were a lush," Cristina said. Then she turned to me and said, "Do you know why Juana opposed the marriage? Because José was a full-time asshole of the worst kind. Am I right, José?" I waited for José to overcome his meekness and strike back, but true to his stoic form, he gave in.

"You are right," José said. In short, José told his mother that if she was in a position to do so, she could host the wedding and send a delegation to Juana. According to Isthmus tradition, the delegation sent to propose marriage is composed of three or more elders from the bridegroom's family and friends. One of the elders, called the *cagoola*, is known for his abilities as a speechmaker or poet, which he uses to convince the bride's mother to give her consent. Out of dignity, the bride's mother is expected to say no the first time they visit her. Then a series of negotiations begins concerning where and when and how the wedding will take place.

The delegation José's mother sent called upon Juana once, twice, and, because of the persistence of José's uncle, a third time. Juana still refused. Then José's uncle confronted Juana. He insinuated that because José and Rita lived together, her virginity was questionable. As a consequence, the clash between the two of them grew even greater. But José's uncle only questioned Rita's virginity so that Juana would give in, and finally she did.

"As a condition of Juana's assent," José said, "we agreed to wait six months before marrying in the church. Even though we shared the same bed, we slept together like brother and sister."

"As brother and sister?" Cristina said. "I doubt it—I *profoundly* doubt it."

"We weren't so brotherly and sisterly," Rita said.

José and Rita were wedded in Juchitán's cathedral on a rainy Sunday morning in August. After the wedding, the newlyweds visited Juana in her home before joining in the celebration that was already underway at José's. At two in the afternoon, the band was playing full tilt, and the wedding party was at its apogee. At seven, when the dancers dwindled away, José's aunts began sweeping out the family storage room. They placed a cot inside the room and covered it with a white sheet. As a final touch, they left two beers next to the cot, one for José, the other for Rita. "Go ahead inside," they said to the newlyweds. "This is where you'll spend your wedding night."

José and Rita entered the room and closed the door. But any hope they had about privacy was soon put to rest. José could hear his friends and family conversing as if they were at a birthday party. But after a time, the conversation ceased. Then a man who did not identify himself began knocking on the door. "Are you done?" he said. At first, José ignored these inquiries. Later, when Rita began crying, José shouted out a plea for peace and quiet, and also for a little privacy.

"I was trying to, to, to, to, court the maiden, but—" José said.

"But you weren't inspired," Cristina said.

"How could we be?" Rita said. "It got so bad that Señora Deci, a neighbor, barged right into the room."

Finally, after Señora Deci had been coaxed out of the room, they made love. But before José could get his pants back on, Señora Deci led another assault on the door. It gave way, and the crowd pushed José aside and stormed into the room. They got hold of the sheet and carried it out for all to see, shouting, "Yes, she was a virgin!" The band played on, and in another minute, you could hear fireworks sounding off from Juana's. In this way, everyone in the neighborhood learned the good news about Rita.

Had Rita not been a virgin, she would have been marched back to Juana's house and her family dishonored. The community would have interpreted the problem as a failure on Juana's part to take proper care of Rita. Ironically, this is the only time when the father becomes directly involved with the wedding rituals. He cancels the festivities and then apologizes to the groom and his family. "It is said that in the old days," writes Covarrubias, "that it was customary to knock a hole in a platter and hang it on the door of the girl's house."

The following day, José's family folded the bloody sheet in such way that only the cloth stained with blood was visible. They put the folded sheet at the center of a platter and placed it on the holy table next to the saints his mother held dear: San Vicente, San Martin, and San Juan. Next to the holy table, they arranged a bed where Rita lay for all to see. And they came in droves, carrying bouquets of red hibiscus and red bougainvillea and red roses. On entering the room, they handed the bouquets over to the woman charged with throwing flowers over Rita while she lay still in bed. In the meantime, everyone crowded around her drinking cups of wine, celebrating her virginity and her marriage to José.

"This is a joyous time," Rita said, "to be shared with all of the friends and relatives of the bride and groom." She said this, however, with an edge of sarcasm. Then she added, "I did all of this for my mother, because she thought in the old way that—"

"You got swept up in the ritual, too," Cristina said.

"No, Cristina," Rita said, "tell your friend the truth. I was afraid and ashamed. Anyway, I had no choice but to follow along. José's family was so enthused that I felt obligated."

Then, for the first time that night, José raised his voice above his usual whisper, and I sat back in my chair. "But what really drove Rita to marry and take part in the rituals was her desire to prove to her mother that in spite of the green mangos, she was still a virgin." For a moment everyone was silent. José the philosopher had stripped the long, elaborate story to its bare essentials, and we saw it for what it was: a protracted struggle between a mother and daughter that had little to do with him.

When I asked about the violent form of *robo*, in which the man literally drags the woman away and has sex with her, José told another anecdote. "This tradition ran very, very deep," José said, "especially in the poorer classes who lived on the periphery of Juchitán." When he was a teenager, a schoolyard friend named Gaspar approached José to ask for help in abducting his girlfriend. José agreed. Then, with four other friends, they looked for a taxi. The first taxi driver they approached told them that he didn't want to get involved. The second driver said, "Abductions are my specialty. Hop in." Inside the taxi, they made plans to grab the girl and then leave her somewhere—maybe in a hotel. They drove to the top of a ridge overlooking the river and told the driver to stop. It was two in the afternoon, and the boys sat scanning the river, waiting for Gaspar's girlfriend to pass by. After a time, Gaspar spotted a girl crossing the shallows of the river. "That's her," he said. But before the boys could get close enough to grab her, she realized what was going on and ran up the riverbank and into her barrio. Gaspar and friends were combing the streets for her when a man who knew them said:

"What are you doing here?"

"Gaspar wants to abduct his girlfriend," one said.

"The girl who came running by?"

"Yes," Gaspar said, "but she's not really my girlfriend. I work in Minititlán. I got here a couple of days ago."

"You're too late," the man said. "She just got married."

"Maybe she got married," Gaspar said, "but I'm not finished with her."

What happened next was this: The man told the girl that Gaspar was looking for her, and that Gaspar thought that she still had a commitment with him. The following day, when the boys returned to the neighborhood to give the abduction another try, a woman came up to them and said:

"Who's Gaspar?"

"I am," Gaspar said.

"I'm here to tell you that my daughter got married."

"But she didn't finish with me."

"If she didn't finish things with you, I am here to finish them for her." Then her mother took Gaspar's hand and squeezed it, but hard.

"With this," she said, "we are ending the commitment."

When I asked how common *robo* was, Rita spoke first. "At least 50 percent of Juchitecos marry in this way," she said, "but in the past abductions of this sort were even more common." All of Rita's aunts were married through force, her mother too. Groups of male friends would get together, and one of them would say, "Let's abduct so-and-so." To escape the consequences, the men abducted women outside their barrio. The men from Chegigo would abduct women from the seventh ward, and the men from the seventh ward would do the same in Chegigo. This put the young men from these barrios in a constant state of conflict. "But if you are to understand this ritual," Rita said, "you must know that our parents were so strict that the only way you could get married was to run off together."

"Fifty or sixty years ago," José said, "almost all Juchitecas were abducted, my mother included." During the Mexican Revolution soldiers would sometimes kill a woman's mother and father and then take her by force. "When the revolution ended," José said, "the same couple could be found living together with children conceived after the abduction."

"*Robo* accounts for many, many marriages," Cristina said. "When we were eating breakfast this morning at Los Mangos, Mario, one of my brother's friends came by." Mario was from a well-to-do family, as was his wife. Mario's parents refused to agree to a traditional marriage. "She was too young," Cristina said, "and he was still a student. So he married her through *robo*, and his parents were forced to accept it."

The following day, I joined Pablo and family to celebrate his forty-first birthday at Rosa's taqueria near Juchitán's bus terminal. The drinking started early. I opened the first bottle of tequila and attempted to pour it into a thimble-sized shot glass Pablo had set on the table. Nothing came out. "Hit it," Pablo said. "Hit it one good." I ignored the advice and waited. Pablo's plastic thimble filled, and he was the first to drink.

He took it in one gulp and passed the thimble back to me. We traded shots and stories until Rosa's boyfriend put a tall shot glass on the table in front of me. When I began filling it for Pablo, he and Sonia screamed in unison: "Eso no es la medida—usa la misma copita" (That's not the measure—use the same cup). We continued drinking in this way until Sonia stood to attend to her children. I took her seat next to Pablo and described the mutiny at mass in Los Mangos the day before.

"Would you have confronted the priest in this way?" I asked.

"No way," he said. "Not on your life. And what about you?"

"Impossible," I said. "I couldn't even imagine it."

Several shots of tequila later, I stood to leave. But why are you leaving, they asked, at least tell us the reason. Then they guessed. "It's a woman," someone said, "I know him, it's some woman."

Half an hour later, Cristina and I were driving west along the Pan-American Highway to the four-star Cali Hotel, one of the most expensive hotels in the Isthmus. This expense, however, had an up side. The price of a meal or room was so prohibitive that the vast majority of Istmeños and low-budget travelers never got as far as the parking lot. This, together with the fact that the hotel was set back from the Pan-American and surrounded by towering trees, made it one of the most private places in the region.

By the time we reached the Cali, it was six thirty. As we crossed the parking lot, the sunset brought out the gloss in Cristina's gold Chrysler and the square-faced diamond ring she wore on her left hand. She was so clean and shiny that I felt grubby whenever I stood next to her. My Levi's were unwashed, and the collar of my shirt was frayed. My shoes were black and worn out, and the right one was tied with half a shoelace. Polishing them, I knew, was a waste of time.

The Cali's restaurant was very big and very empty—except for a table of pale Germans who looked as though they had boarded the wrong plane and become stranded in the Isthmus, afraid to go outside for fear of sunstroke. We sat opposite them, twenty feet away, near a window overlooking Cali's grassy patio. At the far end of the patio a blue swimming pool reflected light from overhead, and a hammock slung between a pair of palm trees lay still. The qualities that made the Cali attractive were same ones that made it undesirable. Sitting in the

Cali Hotel, I felt that my trip to the Isthmus had come to a sudden close, and that I had returned to the world I was intent on escaping.

When compared with the restaurants in other Mexican hotels, the Cali restaurant was fairly ritzy. The tables had white linen tablecloths with matching napkins and silverware that was genuine silver. The menus on our table were voluminous, and we both took our time reading them. When it came time to place our orders, the waiter looked at me, and I ordered in quantity: salad, soup, an entrée, and dessert. Cristina declined ordering food altogether, asking only for a non-alcoholic beverage. I asked why she hadn't ordered anything. "I'm not hungry," she said. This was a first for me. A dinner date in which one of the participants refuses to eat. This put me off. Possibly, she was retaliating for my refusal to eat at Los Mangos the day before.

While we waited for our orders to arrive, Cristina grew unusually quiet, not at all her effervescent self. It occurred to me that I might draw her out with questions about her family, a favorite topic with all the Latinos I know. And for a time, this worked. When it became clear that I had forgotten some of the names of the dozen relatives I met at Los Mangos, she appeared to be disappointed. I had confused her brother with a brother-in-law and an aunt with a niece.

Our waiter brought my soup and salad. I began eating. The silent Cristina had nothing better to do than watch me shovel food into my mouth, and this made me nervous. Between bites, I wiped my mouth and mustache compulsively, sure that I had smeared them with salad dressing or soup. This would not have been so worrisome if Cristina were eating, too. But she was neither speaking nor eating, and this allowed her all the time in the world to watch and be sickened. Cristina continued her silent vigil through the entrée and into dessert. Ten minutes into my meal, she was so silent that I moved my chair back a foot or two and turned sideways so that I was facing the Germans. Though they were twenty feet away, they were eating and conversing, and this arrangement suited me better than my own.

By the time I had finished eating, Cristina's silence had worn me down so completely that I did something foolish. I knew that by revealing something intimate about myself, I could lure her into asking questions and maybe from there, we'd enter into a conversation. "Last night," I said, "I had a dream about my girlfriend that woke me and kept me up for several hours. I remember little about the dream except that its message was clear. My girlfriend, Esmeralda, was sleeping with other men."

"But this was just a dream," Cristina said.

"No, it was not," I said. "Five years ago, Esmeralda and I visited my mother in Los Angeles." Esmeralda had always been emotionally explosive. On this occasion we were in bed, and I had fallen asleep when she went off. She was angry, she said, because of the lack of sex in our relationship. "There has to be something wrong with you," she said. Then, as if to prove her point, she got out of bed. She opened her suitcase, stripped off her pajamas and put her black swimsuit on. Then she stood in front of me at the foot of the bed. "Look at this body," she said. "How can you not be excited?" Her body was always worth looking at so I did look, and, yes, she was in great shape. She got back in bed. "And if you want to know the truth," she said, "I have a lover." I said nothing. I tried making love to her, but she resisted. When this failed, I passed my hand through her hair. This soothes her, and soon she fell asleep.

"I believe the dream was a warning from my subconscious," I said. "Since that night five years ago, we've never spoken about her lover, if he indeed exists. But I worry from time to time that my failure to confront her has been a kind of silent consent."

"The way I see it," Cristina said, "you have two options. Either you close your eyes and mouth and reconcile with her, or you leave her."

"This is the decision I have to make," I said.

"If I were you," she said, "I'd hire a private detective." I controlled the urge to laugh, but at the same time I regretted my confession as soon as it was out of my mouth. In Mexican terms, I was a *cabrón*, a cuckold, a man too weak to confront a woman who's been cheating on him, and I knew Cristina's estimation of me fell with what I had revealed.

After I paid the bill, Cristina asked if I'd like to walk through the patio. This seemed an odd request. We had already seen everything worth seeing in the patio from our table. Nonetheless, I agreed, and we walked along a stone path to the pool. She lingered at the pool's edge, trying to make eye contact with me. Then the breeze moved the water, and the light in the pool cast reflections across Cristina's face, and I saw again that she was beautiful. But I stepped back, and we walked toward the hammock, where it was darker still. "Don't you want to try the hammock?" she said. Rather than respond, I turned away and looked in the direction of the restaurant. Our walk in the patio was as close as Cristina would come to making a pass. It was as assertive as she would get in the way of making herself available to me.

Understanding this, I then realized what her silence had been about. She knew I wanted to hear her talk, to find out what made her tick, and what made Isthmus women tick in general. I wanted talk; she wanted a fling, and either I gave myself to her or she'd have nothing to say. But don't get me wrong. I took no pleasure from her desire to have me, because I doubt it was me she was after. Long ago, at a flop house in Mexico City that catered to young Europeans, I learned something important about a certain class of educated, well-bred women: They loved little more than a brief affair with a man who's about to leave town. "I would have loved you longer," I often heard them say and smile, "but you had to leave." A woman's behavior—especially of the amorous kind—is more often and more carefully scrutinized than men's. But if a man is not a part of the community, or is about to leave it, there is less to scrutinize, and as a consequence, women act more freely on their desires.

Cristina and I walked along the stone path back to the restaurant and then crossed the parking lot in silence. When Cristina unlocked the door to her car, but before she had gotten in, she half-spoke, half-sang a kind of lamentation she would repeat several times over the next twenty-four hours. "Y tú a la reconciliación" (And you to the reconciliation).

The Investigator

That night, I finished reading Ernest Shackelton's *South* in my room at
the Oasis. *South* was the last of the three books I brought with me from
San Francisco, so I paid Julin a visit, and she lent me *Juchitán, la ciudad
de las mujeres*. It was an odd-looking book. The brick-colored jacket
featured a photo of a cocky Istmeña in huipil and enagua, her legs
spread open and her hands dangling between them in a way that called
attention to her womanhood. As soon as I returned to my room and
climbed back in bed, I did what I always do on discovering a book about
the Isthmus. I checked for the author's stance on matriarchy. Twenty-six
pages into the book, I found this: "In the course of the investigation we
realized that in Juchitán, the attention focused on women in reality re-
volves around the figure of the mother. For this reason, Beverly Chiñas,
the only person who until the present has published an investigation on
the women of this region speaks about 'matrifocality' in a broad and
characteristic sense: 'the culture is centered around the mother.' We will
also use these concepts. The comparison of our results with those of the
investigation of different matriarchies, however, makes us think that it is
precise and legitimate, in the case of Juchitán, to speak of a contemporary matriarchy."

This was a milestone, or so it seemed at first. A book with anthropology written all over it — on the cover and the inside flap and the copy-
right page — made the assertion that Juchitán's society was indeed matriarchal. This assertion refuted Chiñas's claim that anthropologists had
never encountered any truly matriarchal cultures. Published in Mexico
by Consejo Editorial in 1994, *Juchitán, la ciudad de las mujeres* forms part
of the Oaxacan Institute of Culture's anthropology collection. The

authors, who lived over a year in Juchitán, could hardly be called superficial observers or any of the other terms concocted by the supposed insiders. On closer examination, however, the authors weren't exactly
anthropologists. Hidden on the inside flap at the back of the book was
a single paragraph describing the authors as a team of "German investigators." Coordinator Veronika Bennholdt-Thomsen led the team, con-
sisting of Cornelia Giebeler and Brigitte Holzer, also investigators, and
Mexican sociologist Marina Meneses. None were anthropologists.

Putting aside the authors' credentials, I experienced a minor epiphany on reading Bennholdt-Thomsen that night. She addressed a fundamental problem with the conception of matriarchal systems that has
clouded the thinking of anthropologists and non-anthropologists alike.
In contrast with other Isthmus observers, Bennholdt-Thomsen defined
matriarchy *before* she used the term. This might seem like splitting
hairs, when in fact it is crucial. Without knowing beforehand the specific criteria that define a social system such as matriarchy or patriarchy,
identifying the Isthmus as one or the other is meaningless. And though
you might think that everyone has an intuitive idea about the meaning
of matriarchy, the variety of definitions found in common desk dictionaries suggests otherwise. The *Oxford English Dictionary,* for example,
defines matriarchy as "A social organization in which the mother is
head of the family and descent is through the female line." *Merriam-
Webster's Collegiate Dictionary* defines matriarchy as "a system of social
organization in which descent and inheritance are traced through the
female line." The *Oxford American Dictionary's* definition is brief but
muddy: "A society in which women have most of the power." If popular
dictionaries such as these disagree about the definition of matriarchy,
blaming outsiders when they use the term loosely makes no sense.

The only exception to anthropologists' failure to define terms might
be Chiñas, whose definition is circular at best: "[Matriarchies] are cultures in which women's roles are the mirror image of men's roles in
patriarchal cultures." As is obvious, this definition begs the question:
What is patriarchy? In addition to calling into question anthropologists'
failure to define matriarchy, Bennholdt-Thomsen's definition made it
clear that I had made the same error as the anthropologists when I
asked Istmeños their stance on matriarchy. How could Istmeños say yes
or no when neither they nor I had a clear conception of what matriarchy

meant? Quizzing Istmeños about matriarchy was analogous to asking subsistence farmers in Africa or Kamchatka if their form of government was a republic or a democracy. The question would only make sense if both parties agree on the meaning of these terms.

Bennholdt-Thomsen prefaces her definition of matriarchy by explaining that during the last twenty years, feminist research has broadened our knowledge of nonpatriarchal societies. "For example," writes Bennholdt-Thomsen, "Heide Göttner-Abendroth has reviewed the historic literature and existing ethnographic material for East Asia, Indonesia and Oceania. With this comparison as a basis, Göttner-Abendroth brought out and put into relief the common structural characteristics of the societies centered around women and motherhood that distinguish them from patriarchal societies." Bennholdt-Thomsen then points out that some of the traits that make Juchitán stand out so sharply from other cultures can be found in Göttner-Abendroth's list of the characteristics of matriarchal societies.

The first characteristic of a matriarchal society, Bennholdt-Thomsen tells us, is its agrarian nature. The majority of inhabitants in a matriarchal society live from subsistence farming and participate in cyclical celebrations of festivals depending on the seasons of the year. Some, like Chiñas, would agree this is so in the Isthmus: "Zapotecs practice mixed-cash subsistence farming, raising some crops totally for sale and others mostly for home consumption." The cyclical celebrations criterion is also clearly met. May and December, planting and harvesting, are linked in every Istmeño's mind.

The second characteristic of a matriarchal society, according to Bennholdt-Thomsen, is generosity and reciprocal giving such as what can be seen in the organization and staging of Isthmus velas. "Every household must meet ritual expenses some time," writes Chiñas, "often unexpectedly when resources are low." A steady income is something most Istmeños dream of, and as a consequence, most respond to this insecurity with their own mutual-aid mechanism. "One household's ritual contribution to another's will be reciprocated on a similar occasion later." Those who reciprocate in this way are considered *buena gente* (good people), a trait that is at the heart of being an Istmeño. It would be difficult to find anyone, insider or outsider, who would disagree that this criterion is also met.

The third characteristic in Bennholdt-Thomsen's definition is a parallelism with respect to the cult of ancestors and the reinterpretation of the dominant religion, integrating elements of animistic and natural religions. Poniatowska writes at length about the continued presence of pagan attitudes toward totems. "[In Juchitán] the only ones who count are animals. They are the kings, the totems, the signs of identity. Nothing that I do, I do for myself but for the animal I carry inside." John Tutino also addresses this issue directly in a chapter he wrote for *Zapotec Struggles*. Sometime after the arrival of Spanish missionaries, Isthmus Zapotecs began converting to Christianity, even though they continued to negotiate with "the Forces of Nature that ruled their agriculture, their fertility and their health." In the process, they reinterpreted Christianity, creating what Tutino describes as a kind of "Zapotec Christianity." The processions I witnessed in the Isthmus often featured a totem of one type or another bringing up the rear, most often a swordfish, but sometimes an alligator. Most velas honor Christian saints, but Vela del Lagarto (Vigil of the Lizard) is the oldest of all and has a drawing power that rivals the largest Isthmus festivals.

Bennholdt-Thomsen's fourth characteristic is that the line of descent is traced through the mother. Here, Bennholdt-Thomsen flounders, and Covarrubias comes closest to the truth: "[Although women might have] their own lands, houses, jewelry and so forth . . . Many lands are owned communally by an entire family, in which case the property is equally divided among the sons and daughters, but most often it passes from father to elder sons." In the fifty years following the publishing of *Mexico South*, no anthropologist has ever suggested anything to the contrary.

Bennholdt-Thomsen's last characteristic of a matriarchal society is that women are in charge of commerce. This characteristic is open to dispute. Some observers—such as Covarrubias and Poniatowska—would agree, others—including Campbell and Saynes-Vázquez—would not.

Even if one were to assume that all of Bennholdt-Thomsen's criteria for a matriarchy were met, there are other, more fundamental problems with her definition. What first strikes those who read how Bennholdt-Thomsen defined matriarchy is this: It makes no reference to a hierarchical structure in which women occupy positions in the upper echelons. In the pages that follow, Bennholdt-Thomsen's definition addresses this apparent contradiction by explaining that a modern-day matriarchal society—by its nature—would never permit such hierarchies. This, Bennholdt-Thomsen tells us, would only invert the worst element of the warlike and destructive male patriarchy. "Lastly, it is worthwhile mentioning what the experts on matriarchy or non-patriarchal relations accentuate: The search [for a matriarchy] does not imply inverting the common reality, changing it for the domination of the other sex, in this case domination by women. The matriarchal structure, by definition, excludes this type of power relations."

What Bennholdt-Thomsen is implying is that according to her definition of matriarchy, men and women share equal amounts of power. And though Bennholdt-Thomsen does not provide any further detail about men's role in a matriarchal society, Göttner-Abendroth does. "The young men," Göttner-Abendroth writes, "who have left the house of their mother after their marriage, do not have to go very far. Actually, in the evening they just go to the neighboring house, where their wives live, and they come back very early—at dawn. This form of marriage is called *visiting marriage,* and it is restricted to the night. It means that matriarchal men have no right to live in the house of their wives."

What can be made of Bennholdt-Thomsen's definition? In one way, I found it self-serving. For more than forty years, feminists have attempted to locate a matriarchal society in which women truly held power over men. None succeeded, and most feminists admitted defeat. Others, such as Bennholdt-Thomsen and Göttner-Abendroth, redefined matriarchy in such a way that the key element—power—is shared equally between men and women. By this definition, there are hundreds of matriarchal societies, one of which happens to be the Isthmus. For the time being, I suspended my judgment on this redefinition until I could research it and others like it more fully in San Francisco. All the same, Göttner-Abendroth's redefinition reminded me of a story I once heard about a woman who travels the world in search of affordable diamonds. Although she never finds such diamonds, she does find a handful of cut glass that looked very much like diamonds—at least to the uneducated eye. Soon, she gives up and returns home with the cut glass. How does she deal with her failure? She changes the definition of diamonds to include cut glass. Now, at last, she has her affordable diamonds.

The General's Daughter

General Heliodoro Charis—the same general whose loyal patronage and troops brought the fledging Casa Verde to life—had but one legitimate daughter. Christened Lugarda Charis, she was born at home in the general's mansion on May 2, 1938. Her earliest memories were centered around dolls made with twigs called *pancha yagas*. They were a cut above the common plaster dolls other children brought to her home to play with, and at times Lugarda wondered whether the neighborhood children came to visit with her or her dolls. Lugarda's only complaint about her childhood was a cloistered feeling because she rarely left home. Children could visit her, but rarely the other way around.

When it came time to enroll her in school, the general went against the conventions of the moneyed class. Other families with the kind of income her father had would have enrolled her in one of Juchitán's private schools, but Lugarda's father wanted no special privileges for his only daughter. He enrolled her in Centro Escolar Juchitán, an army barracks he had converted into Juchitán's largest school. While there, Lugarda made friends with Delia Fuentes, who remembered visiting the Charis home in those days. "I was always afraid of her father, General Charis, because he was so strict and insisted we study constantly. 'Don't do anything except study,' was one of his favorite expressions." Because Lugarda was the only child, the general was even more rigid concerning her comings and goings from home. If a family member or maid was not available to accompany her, she was not allowed to set foot outside the house.

Lugarda attended high school at Juchitán's School of Special Learning Number Twelve. While there, Lugarda and Delia discovered a passion for basketball that would carry through to their university years. There was a basketball court nearby, and at five foot six, Lugarda was one of the tallest girls in Juchitán. She joined Escuela de Enseñanza's team and competed against other high school teams in the region for the next three years. Once, the city of Juchitán invited one of Mexico City's basketball teams, the Ferrocarriles, to compete with Lugarda's team at the local high school. Some of the players stayed at Lugarda's, the rest at Delia's. Although Juchitán's team lost the game, this exposure to the Ferrocarriles would play a role in Lugarda and Delia's future.

After high school, Lugarda enrolled in the nursing program at UNAM—Universidad Nacional Autónoma de Mexico (National University). At first, Lugarda lived with her mother and father in Hotel Buen Tono, where the general always stayed when visiting Mexico City. He liked its central location on 16 de Septiembre with the doors that opened onto the main plaza, and money was never a question. Lugarda renewed her friendship with Delia, and they began playing basketball together. They contacted the Ferrocarriles and were invited to become part of the team. But the distance from UNAM to the Ferrocarriles gymnasium was great, and the bus ride took forever. Lugarda and Delia had to decide which was more important, their studies or basketball. After they had completed a full year with the team, both chose to apply themselves full-time as students.

Lugarda graduated from UNAM as an obstetric nurse in 1958. She served a five-year internship at the Instituto de Seguridad y Servicios Sociales in Mexico City and then returned to Juchitán. In 1960, against the wishes of her father, Lugarda married Teodoro Altamirano, a left-wing activist and chemical engineer from Juchitán. Lugarda met Teodoro at an Isthmus dance that celebrated his graduation from UNAM. In his student days, Teodoro had been a member of the Partido Popular Socialista, considered by many to be a front for the Communist Party. His membership in the party won him the nickname Rojo, which stuck with him for life.

At the time Lugarda met Teodoro, Lugarda was not politically active, but she was well informed on this topic because of the many politicians who frequented her father's house in Juchitán. Following the example of her father—who refused to be wed in a church—Teodoro and Lugarda married in a civil ceremony. Shortly after the marriage,

Lugarda's mother gave her a piece of land near the general's house. Lugarda and Teodoro built their family home on this site.

When Lugarda became pregnant with her first child, she asked her father to sponsor his baptism. Still angry about Lugarda's choice for a husband, the general refused. Lugarda then approached Delia, who agreed. But when the baby was born, Charis changed his mind and agreed to be the godfather. Lugarda then approached Delia and said, "My father wants to baptize the child, and I feel bad about this." Delia told her not to worry and to use the opportunity to reconcile with her father. You'll have other children, she said. Over time, Delia was proven right: she was godmother for Lugarda's second and third children.

In 1964, the general died from diabetes aggravated by alcohol. In the same year, Lugarda began a twenty-year career as a midwife. In those days, Juchitán had no hospital and lacked physicians, so midwifes were counted upon to deliver babies. Lugarda encouraged her patients to consult with her long before delivery, making pregnant women a common sight in Lugarda's household. When the contractions began, however, Lugarda chose to assist the birth at the pregnant mother's home. The majority of the babies, and by far the easiest to deliver, were those born head first. More difficult were the feet first, but by far the most trying were the *caritas:* babies born face first, who almost always led with their chins. Lugarda would touch here and there, trying to get a grip, but she was never sure if what she was touching was the nose or the eyes or the mouth. Lugarda delivered just two *caritas* in twenty years, both successfully. And though Lugarda assisted in four to five deliveries per week during this time, no child died on Lugarda's watch.

In some Isthmus cities such as San Blas, the father is sometimes present at birth, offering words of encouragement to the mother. Once the baby is born, he is responsible for storing the placenta in a jar and burying it underneath the family patio. In Juchitán, however, Lugarda reported that men were rarely present at birth, and she preferred it that way. Although men meant well, they had the tendency to push at the womb and force was not what was needed. At times the babies were born in seconds, others took hours. In either case the pay was the same, $5 per child.

In the early days of Lugarda's career as midwife, the pain of childbirth was borne with Mexican valor. Pain killers were usually unavailable, and even when they could be found, they were too expensive for the average Istmeño family. The pain was worst for mothers giving birth for the first time, especially when they were teenagers, and there were many of these, as Zapotec custom allowed marriage of girls as young as thirteen or fourteen. Later in her career, Lugarda had access to drugs that helped avoid the hemorrhaging that sometimes occurred after birth. In rare occurrences, she also used a glucose serum with pitocin—a synthetic hormone that stimulates contractions—but this was a luxury for most women and could be purchased only in a hospital. Three days after birth, mothers would bring their newborn daughters to the Charis household, where Lugarda would pierce their ears using a needle and thread.

As the years went by, it became clear that Teodoro was a good father and a responsible husband, even though his excessive drinking was a constant bother for his family and would later cost him his life. In the political arena, Lugarda described him as provocative and combative. Despite his left-wing tendencies as a university student, Teodoro was a registered member of PRI for thirty-three years. Throughout this period, his archenemies were his fellow students who rose to power when they formed a coalition of left-wing parties that included COCEI and PRD. The coalition accused Teodoro of exploiting his marriage to the general's daughter and identifying himself with the Charis's legacy for the sole purpose of winning the votes and support of Juchitán's disenfranchised. In 1988, Teodoro abandoned PRI and joined PARM (Partido Auténtico de la Revolución Mexicana), a coalition that supported the presidential campaign of Cuauhtémoc Cárdenas. Although Cárdenas lost the election, PARM made Teodoro a candidate for federal deputy, and ultimately he won.

In all, Lugarda bore Teodoro four children. Time passed, and the children matured and took on professions. The first became an agricultural engineer, the second a captain in the Mexican army, the third a journalist, and the last a civil engineer. Tragedy visited when the car in which Lugarda's son the captain was driving exploded outside Mexico City. As always in Mexico, the details are vague, the rumors many. Family members describe his death as a car accident. Others, including the Mexican news media, say the captain was deeply involved in the trafficking of narcotics, and the accident was no mistake.

In 1988, PRI invited Lugarda to participate in a primary to name a candidate for mayor of Juchitán. Because of his love of politics, Teodoro encouraged Lugarda to take part. When she was reluctant, he asked Delia to help persuade her to run. Delia did as she was asked, but in the end, Lugarda refused.

In 1997, after a long struggle with diabetes, the sixty-five-year-old Teodoro died. A year later, the governor of Oaxaca asked Lugarda to run as candidate for mayor in Juchitán. After consulting with her children, Lugarda accepted the proposal, though she had the premonition she would lose. Nonetheless, the support prior to the election was strong. In addition to monetary support, she received free supplies, newspaper ads, and commercial spots on the radio. Smaller donations that could be stamped with her name also rolled in: *paliacates,* T-shirts, footballs. She did not use any of her own money for the campaign, but that part was easy. She had no money—other than her husband's pension—she could have used for this purpose. Throughout the campaign, many Juchitecans would approach her, offering her a dollar or two, saying, "Take this, even if it only means a dozen *paliacates.*" Others, who Lugarda believed must have been old friends of her father, would come with loads of foodstuff for the hungry campaigners: sacks of sugar, rice, beans, bottles of beer, cooking oil, and sodas.

What Lugarda brought to the campaign was energy and persistence. She visited all of Juchitán's outlying districts, often soliciting support door by door. Her only complaint about the campaign arose when she was visited at home by certain Juchitecos who would say, "Look, I'll sell you my vote for 200 pesos." This enraged her. "I ran a lot of these people out of my house." On election day, the coalition received 16,000 votes. Lugarda received 14,500—by far the most votes that any single candidate received in Juchitán's elections. Although Lugarda suspected that fraud might have been involved, she refused an investigation. "I've gotten this far because I refuse to quibble. I'm not going to start now."

On Tuesday, my last day in Juchitán, I woke late. Cristina had arranged an eleven o'clock meeting with Lugarda, and already it was half past ten. I dressed quickly, tucked my journal under my arm, and descended the stairs to the Fortress restaurant. I sat at the only available table near the swinging doors and wrote questions for Lugarda. Ten minutes later, Cristina joined me. Her mood had improved; she was as talkative and bright-eyed as the night we met in the lobby. Maybe she dealt well with rejection, or maybe I had imagined her desire for me the night before. In either case, I showed her my list of questions, and she corrected my Spanish and suggested a phrase here and there.

When eleven o'clock came and went, I began to doubt that Lugarda would show. As Cristina and I waited, now in silence, there was the usual flow of businessmen with strained faces and striped ties who gravitated to the Western style of the Fortress restaurant. Though subtle, all the elements of this style were there: the glossy, gray walls and marbleized columns; the waitresses in black and white uniforms; the poorly imitated club sandwiches and continental breakfasts; and the television reciting stock market news over the noise of an air-conditioner. Taken together, these details gave the restaurant a Western feel, as though management wanted to cater to anyone except Istmeños. And, in large part, they had succeeded. I'd never seen a street vendor, male or female, push their way through the Fortress's doors to hawk their goods. There were no men in sandals stopping by for a beer or women in traditional dress eating fried iguana. Other than a painting of a woman in huipil and enagua hanging in the lobby, the restaurant was free of Zapotec tradition.

And so it was that when a middle-aged woman in a bright, full-length skirt and flowery huipil pushed her way through the swinging doors and entered the restaurant, I put down my pen and stared. She was a large woman, possibly the tallest woman I had ever seen in Juchitán. She wore her hair parted down the middle and braided into two strands in the style of a Navajo Indian. Her face was rugged and dark, her nose hooked, and her full-length skirt was tied loosely around a plump belly she made no effort to hide. For a moment, the woman stood still scanning the restaurant for a familiar face until her gaze fell upon Cristina, and she turned in our direction.

Watching her cross the room was a revelation. It did not seem to matter to her that she was the only woman in the room with pigtails, or that her dress was one hundred years out of style with what the other women in the restaurant were wearing. And the more I watched her walk, the more I was reminded of the confidence with which the women had confronted Father Ben the day before. The women at the blockade also came to mind, especially those who stood in the path of the renegade truck, and the women from Ixtepec who'd knocked Governor Ruiz Jiménez to the ground.

According to outsiders, this self-assurance—which at times borders on audacity—is a key characteristic of Isthmus women. Poniatowska and her photographer, Graciela Iturbide, were well aware of this trait. The photographs of women in *Juchitán de las mujeres* provide a kind of visual evidence that Isthmus women are matriarchs. One of Iturbide's most suggestive photos captures a plump, self-assured mother nursing her tiny male infant; another shows elderly women marching fearlessly at the front of a demonstration while the men follow at a distance somewhere behind. Bennholdt-Thomsen, in *Juchitán, la ciudad de las mujeres,* was also aware of imagery's power. Although works of anthropology like hers usually feature a negligible number of photographs, Bennholdt-Thomsen hired photographer Cornelia Suhan to shoot eighteen photos of more than forty Isthmus women—all of them posed, all of them self-assured.

When the woman reached our table, Cristina introduced her as Lugarda. For a time, Cristina and Lugarda exchanged news and gossip. Then Lugarda turned to me and spoke about General Charis's childhood. "My father was an illiterate child who never lived with his parents," Lugarda said. "His grandmother raised him, and he spent his time hunting iguanas, rabbits, armadillos, and deer." In 1916, when he was twenty, he enlisted in the rebel army under Felipe López and eventually rose to the level of general. Four years later, the revolution ground to a halt. Charis returned home in control of Juchitán's spoils, which he used to buy a large amount of terrain adjacent to Juchitán. "His first act as leader was to reward each of the soldiers [with] a piece of land," Lugarda said. "The soldiers used the land as a place where they could build a home, plant seeds, and cultivate crops."

Charis next approached the secretary of the Republic with his plans for building schools. "Why do you want schools if there are no teachers?" the secretary asked. "Because," Charis replied, "you are going to give me teachers and materials as well." When the schools were completed, Charis scoured the Isthmus and later the state of Oaxaca to bring students to the newly built schools. Lamentably, he found no more than twenty students. "They stayed at our house," Lugarda said. "He maintained them and fed them as they studied. He did not want other children to suffer what he did as an illiterate peasant." In addition to the Centro Escolar where Lugarda went to school, he built a secondary school that now houses the Casa de Cultura.

"There was one thing he did that might have been wrong," Lugarda said. "He took advantage of the fact that Lázaro Cárdenas had shut down the churches. He took the land on which he built the high school away from the church."

"What was his attitude toward women?" I asked.

"He had lots of women," Lugarda said and smiled.

"He also had many, many children," Cristina said. Then Lugarda thought a minute, and answered my question more directly.

"I would say he wanted women to join the struggle for Juchitán. Because in the epoch of the revolution there were many, many female comrades who followed him all over Mexico."

"Were these women soldiers," I asked, "or camp followers?" Here Lugarda paused as if she did not understand me. Cristina motioned to my journal where I kept the photo of the women with the Winchester rifles in their laps. I took the photo out of my journal and showed it to Lugarda. She studied it for a moment.

"This was taken in 1912," she said, "during the time of Ché Gomez." Given the date Lugarda provided, and a little research, I was later able to identify the women in the photo. Both belonged to the liberal Green Party, founded by Ché Gomez in opposition to the conservative Red Party. In order to identify themselves on the streets in Juchitán, the men who were Greens tucked a sprig of leaves into their hat, while the women would wear green ribbons. The Reds, on the other hand, would wear a red hat band if male or a red flower in their hair if female. As tension between the two parties grew, the women began wearing matching huipiles and enaguas in solid red or green, depending on their political affiliation. Heated arguments between one woman wearing green and the other red became commonplace in the market or along the way to it. As time passed, the two groups took up arms, and the heated arguments became bloody battles, hence the photo of Juchitecas with Winchesters.

To calm the increasing violence, police began snatching red flowers and greens sprigs out of women's hair. They also confronted women wearing red or green clothing and asked them to change it to a less provocative color. This enraged the women of Juchitán. They marched on city hall, drew up a document outlining their complaints, and sent it to the governor of the state of Oaxaca. He in turn exerted pressure on the local chief of police, Antonio Escobar. Rather than deal with the difficulties case by case, Escobar issued a regulation banning the use of red or green: "All persons, whatever their sex or age, are completely prohibited from wearing in public places red flowers or green sprigs, whether in a hairdo or on their clothing. Likewise, the use of green or red colored huipiles, enaguas, and bows is prohibited."

When Lugarda handed the photo back to me, she added, "Many women like these in the photo accompanied their husbands into war. Captain Victor Jimenez left with his wife for the revolution, and lots of others followed his example." In all, there were four battalions of Juchitecan soldiers who fought throughout Mexico during the 1910 Revolution, primarily in support of Álvaro Obregon. "Many Juchiteca *soldaderas* also went on these campaigns," writes Campbell, "performing vital tasks such as cooking and smuggling messages in their huipiles and sometimes engaging in the fighting, although they were seldom rewarded for their efforts." Juchitán's women have had a long history of participating in Juchitán's armed struggles, even before the Mexican Revolution. In 1866, for example, women of Juchitán did their part by egging on local men to do battle with the French troops in 1866. "When the French entered Juchitán, these women climbed to the top of the church and saw that they were under siege on all sides," said eyewitness Anastasia Martinez. "They were the ones who rang the church bells and cried out that the Juchitecos should attack the French, who were in retreat. They defeated them over there by the lagoon."

In the years after the revolution, General Charis's ranch provided the income necessary to keep the family intact. "But when times were tough," Lugarda said, "my mother sold meat and milk in the market to help him out like many Isthmus women do for their husbands." Lugarda went on to reiterate what had become a persistent theme with every man or woman I'd spoken to in the Isthmus. "Women don't wait for men to turn money over to them." They work hard also, often harder than their men, but this doesn't make them matriarchs. "What happens is that only women are seen in the market, and that's why we have this myth." But Lugarda had her own spin on the underlying motivation for all of the hard work women did. "Women work hard because we love gold," she said, touching her necklace. "That's why we work, to show off our pride, which is gold."

What I remember most about that morning was Cristina's and Lugarda's reaction to my retelling of the "don't invent" incident at Los Mangos. Although I am not entirely sure why I told Lugarda the story, I would venture to say that I came to respect her quickly and thought that she might provide insight into the nature of the disagreement. I told the story in detail over the course of the next several minutes: how I had tried to fill in the gaps about what I knew about Santa Inés with a little guesswork, and Cristina's aggravating response. "I hadn't known Cristina for more than five hours," I said in closing, "and there she was, telling me what to do."

What came next was unexpected. Lugarda and Cristina looked at each other, and a laugh that began low in their throats bubbled up and became so loud I looked away in embarrassment. And every time their laughter would die down, they'd look at each other, and then at me, and start laughing all over again. Why they laughed, I failed to see, unless they caught a glimpse of themselves in my story as complex, and at times contradictory, women about whom generalizations were unwise. And it came to me then that apart from marrying an Isthmus woman, no number of return trips, interviews, or analysis would get me any nearer to understanding them. Then the laughter subsided, and when I shook hands with Lugarda, I studied her eyes and saw in them something neither insiders nor anthropologists had accounted for. Clearly, as the tourist myth explained, outsiders had based their opinions on the abundance of women hard at work and the scarcity of men in Isthmus towns. But neither anthropologists nor insiders had considered that intuition was also at play. Even though the tourists—most of whom were Mexican—had little contact with Istmeñas, they were not blind to the confidence in their eyes and the freedom with which they joked and cursed and laughed as they sold their goods in the market. And when they made the comparison between Isthmus women and their own, they found the gap so wide that they went home saying Amazon to anyone who would listen. This was a worthy thing, I decided, and I resolved to do the same.

Epilogue

The epiphany I experienced on reading *Juchitán, la ciudad de las mujeres*'s redefinition of matriarchy deepened when I returned to San Francisco. The more I researched, the more I learned that everyone but Bennholdt-Thomsen relied on a common understanding of the term *matriarchy* when no such understanding existed. And so it was clear to me, that before I could voice an opinion about the quality of life in a matriarchy, I would first have to find a suitable definition of the term. If Bennholdt-Thomsen could define matriarchy for her own purposes, I reasoned, then surely there would be other definitions, one of which might appeal to my understanding of the term. And so I began my hunt, convinced that research would soon reveal a commonsense definition of matriarchy that would show Bennholdt-Thomsen's characterization—with egalitarian relations for the sexes—to be an anomaly.

At the beginning of my research, I had the good luck to come across a book by anthropologist Peggy Sanday, who shared my concern about inexact use of the term *matriarchy*. Published in 2002, *Women at the Center: Life in a Modern Day Matriarchy* documents the unusual traditions of the Minangkabau, one of Indonesia's largest ethnic groups. "On my first visit," writes Sanday, "I encountered many people who proudly referred to their society as a *matriarchaat,* a term used by Dutch colonial officials in the nineteenth and early twentieth centuries to describe the Minangkabau." Like the Zapotecs, the Minangkabau have resisted outside influence, and many of their traditions governing gender relations are intact. "My journey into the heart of the Minangkabau," Sanday writes, "has convinced me that a challenge to the Western definition of matriarchy—rule by women—is long overdue. This vision of matriarchy has produced more than a century of squabbling. It arose in the nineteenth century by analogy with 'patriarchy' or 'father right,' not from ethnographic studies of female-oriented social forms." Using this rule-by-women definition, Sanday explains, "countless scholars went looking for primitive matriarchies . . . but they turned up nothing." She laments the fact that because no matriarchies were ever found, many feminist writers within and outside anthropology have avoided the term *matriarchy*.

And then, unexpectedly, Sanday, like Bennholdt-Thomsen, insists on using the very term she blames for the squabbling, even though her book jacket states that the Minangkabau are known in Indonesia for their "egalitarian, democratic relationships between men and women." Why has she chosen to describe Minangkabau society as matriarchal? "I prefer to retain the term matriarchy out of courtesy and respect for the Minangkabau usage." Both Bennholdt-Thomsen's and Sanday's definitions seem counterintuitive. At its very core, matriarchy pertains, as feminist historian Gerder Lerner pointed out, "only when women hold power over men, not alongside them."

Of all the definitions I examined, and there were dozens, *Encyclopedia Britannica*'s appealed to me most because it defined both matriarchy and patriarchy as *hypothetical* social systems. The implication here is that a true matriarchy, in which women hold absolute power over men, could only occur hypothetically. Anthropologist Ellen Gruenbaum sees patriarchy in much the same way: "There is of course no society in which all males have power over all females. Think of the male two year old and his competent older sister, adult mother, and grandmother. Each of these females no doubt has significant say over the small boy. And yet that same small male child when older may well move into a position of power and authority over women as the boys become men." Treating matriarchy and patriarchy as hypothetical opposites also agreed with what I heard from the men and women of the Isthmus. Although every now and then I encountered a relationship in which a woman seemed to dominate, I found none in which a woman held absolute power over her husband. "That would be slavery," as one Istmeña put it, "and there are no slaves in the Isthmus."

At about the same time I found *Britannica*'s definition of matriarchy, I came across an article written by Howard Campbell that examines the observations of European travelers who visited the Isthmus during the colonial period. "Colonial era reflections on Zapotec people are examples of the growing 'planetary consciousness' of Europeans who sought to categorize unfamiliar animals, plants, and people in terms of concepts understandable to them while they simultaneously harnessed the economic potential of the new lands they explored and colonized." This tendency to categorize is at the root of the controversy over Isthmus women in that it attempts to fit Isthmus society into one of the Westerner's predefined categories such as matrilineal, matrifocal, or matriarchal. A much better way to conceptualize Isthmus gender relations that avoids categorization is a model suggested by Chiñas in *The Isthmus Zapotecs:* "[There is] great variation from one society to another in the status of women as a group compared to men—from equal at one pole to grossly unequal at the other pole. Theoretically one might place all societies on a continuum designating the status of women as compared to men from equal on one side to grossly unequal at the other end of the pole."

Chiñas would place the Yanomamo of South America—who practice polygyny and female infanticide—near the low-status pole for women. "The Isthmus Zapotecs," Chiñas writes, "would be near the high-status or equal pole. Where our own society in pre-1970 times would have fallen I am not prepared to state, although I perceive it as having been lower than that of the Isthmus Zapotecs."

The beauty of Chiñas's model is that it avoids categorization and works even better if you extend it, placing the hypothetical pole of patriarchy at one end and the hypothetical pole of matriarchy at the other. Using this extended model, Chiñas would place Zapotecs midway between the two poles. I would suggest that Istmeños are nearer the matriarchal pole, while others, such as Howard Campbell or Saynes-Vázquez, would place Isthmus society nearer the patriarchal pole.

Given this redefinition—that matriarchies are hypothetical—the answer to my question about life being any better in a matriarchy became moot. We can, however, rephrase the question in a way that preserves some of the original meaning: Is life any better when women play a strong role when compared to the male-dominated regions that surround it? Although it is difficult to quantify a quality-of-life question such as this, the World Bank has tracked infant nutrition, which helps shed light on this question. This institution characterizes any child born weighing less than 5.5 pounds as malnourished. In the 1990s, the average weight at birth for Mexican children was 6 pounds at birth, a figure which is reduced substantially in Mexico's poorer states such as Oaxaca and Chiapas and even more so among the rural indigenous, where close to 80 percent of the babies fall into the World Bank's malnourished category. In Juchitán, on the other hand, the average weight in 1989 was 7.3 pounds—one-tenth of a pound less than the U.S. average.

From my own experience, I can say that life in the Isthmus is substantially better when compared to the surrounding regions, especially for women past their childbearing years. Women in this age bracket can attend velas and *lavadas* alone and travel as far and as often as they like unaccompanied by husband or children. Daughters and daughters-in-law increase a middle-aged Istmeña's standing in the community, especially when they can be seen helping with household duties and providing economic support. This help at home allows mature Isthmus women time to devote to making extra money by selling door-to-door or in the marketplace. Women spend this additional money on favorite activities, which often means contributing to a vela for food, beer, or rental of an appropriate site. After menopause, the carefully drawn line between the sexes begins to blur, if not disappear altogether. "Elderly men and women, perhaps lifelong compadres or neighbors," writes Chiñas, "lend one another comfort and moral support during the trying periods of illness and death. These tender relationships between the aged are among the most poignant in the Isthmus Zapotecs."

But how have men fared in Isthmus society? Jorge Contreras, Julin's father, lived through the time when women had complete control of the market. He suggested that the ban on men in the market had a broad range of implications. The most obvious was that men were deprived of learning the art of bargaining, an important skill in a country that had no fixed prices. Though not as important as bargaining skills, there were other implications of the ban. Men were not allowed the luxury of entering the market and considering alternatives before making a purchase. They could only describe what they wanted and hope for the best—if and when they could find a woman to do their buying. The market also represented a missed opportunity to learn and use Spanish with other ethnic groups or foreign traders. Ironically, Isthmus men were allowed to enter foreign-owned shops, but it did them little good. They could not speak Spanish with the owner, nor could they bargain for what they wanted. The end result is that Isthmus men tend to be reserved, while the women, who learned Spanish and developed their skills as traders, are considered assertive.

Though I now find myself in the camp of those who feel Isthmus matriarchy is myth, some small part of me feels that were I to return to the Isthmus once more, I might unearth evidence that would steer me back into the camp of the believers. In his book *In Southern Light,* Alex Shoumatoff describes his 1990 journey to the Amazon River in search of a matriarchal society. At the end of his journey, when he abandoned hope of finding any such women, he posed some of the same questions that still nag at me. "If, as all the evidence seems to indicate, the Amazons or the women without husbands never existed except in the various guises of a universal myth, one question remains: Why do so many of the stories say that the women lived on the Nhamudá? What could be up there? Could there be an undiscovered basis of truth to the stories?" In the end, we are left with what Chiñas calls "the elusive quality of relationships between the sexes." We peel back layer after layer of evidence, finding not what we set out to find, but always something unexpected, and never quite enough.

BIBLIOGRAPHY

INDEX

Bibliography

Agosín, Marjorie. *A Dream of Light and Shadow: Portrait of Latin American Women Writers.* Albuquerque: University of New Mexico Press, 1995.

Albers, Patricia. *Shadows, Fire, Snow: The Life of Tina Modotti.* New York: Clarkson Potter, 1999.

Augur, Helen. *Zapotec.* Garden City, NY: Doubleday, 1954.

Bennholdt-Thomsen, Veronika. *Juchitán, la ciudad de las mujeres.* Oaxaca: Instituto Oaxaqueño de las Culturas, 1997.

Brasseur, Charles Etienne. *Viaje por el istmo de Tehuantepec.* Mexico City: SEP, 1981.

Brown, David Jay, and Rebecca McClen Novick. *Mavericks of the Mind: Conversations for the New Millennium.* Freedom, CA: Crossing Press, 1993.

Burke, Pam. *Zapotecs of Mexico.* Center for International Development and Conflict Management, University of Maryland. 1995. http://www.cidcm.umd.edu (accessed 2002; document no longer available).

Campbell, Howard. *Mexican Memoir: A Personal Account of Anthropology and Radical Politics in Oaxaca.* Westport, CT: Bergin and Garvey. 2001.

———. *Zapotec Renaissance: Ethnic Politics and Cultural Revivalism in Southern Mexico.* Albuquerque: University of New Mexico. 1994.

Campbell, Howard, and Susan Green. "A History of Representations of Isthmus Zapotec Women." *Identities* 3, nos. 1–2 (1996): 155–82.

Campbell, Howard, et al., eds. *Zapotec Struggles: Histories, Politics, and Representations from Juchitán, Oaxaca.* Washington, DC: Smithsonian Institution Press, 1993.

Castillo, Ana. *Goddess of the Americas.* New York: Riverhead Books, 1996.

Charlot, Jean. *An Artist on Art: Collected Essays of Jean Charlot.* Honolulu: University Press of Hawaii, 1972.

———. *Mexican Mural Renaissance.* New York: Hacker Art Books, 1979.

Chiñas, Beverly Newbold. *The Isthmus Zapotecs: A Matrifocal Culture of Mexico.* 2nd ed. New York: Holt, Rinehart, and Winston, 1992.

———. *La Zandunga: Of Fieldwork and Friendship in Southern Mexico.* Prospect Heights, IL: Waveland Press, 1993.

Covarrubias, Miguel. *Mexico South: The Isthmus of Tehuantepec.* New York: Knopf, 1946.

Dibble, Sandra. "The Song of Oaxaca." *National Geographic* 186 (1994): 60–63.

Elena de Valdez, Maria. *The Shadowed Mirror: Representations of Women in Mexican Literature*. Austin: University of Texas Press, 1998.

Fisher, John. *Mexico: The Rough Guide*. London: Rough Guides. 1999.

——. *The Rough Guide: Mexico*. London: Rough Guides, 1985.

Franz, Carl, Lorena Havens, and Steve Rogers. *The People's Guide to Mexico: Wherever You Go — There You Are!!* Santa Fe, NM: John Muir, 1998.

Garcia Pinto, Magdalena. *Women Writers of Latin America: Intimate Histories*. Austin: University of Texas Press, 1991.

Geduld, Harry M., and Ronald Gottesman. *Sergei Eisenstein and Upton Sinclair: The Making and Unmaking of* Que Viva Mexico! Bloomington: Indiana University Press, 1970.

Goodison, Lucy, and Christine Morris. *Ancient Goddesses*. London: British Museum Press, 1998.

Gosling, Maureen. *Blossoms of Fire*. Videocassette. Directed by Maureen Gosling. Oakland, CA: Intrépidas Productions, 2000.

——. "An Indomitable Culture." Interview by Belinda Acosta. *Austin Chronicle Screens*, May 4, 2001. http://www.austinchronicle.com/issues/dispatch/2001-05-04/screens_feature.html.

Göttner-Abendroth, Heide. *The Goddess and Her Heroes*. Stow, Mass.: Anthony Publishing Company, 1995.

Gruenbaum, Ellen. *The Female Circumcision Controversy: An Anthropological Perspective*. Philadelphia: University of Pennsylvania Press, 2001.

Hamovitch, Eric. *Southern Mexico and Yucatan Guide: Your Passport to Great Travel!* Washington, DC: Open Road, 1995.

Henestrosa, Andrés. "The Forms of Sexual Life in Juchitán." In *Zapotec Struggles: Histories, Politics, and Representations from Juchitán, Oaxaca*, ed. Campbell, et al. Washington, DC: Smithsonian Institution Press, 1993.

——. *Los hombres que disperso la danza*. México: M.A. Porrua, 1997.

Herrera, Hayden. *Frida, a Biography of Frida Kahlo*. New York: Perennial Library, c1983.

Iturbide, Graciela, and Elena Poniatowska. *Juchitán de las mujeres*. México City: Ediciones Toledo, 1989.

Jiménez López, Gonzalo. *Historia de Juchitán*. Oaxaca: Carteles Editores PGO, 2000.

Jorgensen, Beth E. *The Writing of Elena Poniatowska: Engaging Dialogues*. Austin: University of Texas Press, 1994.

Krauze, Enrique, and Hank Heifetz. *Mexico: Biography of Power*. New York: HarperCollins, 1997.

Lederer, Jaime. "The Personal Is Political: An Oral History of an Anthropologist." Photocopy. Department of Sociology and Anthropology, University of Texas at El Paso. December 2002.

Leslie, Charles. *Now We Are Civilized*. Detroit: Wayne State University Press, 1960.

Let's Go: Mexico. New York: St. Martin's Press, 1985-.

López, Kimberly. "Internal Colonialism in the Testimonial Process: Elena Poniatowska's 'Hasta no verte, Jesús mío.'" Paper presented at Comparative Literature Symposium on Latin American Women Writers: Canons, Traditions, Revisions. Texas Tech University, Lubbock, January 26-28, 1995.

———. "Internal Colonialism in the Testimonial Process: Elena Poniatowska's 'Hasta no verte, Jesús mío.'" *Symposium* 52, no. 1 (1998): 21-39.

López Chiñas, Gabriel. *El concepto de la muerte entre los Zapotecas.* México: Revista Folklórico de México, 1948.

Marcus, Joyce, and Kent Flannery. *Zapotec Civilization.* London: Thames and Hudson, 1996.

Miano Borruso, Marinella. "Hombres, mujeres y muxe en la sociedad zapoteca del Istmo de Tehuantepec." PhD diss., Escuela Nacional de Antropología e Historia. Mexico City, 1999.

———. *Hombre, mujer y muxe': En el istmo de Tehuantepec.* Mexico, D.F.: Instituto Nacional de Antropología e Historia, 2002.

Parsons, Elsie Clews. *Mitla: Town of the Souls and Other Zapoteco-Speaking Pueblos of Oaxaca, Mexico.* Chicago: University of Chicago Press, 1936.

Perez, Esther R., James Kalas, and Nina Kalas. *Those Years of the Revolution, 1910-1920, Authentic Bilingual Life Experiences as Told by Veterans of the War.* San Jose, CA: Aztlan Today, 1974.

Poniatowska, Elena. *Here's To You, Jesusa.* New York: Penguin Books, 2002.

———. "Juchitán, a Town of Women." In *Zapotec Struggles: Histories, Politics, and Representations from Juchitán, Oaxaca,* ed. Campbell, et al. Washington, DC: Smithsonian Institution Press, 1993.

Ruiz Campbell, Obdulia. "Representations of Isthmus Women: A Zapotec Woman's Point of View." In *Zapotec Struggles: Histories, Politics, and Representations from Juchitán, Oaxaca,* ed. Campbell, et al. Washington, DC: Smithsonian Institution Press, 1993.

Salas, Elizabeth. *Soldaderas in the Mexican Military: Myth and History.* Austin: University of Texas Press, 1990.

Sanday, Peggy. *Women at the Center: Life in a Modern Day Matriarchy.* Ithaca, NY: Cornell University Press, 2002.

Saynes-Vázquez, Edaena. "Galán Pa dxandí. 'That Would Be Great If It Were True': Zapotec Women's Comment on Their Role in Society." *Identities* 3, nos. 1-2 (1996): 183-204.

Shoumatoff, Alex. *In Southern Light: Trekking through Zaire and the Amazon.* New York: Vintage Books, 1990.

Spicer, Edward H., and Russell C. Ewing. *Six Faces of Mexico: History, People, Geography, Government, Economy, Literature and Art.* Tucson: University of Arizona Press, 1966.

Steininger, G. Russell, and Paul Van De Velde. *Three Dollars a Year.* New York: Diamond Press, 1935.

Stephen, Lynn. *Zapotec Women*. Austin: University of Texas Press, 1991.

Sternburg, Janet. *The Writer on Her Work*. New York: Norton, 1980–91.

Stoppleman, Joseph Willem Ferdinand. *People of Mexico*. New York: Hastings House, 1966.

Terry, T. Phillip. *Terry's Guide to Mexico*. Garden City, NY: Doubleday, 1947.

Theroux, Paul. *The Old Patagonian Express: By Train through the Americas*. Boston: Houghton Mifflin, 1979.

Vasconcelos, José. *A Mexican Ulysses*. Trans. and abridged by W. Rex Crawford. Bloomington: Indiana University Press, 1963.

———. *Ulises criollo*. México: Secretaria de Educación Pública: Fondo de Cultura Económica, 1983.

Vaughan, Genevieve. *The Gift, Il dono: A Feminist Analysis*. Rome: Meltami Editore, 2004.

Weston, Edward. *The Daybooks of Edmond Weston*. Vol. 1: *Mexico*. New York: Aperture, 1990.

Williams, Adriana. *Covarrubias*. Austin: University of Texas Press, 1994.

Index